I Never Met My Mother

A true story dedicated to each and every child who was deprived of love, who was abused or simply ignored by their parents – and what one can do in life in spite of it.

JANNA SOSENSKY

Copyright © 1998 # 471858

Janna Sosensky

All rights reserved.

ISBN: 1482516837

ISBN 13: 9781482516838

Library of Congress Control Number: 2013903118
CreateSpace Independent Publishing Platform
North Charleston, South Carolina

Dedication

This true story is dedicated to each and every child who was deprived of love, who was abused or simply ignored by his or her parents—and what one can do in life in spite of it.

Author's note

In this book, some names and other identifying information have been changed. Other than the alteration of such information, the events and locales are presented as they occurred.

Acknowledgements

This project has been in the works for twenty-one years. I wish to acknowledge and thank the following people:

The late Jack Hutchinson, CBC producer who took me to Moscow, seventeen years after I left, as a guide, just prior to the collapse of the Soviet regime. He suggested that I write my story as a comedy.

Margaret (Nonni) Griffin, prominent Canadian actress, whose talent I admire and who played a significant role in encouraging me to complete this project. To her I owe my heartfelt thanks.

Thelma Barer-Stein, PhD, editor from Culture Concept Books, who provided valuable insight and remarks.

Anna Bortolus, who read this manuscript and contributed valuable comments. Thank you, Anna, for your encouragement.

My dear friend Wes Stewart, for supporting me and helping me in the final phase of publishing this book.

Finally, my son, who has made me so proud.

About the Author

Janna Sosensky's life-long search for a reason WHY she survived after her mother's death when she was just three months old has been the main driving force behind most of the major decisions and changes she has made at every step of her life's journey.

Born in the former USSR in 1941, Janna was raised in an orphanage but was eventually released to her motherless family at the age of six years.

On a freezing winter night in Moscow, as a young teenage girl, she ran barefoot through the snow. She ran for her life, away from her abusive father. She kept running until her feet got numb with frostbite. She was not afraid to endure the pain. She was running toward her life of freedom.

For many years, back in the place of her birth, Moscow, she struggled. She worked by day from a very young age, while completing high school and attending university by night to make something of herself and become a "somebody."

Eventually, Janna graduated from journalism school (an interesting occupation in a Communist country where freedom of speech didn't exist at the time), only to find out that the field that she thought would allow her creative expression held no interest or excitement for her, let alone creative possibilities.

When asked about her long-term vision, she always answers without missing a beat. She wants to go, to play, to live at 100 percent. She wants to feel fully engaged and excited at every age. She wants to live a life of choice. That's life! That's freedom!

Janna emigrated from the Soviet Union in 1974.

Chapter	1	Born The First Week of The War	1
Chapter	2	Always Hungry	5
Chapter	3	The Orphanage	7
Chapter	4	My Father's Boy	13
Chapter	5	My Two Older Sisters Arrive	15
Chapter	6	My Father Gets Married	19
Chapter	7	Two Enemy Camps	23
Chapter	8	Misfit And Outcast	27
Chapter	9	My Eleventh Birthday	35
Chapter	10	Summer Camp	39
Chapter	11	My Sister's Coat	43
Chapter	12	Enough! I'm Leaving	49
Chapter	13	Moscow Meat Plant	55
Chapter	14	My First Date	59
Chapter	15	Is It Over?	65
Chapter	16	You Don't Belong With Workers Like Us!	77
Chapter	17	My Accident	91
Chapter	18	How I Fooled Them	101
Chapter	19	At The Top	113
Chapter	20	My Boss	127
Chapter	21	In Hiding	133
Chapter	22	Still A Virgin	137

Chapter	23	Wrong	147
Chapter	24	New Year's Eve	153
Chapter	25	My Father's Divorce	165
Chapter	26	Frozen Ears	173
Chapter	27	The Magic Is Gone	181
Chapter	28	I Have To Make It	187
Chapter	29	Courtship And Marriage	197
Chapter	30	The Reality Check	205
Chapter	31	What Do I Do?	209
Chapter	32	The Baby	221
Chapter	33	Masha	225
Chapter	34	Raya	233
Chapter	35	The Fire	243
Chapter	36	The Discovery	247
Chapter	37	Life As It Goes	255
Chapter	38	The Orphanage Counselor	261
Chapter	39	The Important Decision	265
Chapter	40	Applying For Emigration	273
Chapter	41	Finding My Mother's Friend	279
Chapter	42	The Last Thirty Days	285
Chapter	43	Goodbye, Father	289
Chapter	44	Goodbye, Valentin	291
Chapter	45	Goodbye, Russia	295
Epilogue			301

CHAPTER 1

Born the First Week of the War

I was born on the first of July in 1941 in Moscow, USSR. My parents had two daughters before me. The oldest, Tania, was seven years old and the middle one, Sema, was five. My father wanted a son. He told my mother that if she had another girl, he wouldn't even take the baby home from the hospital.

On June 22 of that year, Stalin went on the radio and announced to the Soviet people that the USSR was at war. The German fascists had invaded Russia. It was just eight days before I was born, and my father was called up to serve in the army and had to leave Moscow. My mother was left with her two daughters and the new baby, me. What do you know? "Another girl!"

During the first couple months of the war, the citizens of Moscow were in a panic. Word went around that the Germans would take Moscow in no time and would do terrible things to the people.

My father's whole family lived in Moscow. He had one sister, who was the eldest, and eight brothers. None of them went to war except my father and his youngest brother Uri, who had no children. Nevertheless, none of my father's family offered to help my mother with her children, so she felt very much alone and in danger. She had a friend in a similar position, whose husband had gone to the front leaving her with their two children, a girl of thirteen and a boy of eleven. The two women decided to leave Moscow before it was too late.

The only help my mother got from my father's family was through his eldest brother, David, who had an important post with the Ministry of Transport. He provided her with access to a railway car, the kind used to transport animals. It was all he could manage since almost all the passenger trains had been commandeered by the army.

The wagon was hooked up to another twenty or more cars of different kinds, carrying animals, machinery, chemicals, and thousands of refugees heading east. The whole railway system was in total confusion. There were delays and long stops, endless days and nights spent on railway sidings, cars hooked up and then disconnected, sudden changes in orders, trains rerouted at the last minute, and sometimes whole trains literally going around in circles.

My mother and her friend often had no idea where they were going or where they were. It took them more than two months to reach Bugulma in the Tatar Republic, a little more than a thousand kilometres from Moscow. There they were told they could settle in one of the nearby villages.

My mother became very ill on this long journey, and, of course, there were no doctors on the train or in the villages where they stopped. The army had called up most of them as well. She was getting worse and worse, and by the time the two women arrived in the village about fifty kilometres outside the city of Ufa, she was in terrible pain and could no longer walk.

Her friend did her best to look after her and all five of the children. As soon as they were settled in the village, she decided to take my mother to the hospital in Ufa, but the problem was transportation. There were no cars or trucks, only horse-drawn carts but no horses, which, along with nearly all of the men, had been taken by the army. The villagers provided her with one of the carts and also collected a little money for my mother.

She started on her journey at about four o'clock in the morning, pulling and pushing the cart by herself with my mother unconscious most of the time. It took them until midnight—twenty hours—to get to the only hospital in Ufa. A clerk at the front desk told my mother's friend, "No beds!" slamming the little window shut in her face. The poor woman didn't know where to turn. She offered money to some of the nurses, but they said there was nothing they could do; there were just no beds available. She would have to wait her turn, and the waiting list was a long one. Some people had been waiting for as long as two months, she was told, so they couldn't possibly make an exception for my mother.

What was she to do? Should she take my mother back to the village and let her die there? She herself was exhausted, hungry, and at her wit's end. Suddenly, an older woman who had been washing the hospital floors and who up to then had seemed to pay no attention to this woman with her dying friend, put her mop down and went up to her.

"Listen to me!" she whispered. "Leave your friend here on the floor and go! I'm sure they will find a bed for her. Don't worry! Just go!"

And that's exactly what she decided to do. She hung around outside the hospital for a few hours to make sure my mother was taken care of. When she went back in, there was no one in the hall where my mother had been left. Sighing with relief, she started back to the village, pulling her cart the fifty kilometres. Five children were waiting for her, and she had to get back to them. She thanked God that her two children were at least old enough to help with the three younger ones.

When she returned, the first problem to deal with was me. I was barely three months old and needed the most care. There were a couple of mothers in the village who were breastfeeding their babies. One of them agreed to feed me as well, especially after the villagers offered extra bread and food to help feed her own children. So I was placed with her immediately. One problem solved.

Shortly after that, my mother's friend walked back to Ufa to see how my mother was doing. She found that she wasn't getting any better and nobody seemed to know what was wrong with her. On top of that, someone had stolen all her money and so she couldn't pay for the extra attention she needed. She was, in fact, dying. The two friends had what they knew was to be their last conversation. They talked and cried, and then my mother's friend had to trudge the long way back to the village.

The next time she went to visit my mother, she was told that the patient by that name had died. Nobody knew anything more than that—not even where she had been buried.

Two other families in the village took in my two sisters.

My mother's friend never returned to Moscow after the war.

CHAPTER 2

Always Hungry

My very first memory goes back to when I was three or four years old. This period of my life made such a vivid impression on my mind that I've remembered it all my life. Even now I can visualize the episode; I can hear a child's scream and almost physically feel the pain.

The episode was very short. The woman who breastfed me and took care of me at some point could no longer feed me with her own milk. She had no interest in an extra hungry mouth anyway when she didn't have enough for her own children.

I remember being hungry. All the time.

Sometimes I couldn't fall asleep because of hunger pains, so I started to make deals with the children in the household. I was quite successful. I would volunteer to do some little thing for them, like bringing them pieces of newspaper (what we used instead of toilet paper) and asking for half a piece of bread in return. I would run and pick up the ball when they played outside and were too lazy to run after it. I cut these little deals so that the children would give me bits of their rations.

Their mother noticed what I was doing, and she warned me that if she ever caught me again, she'd throw me out of the house.

I remember holding my hand out to receive a piece of the bread I had earned and that I deserved. At that very moment the woman (I don't even know her name, although thanks to her I am alive) grabbed me by the neck and before I knew it I was flying out the door, landing like a stone on a pile of wooden logs.

It must have been late fall because I remember that when I landed, the logs were slippery and my body was immediately covered with freezing rain. The landing was painful. I remember my own scream. That is all.

CHAPTER 3

The Orphanage

The next memories I have are when I was around five, and they are my happiest ones.

I had been sent to an orphanage near Moscow in a little town called Serpukhov. One thing I made sure of—to never to be hungry! In order to do this, I always made myself useful in the kitchen. By the age of six, I knew, or thought I knew, how to cook. Since that time, cooking has been my lifelong passion.

I remember when the chef was making borscht. It fascinated me to watch her. Every move was sure and quick. Real Russian or Ukrainian borscht is a meal in itself, and the longer it's around, the better it tastes. Chefs from all over the world have tried to reproduce this famous soup, but it has never even come close to the original, and I'm sure it's because the chefs, trying to replicate it, prepare it with a recipe, not with the heart.

Real borscht smelled of warmth, home, peace—and it always made me feel safe.

I was always in charge of some part of the preparation for the borscht. They trusted me to wash the carrots, beets, peppers, potatoes, and onions, and I would sit with the chef's actual helper to peel and work as an equal.

They even gave me an apron. I took the job seriously, making sure I did a good job.

The queen of this heavenly soup was cabbage, and of course the spices were essential. The chef was in charge of chopping vegetables—an art in itself. Only a good chef knew how to dice them properly and efficiently. At the end of this part of the preparation, the chef would reward me with cabbage sticks, which were crunchy and juicy.

In my mind, our chef was like other people's image of a grandmother, a loving and caring person who brought to mind mouth-watering taste and warm comfort.

Another dish I loved, another one I considered a magic meal, was cream of wheat. It was served for breakfast almost every other day. I always knew the menu, so when there was to be cream of wheat, I would get up extra early before anyone else, wash my hands and face, and put on my orphanage uniform. I didn't have to spend time brushing my hair because our heads were shaved, so I was ready in five minutes. After making up my bed, I'd appear at 5:00 a.m. sharp in my favorite place—the kitchen!

The preparation of cream of wheat always started with boiling a huge pot of water. After all, the kitchen had to feed two hundred children from age two to sixteen.

Standing by my post, I would patiently wait for the water to boil. It took a while because the huge stove was fueled by a wood fire. In the meantime, the chef would be busy organizing the next meal, a snack after our midday nap. When the water was almost at the boiling point, she would allow me to pour three or four jugs of milk into it, so the colour of the cream of wheat would be kind of bluish – she wouldn't allow me to use more because of the shortage of milk

After I carefully poured the milk into the water, I was in charge of watching it gradually start boiling. The chef entrusted me with stirring it from time to time with a big wooden spoon to make sure the milk mixed evenly in the water. When it came to a boil, my responsibility was to call the chef who would then do her finishing act. She would hold a large bag of wheat and pour it very slowly into the water. The secret to good cream of wheat was to end up with no lumps, and she knew just how to do it perfectly, to make it very smooth and not too thick, creamy, almost like a milkshake. Of course, the wheat had to be used very economically, and she knew the exact amount that would make a meal for two hundred children and the entire staff.

Her method was to hold the bag in her right hand, propping it up on her right breast, while using her left hand to stir the cream of wheat with a long wooden spoon. Slowly she poured out the wheat until the bag was empty. Afterwards, she continued stirring for some time, but not too long. It came out beautifully each and every time. After that she would add a little sugar and salt, and the end result was always perfect, neither too sweet nor too salty. Her final touch was to add a chunk of butter, which sat on top and gradually melted into the mixture, so that the top of the cream of wheat was always golden.

She appointed me first taster. She would give me a dollop right from her magic wooden spoon, and I would close my eyes, wrap my tongue around the delicious mixture, and cry, "Whoa!" which never failed to put a smile on the chef's face. It seemed to make her day! Those hours spent helping prepare cream of wheat for the orphanage are unforgettable to me.

Another task the chef entrusted me with required two important qualities: counting skills and honesty. I never failed in either of them—to make sure she kept me on the job. It was my task to count cookies and cubes of sugar. Children received one of each after their nap. I was very proud of myself when everybody sat down for their tea and no one was ever short of anything.

I was practically a permanent part-time kitchen worker with one condition: everything outside of the kitchen had to be perfect, with no complaints about my behavior. This was easy for me because I had a counselor I adored. Her name was Anna Ivanovna, and I remember her clearly to this day.

She had a lovely soft voice and a very gentle way of speaking. How I loved her! When she spoke to me, I felt very important and would do anything she asked, and more. She was a goddess to me. "Ania" was very tall and quite large. My dream was to grow up to be big like her and be exactly like her.

Life in the orphanage was happy and peaceful with only one upsetting episode.

In the middle of the night one night I heard a girl screaming at the top of her lungs. The scream was some distance from our room, which slept about forty girls, and seemed to be coming from underneath a bed or behind something. The screaming girl didn't seem to take a breath, even for a second, and I began to feel very frightened. Everyone else was sleeping, so I got up very quietly and tiptoed out of the room.

It was dark and cold in the hall, but I could tell a little better where the sound was coming from, which was near the staircase. I started to move towards the voice, but I couldn't make out much in the dark. Then one of the other doors opened, and a boy came out and almost bumped into me, but I moved away in time. He was heading in the opposite direction from the sound, and it looked as though he knew where he was going. He was moving towards a room where no one was allowed to go, which was where off-duty counselors went. We were trained never to knock on that door and to keep quiet when passing by because even during the day one of them could be with a visitor or resting.

As this boy moved closer to the door, the screaming became a bit subdued, and then it got louder again and sounded even more terrified.

A few people were beginning to emerge from their rooms, and when the boy saw them he became panicky, as though he didn't know what to do or where to turn. He hesitated, and then he began to run. By this time, the screams had become hysterical. All of a sudden someone turned the lights on. I stayed where I was and watched the whole scene unfold.

One of the counselors ran quickly after the boy and grabbed him. As she did so, a large butcher knife dropped from the boy's hand. It was terrifying. The hall was now full of children standing there looking half-asleep with their shaved heads and in their bare feet. Strangely, the screaming didn't stop when the lights came on but instead became even more piercing. I thought I knew where the voice was coming from and I called for someone to help me find the child whose screams were coming from under the stairs. All we could see was a box.

A woman calmly went towards the box and discovered a little girl hiding inside. Even then she continued to scream, but her body was so stiff she couldn't be removed from the box. The whole box had to be pulled out and finally she was lifted from her hiding place. I immediately recognized her.

She was the same age as I was. We had played paper dolls together, cutting them out of newspaper and making all kinds of dresses for our cardboard dolls. I called her by her name, but she didn't seem to hear me and continued screaming. The sound was unbearable.

Then my dear Anna Ivanovna's calm, quiet voice was gently saying, "Come with me, Janna." I immediately turned and followed her. She tucked me in and told me a soothing bedtime story. Every time I opened my mouth to ask her what had happened, she told me something so interesting that I finally gave up until I could no longer keep my eyes open. When I woke up, it was too late for me to go to the kitchen to help prepare breakfast. I was very upset to have missed my cream of wheat fun for that day.

CHAPTER 4

My Father's Boy

I remember this particular day as though it were yesterday. It was bath day at the orphanage. All of the children, no matter how good or bad they were, loved it. It was like a holiday or celebration, and every one of us looked forward to the fun.

Our baths took place every two weeks. We were divided into five groups of forty, and each group was given a whole bar of brown soap and our own appointed time. Before their baths, all of the children had to change their bed linen, and each was given a clean flannel nightgown that felt warm and cozy as well as a clean dress. Our uniforms were made of stiff fabric, and at bedtime some of the girls liked to stand their dresses up against their headboards. When the counselor came into the room to make sure everyone was there, it would startle her because in the dark these standing figures looked a bit scary!

The bath procedure involved warming up a huge tub of water on the stove. The large aluminum basin was placed on a sturdy wooden bench, and each of the five groups was given two large flannel blankets for drying all forty kids. When the counselor gave the signal, my job was to pour water over the girls' heads. It was a job I loved. It made me feel useful and important. Because of it, I was bathed last, and by then I was good and tired and looked forward to the afternoon nap.

On this particular day, it took a little longer because the flannel blankets were damp and Anna Ivanovna had to use both to dry me off thoroughly.

I felt so clean and tired that I almost fell asleep the minute my head touched the pillow, but I took a little longer, enjoying this moment of total bliss. I had just fallen asleep when I felt a gentle touch and the soft voice Anna Ivanovna.

"Jannachka! Get up! Your father is here!"

When I opened my eyes, I saw her smiling and looking very happy. "What is it, Ania?" I asked sleepily. I figured it was good news, but I had no idea what it meant—especially the word "father" that sounded so unfamiliar to me.

I wanted to go back to sleep, but I couldn't let her down. I got up and put my dress on. She was scrutinizing me, as if to make sure I had everything in place, but I still had both my arms and legs! My hair didn't need to be combed out because there was no hair to comb.

She took me by the hand and led me to the hallway where I saw two people standing in the middle of the room. One was an old woman not much taller than I was. She had silver-grey hair pulled into a tight knot at the back of her head, and she was holding a large bag in each hand. I also noticed that she had thick veins on her hands. She was very old, but I liked her. She had a kindly smile on her wrinkled face.

The man standing there wore a stern expression on his face, which frightened me so I pulled back, but Ania held my hand tighter and edged me forward a little. At that moment, I knew that Anna Ivanovna wanted me no more—that I had to go to these two strangers. I certainly didn't want to go near the man, so I decided to go to the old woman and for some reason she cried. But the man pulled me away from her. He grabbed me as if I were a package. In a moment I was put on top of the table, but that wasn't the worst part of it. The worst was that he stripped my clothes off and I stood there naked and vulnerable as these two complete strangers continued to examine me.

From the two large bags they had brought, they began to take out different trousers, shirts, and shoes until they were satisfied. Then they dressed me and put me down on the floor and I stood there frightened and awkward in this strange clothing. I didn't look like the five-year-old little girl that I was. I looked like a boy!

CHAPTER 5

My Two Older Sisters Arrive

We took the train to Moscow, and when we arrived at the station the old woman smiled at me, told me to call her grandmother, and left us. My father and I walked in silence to his house. It was getting dark, and when we got inside my father told me I had to go to bed, but before I did I must pee, otherwise an accident could happen.

"The washroom is outside, at the far end of the garden," he said roughly. "You can't go there at night. There are wolves there that would eat you alive, so you must pee in the house."

I tried to say something. "But—I don't need to—"

"Here!" he said, pulling out a large laundry tub. "You pee in this right now. Come on! Do it!"

How could I? First of all, the basin was so big that it scared me to death, and secondly, my knees were shaking, and it felt as though I were about to lose my balance. I was terrified my father might punish me for being clumsy. I couldn't let myself fall and I couldn't do what he was demanding I do either, so I stood there shaking like a leaf for several minutes. Finally, instead of peeing I began to cry. I cried and cried and cried. I knew that my happy life was over.

My two older sisters arrived a couple of months after me. Apparently, after my mother's death they had been placed in different homes so that when my father returned from the war nobody knew what had happened to his family. All he knew from his older brother was that his wife had been evacuated out of Moscow, but he had no idea where she had ended up. He put out a search for his wife and children but received no information until one day a letter arrived about me in an orphanage in Serpukhov.

I learned that he was greatly disappointed that he had another girl and not the boy that he had wanted so much. But at that point, with very little hope of finding his other children, he decided to pick me up, still continuing his search for the rest of his children.

My eldest sister, Tania, was about thirteen years old by then and Sema was about eleven. "Sema" was her nickname. Her real name was Fera or Esfir, which she hated. Under no circumstances would she allow anyone to call her by that name. If anyone did, she would become so enraged she seemed like she could almost commit murder.

Tania and Sema screamed at each other constantly and also at me because I seemed to be always doing something wrong. Sema said I had two left hands and that I was good for nothing. I ended up sleeping in the same bed with her and the rule was never to touch her during sleep. I don't know how I did it, but somehow I managed. I think I simply trained myself not to go anywhere near her!

In my new life we were on our own most of the time. Our father went to work every morning early, but from time to time my father's mother, whom I liked, would come to our house and cook for us. At other times, my father brought home all kinds of cold cuts and other delicacies, like black and red caviar. All sorts of goods were available in Moscow after the war—tasty things that I had never seen before.

He also brought big chocolate bears and rabbits once in a while. My sisters always argued over them. When Tania wanted a rabbit, Sema would want it too. I didn't understand this at all because at least they were getting something while I got nothing. I would ask them to let me have one of the ears or the tail, which they made me beg for. Eventually, one of them would give me a piece in exchange for washing dishes for them. Washing dishes was the big issue in our house. We didn't have running water. It had to be brought all the way from down the street and then heated on the stove or on a little kerosene burner.

I remember very well that someone gave me my first and only real toy, a boy doll I called Andrey. He was beautiful with his shiny face and silky hair and was dressed in blue pants and a red shirt. He looked as though he were always smiling at me. How I loved this beautiful doll, and he was no one else's. He was mine. I would feed him and put him to bed with me, and I was very careful not to crush Andrey while I was asleep.

One day I was playing outside on the street when I suddenly dropped him on the sidewalk. When I picked him up there was a big hole right in the middle of his forehead! And he didn't seem as pink and shiny anymore either. Oh my God! What was I to do? My best friend was ruined, and I was miserable. I couldn't move for a long time, and then I went to the garden as my tears fell onto Andrey's poor broken face. He looked dead, and the only thing I could do was to bury him.

I dug a hole in the garden as deep as I could, which wasn't difficult. The ground was soft because my father had just hired a man to work on our vegetable garden, digging up the entire area for planting potatoes. After digging the hole I put my little Andrey in and covered him up so he would be warm.

My grandmother was cooking for us that day, and I ran to her, crying. "Baba! Baba! My Andrey is dead! My little Andrey is dead!"

My grandmother looked at me with a smile on her face. "You silly child! Don't you know that dolls don't die? What happened? Show me!"

"I have nothing to show you!" I sobbed. "I've already buried him!"

"Where?"

"There, in the garden!"

"Now Jannachka, stop crying! Here's some stewed fruit for you. Enjoy it, and then we'll go out to look for your doll. I'll patch him up for you, and he'll be as good as new. And next time you'll know that dolls never die."

After I had a few spoonfuls of fruit, I rushed out with her to the garden and took her to the spot where I had buried him, but my doll was not there. Then I thought he was "over there," and my grandmother dug some more, but there was no sign of my Andrey. We dug five or six holes and we could not find him. He was gone.

I never had another doll. Nobody ever gave me one. Perhaps they thought I was too stupid to have one.

Our lives went on. That is to say, I lived my life while my sisters lived theirs. Mine was a street life. I was beginning to be accepted by the neighbourhood boys almost as an equal. After all, I was dressed like them and I had very little hair underneath my cap. I was learning how to whistle with two fingers and to climb trees. I made sure I did everything as well as the boys or better. I could run so fast that some of them gave up trying to catch me. I had only one problem: I didn't have a ball of my own.

So I couldn't practice, and the rule was that whoever owned the ball got to play the most.

CHAPTER 6

My Father Gets Married

My father came home one day and announced to all of us that he was getting married. "She is coming for dinner tomorrow to meet all of you," he said in a casual, indifferent way.

I was so excited! I hoped with all my heart that she would be like Anna Ivanovna—warm and loving and that I could be happy again. I washed myself extra carefully the next morning, even washing my neck, and I decided not to put my cap on so I'd look more like a girl.

To add to my excitement, my grandmother had come over to cook dinner for us and had promised to make my favorite dish, the cream of wheat that I missed so much. I hadn't had it since the orphanage, the place I secretly considered my real home.

I thought dinnertime would never come, but finally everyone seated themselves around the table. My father sat at the head of it in his usual spot, Tania on his right and Sema next to her. I was at the other end of the table, across from my father with my back to the kitchen, where my grandmother was cooking my cream of wheat. I could hardly wait for it to be ready.

While we waited for this woman to arrive, my father read his newspaper, *Pravda* ("Truth"). It was the only thing he ever read.

At last my grandmother served me my bowl of delicious cream of wheat. I had just started to eat it when there was a knock at the door and this woman walked in. She was not alone. She had an absolutely beautiful little girl with her who she told us was her niece, Lusia.

The girl was breathtaking! I had never in my life seen anyone so beautiful! She had thick braids tied with white satin ribbons that looked like flowers and she had small bright brown eyes and the longest eyelashes I had ever seen. Looking at her, I wanted to hide under the table. She had on a silk dress and black patent leather shoes, and she looked like a beautiful doll. The woman held this gorgeous little girl by the hand, and I could see that she was about my age or maybe just a little older.

My father got up and said, "Meet my children." He pointed us out: "This is Tania, and next to her is Sema." And then he just waved his hand in my direction as though I had no name. After that he said to the woman, "Sit down!" and showed her to the couch. "Dinner will be ready soon," he said and went right back to his newspaper.

There was total silence in the room. My two sisters stared at the woman my father called Polia. Their expressions were anything but warm and friendly.

My first thought was, "Why would this woman in such a nice peach blouse come to us when she already has this sweet little girl?" My second thought was that this woman was never going to love me—an ugly little nobody. How could she when she already loved this other little girl, her niece?

And I was ugly. I had huge eyes and a mouth that was so big I had a hard time keeping it closed. Sema often told me, "Keep your mouth shut! It's so big a crow could fly into it!" Also my ears stuck out and my hair sprouted in little clumps that pointed in different directions, and it never seemed to grow. On top of this, my pants, torn from falling out of trees, had been patched up without much care by my older sisters using different colored fabrics. My shirt had one pocket halfway off and had at least three buttons missing.

Why would this nice, warm-looking woman love me?

Now I was faced with a dilemma. What was I to do first? Go to this woman who was sitting on the couch looking somewhat uncomfortable and beg her to stay? Or finish my delicious cream of wheat?

I decided to do both. First finish my cream of wheat. Spoonful after spoonful burned my mouth, but I did not even feel the pain as I worked my way down to the bottom of the bowl. As soon as I finished I got up, went over to the couch, and climbed up on the woman's lap. I put my arms around her and hugged her tight.

"You are going to stay with me, Mama, aren't you?" I pleaded, looking at her longingly. "Please say you are! Please!"

CHAPTER 7

Two Enemy Camps

Within the next couple of days a new kind of life began in our house. I was the only one who called my father's wife "Mama." My two sisters didn't even call her by her name. Amongst themselves they referred to her as either "she" or "Polia."

The first thing Mama did was to turn the entire house upside down. She washed everything, starting from the ceiling to the floor, polishing all the windows and doors. She took every mattress outside and beat and washed it. She laundered every piece of linen several times over, boiling it in a large basin and afterwards taking it outside and rinsing it over and over again. Afterwards, she brought everything back into the house and starched it before hanging it outside to dry on thick rods. Then she began a very special procedure.

Every piece of linen had to be slightly dampened before being folded carefully for ironing. First came the pillowcases, followed by the linen towels, which I had to fold by myself. The large sheets and the blankets, Mama and I did together.

Mama and I held the opposite ends of the sheet and stretched it as much as we could, making sure the corners weren't wrinkled or over-starched. Then both of us met in the middle to fold it in half, stretching and pulling and folding it until it was almost the size of a pillowcase. In the meantime the iron was waiting to play its role. It sat on the table with its nose up, looking very pleased with itself. Our dining table looked very different now. It looked more like an ironing station.

Ironing was a skill I had to learn very thoroughly. Only after the learning process would Mama trust me to iron on my own. The finished product was supposed to look so perfect that if you held it in your hand it would sit there stiffly like a piece of metal and shine like one as well. When all the pieces were ironed, we piled them on top of one another according to size, each one its own tower. Then we placed them on separate shelves of the redwood dresser in the bedroom, a giant piece of furniture that had a mirror in the center and shelves on both sides to hold the clean linen.

This cleaning fit lasted the entire week, during which our family war began.

My sisters wanted no part of this cleaning madness. They wanted to sleep late, and they had their own thing to do, which consisted of walking around the house like zombies in their nightgowns with their hair uncombed.

When Mama asked them to help, they would object so loudly that they could be heard from outside the house, and the conversation always ended up with them throwing things around. When they got tired of arguing, they would quickly get dressed and leave the house. This left Mama and me in peace so we could continue our work.

One evening when the whole house was nice and clean, we sat waiting for my father to come home from work so we could all have dinner. That evening Mama had prepared a special dish and even baked a cake, so the whole house smelled clean and delicious.

When she finished preparing everything, she changed into a pretty coral blouse and a silky skirt and combed her hair. Before putting the finishing touches on her face, she took a little fresh milk and dabbed her face with it. She believed that milk was good for the skin, and at the age of forty-five she hardly had a wrinkle and her skin was a fresh pinkish color.

"I never wash my face with soap and water," she told me. "I only use milk!"

All of a sudden, I noticed vicious looks on my sisters' faces. They started to whisper to each other—what about, I had no idea. It didn't take long to find out. They rushed from the house very early the next morning, and we didn't know where they had gone. But we found out when our father came back from work and started to yell at Mama.

"Don't you dare think for a moment that you can come here to hurt my poor orphans and push them out of the house so that you can sit here like a queen!" he shouted. "If I hear one more time that you've taken their milk to bathe yourself in, you'll be thrown out of this house! Do you hear me?"

Apparently my sisters had run to our grandmother and Aunt Rita's house to tell them that Polia wasn't feeding them properly, that they were always hungry, that she forced them to work so hard cleaning the house that they didn't have time to study. On top of it all, they said, she was bathing in the milk they needed! Aunt Rita, who cast herself in the role of judge, called an emergency meeting with our father and gave him an ultimatum:

"Listen, Boris," she said, "if you think we'll allow this witch to abuse these poor orphans and send them out of the house so that you two can be alone like lovebirds, you're mistaken! We'll kick her out first, before it's too late."

And so, the war in our family worsened.

In one camp was my father and sisters; in the other, Mama and me.

You might think that two against three didn't stand a chance, especially if one of the two members wasn't yet seven years old. True, perhaps. But even if we didn't have a chance of winning, we certainly had a chance of keeping the war going! And that was how it went.

When I heard my father's accusations about the milk and other things, I spoke up. Unfortunately, he wasn't interested in the truth and kept interrupting me with all kinds of pounding on the table and savage shouts. Nevertheless, I held my ground and kept saying, "No! That's not true!"

One thing was for certain: my father continued to hate me, not only for the fact that I wasn't a boy and that I was to blame for his wife's death (as he thought) but also for standing up for the truth that he wasn't interested in hearing.

CHAPTER 8

Misfit And Outcast

It was the first of September, the biggest day for a seven-year-old, the day when every child in the Soviet Union started school.

In the Soviet school system, everyone wore uniforms. The girls wore brown pleated wool dresses with white collars that were supposed to be fresh every day. We also had to have two aprons, one black and the other white. The black was for every day and the white for important events.

The boys wore blue wool suits with white shirts, and up until grade five their hair had to be cut very short: a brush cut with bangs. After grade five, they were allowed to have a proper haircut. Girls had to wear their hair braided with black ribbons.

My family had to prepare three school uniforms for that first day of school, and I waited with mounting excitement for the day to arrive. I counted the hours until I could join other children. For some reason I thought going to school would be a little bit like the orphanage where I had been so happy.

The evening before that first day, we pressed our uniforms. I did mine first and did an excellent job. After I finished, I carefully laid it on top of our sewing machine, after which Mama gave me a glass of milk and sent me to bed early so I'd be well rested.

The next morning, I jumped up and helped Mama prepare breakfast for my father. After he left for work, she and I made sandwiches for the three of us and I had a bath.

As soon as Sema and Tania got up, they started to argue. Apparently, Sema found out that Tania was wearing her new stockings without asking, and it turned into a row. Both of them began screaming at each other, and then they turned on Mama. As a result, she became upset and went out to the market for some fresh chicken for dinner. She did this every morning because our father had an ulcer and she wanted to make sure he was on a proper diet. Nobody had refrigerators, so the shopping had to be done almost daily, especially in the summer.

When the time came to leave for school I put on my uniform with my beautiful white apron, and I went to the mirror to see how I looked. It was the first time since the orphanage I'd worn a dress and it felt rather strange. As I looked at myself, I noticed my collar was all wrinkled! I had done a perfect job the day before. Even Mama, who was such a perfectionist, had praised me. I found out that Sema had put her uniform on top of mine and my collar had somehow gotten crumpled. I panicked. I didn't have time to take it off and iron it again, and, besides, Tania was furiously ironing her own uniform.

She gave me a hateful look and screamed, "I'll do it for you so I can get you out of my way! Come here and hurry up!"

She grabbed a book, placed it under my collar, and asked me to hold it so that she could iron the collar without my taking it off. As she did, the iron touched my neck and I shrieked so loudly that she lost control of the iron and burned my neck again. I was in excruciating pain.

Tania shouted, "This is all your own fault, and now I'm going to be late for school!" My burned neck was of no importance to her.

And thus my school life began.

The next five years were wretched. Many nights I couldn't sleep because of the terrible rows at home. My father always managed to start an argument. Almost every night he would pick on something. One day it would be the soup, which was too salty. The next day it would be an overstarched shirt. Often he would come home in a state of fury because Tania had waited for him outside on the street somewhere and had told him stories of how Polia had mistreated her, stories that were all twisted lies.

During those terrible times, Sema was usually seated on the couch, pretending to read. In actual fact, she was staring at the same page for the longest time, preferring not to say anything.

I tried to keep calm until I couldn't take the lies anymore. Then I'd speak up. My father hated me for it and would find ways to punish me by taking away things that were important to me.

For instance, I wanted to learn to play the piano. Eventually he said to me, "All right. Find yourself a teacher who'll let you practice in her home because I'm not about to buy a piano for you."

I knew that if Tania had wanted to learn the piano, or any other instrument, he would have bought one for her in five minutes. He bought many expensive things for Tania and not as much for Sema; he really wasn't sure which side Sema was on because of her silence. Tania was definitely on his side.

About my piano lessons he said, "There is one condition you had better follow. If you open your mouth one more time the lessons will be cut off!"

In the following weeks I found a teacher who was good enough to take me on as her pupil. For a very small charge she allowed me an extra hour of practice after my lesson. I hoped to be a worthwhile pupil and tried to be helpful to her while I was there. I offered to wash dishes and iron because she always had a kitchen full of dirty dishes and a pile of wrinkled clothes. If Mama had seen it, she would have fainted!

But the lessons didn't last long. I did my best to keep out of the fights and accusations and every time I came home, I would put my ear to the door to see if it was quiet or not. I'd walk in only if it was peaceful and get to bed right away.

At other times, if I heard screams, I wouldn't go in the house. I'd sit on the bench under our two maple trees in the garden, scared of the darkness and crying. Sometimes I sat in the dark for two or three hours.

One time I was fooled by the silence in the house and walked in to find that my father was about to hit Mama with a chair. She was lying on the bed. My father, in his long underwear looking like a devil in white, was in a complete rage. It was lucky for her that I walked in when I did: the chair was about to land on her head. I took my father by surprise and grabbed the chair from behind him. He was so shocked, he nearly fell down, but he quickly regained his balance and turned to strike me. Without thinking, I hit him first, right between his legs. He doubled up, and Mama and I took the opportunity to run. We spent that night with her sister Luba.

To this day I have no idea how I managed to do what I did, and without hesitation, but as a result of this episode, he cut off my piano lessons.

Taking away my skates was another punishment. When he bought skates for all of us, I was so happy! But it didn't last for more then three sessions before I again opened my mouth and told him the truth of what had happened during a quarrel between Mama and Tania.

He grabbed my skates and hit me with them, shouting, "That's it! You are never going see these skates again!" He grabbed my hand, dragged me outside to our toilet in the garden, and threw the skates right in the pile of filth below. He then pushed my head down into the vile-smelling hole to make sure I saw my skates disappearing into the pile of excrement.

In a state of hysteria I collapsed, having no idea where I was, who I was, or what had just taken place. I pulled away from him and ran and kept on running for a long time until I realized that all I had on my feet were socks.

It was a very cold winter night with a temperature of around minus thirty degrees Celsius. I don't remember when I returned to my house. All I know is that ever since then I have suffered pain from the deep frostbite in all of my toes.

Life at school was not happy either, especially after an episode that had to do with the Soviet regime. One might wonder what a little person of nine and a half had to do with the Soviet regime.

To start with, I have to describe the structure of the Soviet school system of the time. From the age of seven, every child in the Soviet Union was required go to school for ten years until high school graduation. In the beginning of the first year each pupil had to join the Elementary Organisation in Memory of the October Revolution, or the "Octiabrenok," and wear the red star on his or her uniform.

"Pioneer" was another organisation that was mandatory for everyone to belong to. The designation was a red tie. Every pupil from age nine to fourteen was encouraged to be proud of belonging to the "Pioneer Organisation."

The next step was "Komsomol," which required a specific pin on the uniform as well. Finally, there was membership in the Communist Party, which was geared towards those who were the highest achievers. The party membership was for all intents and purposes a ticket for better future positions and careers.

Since the October Revolution in 1918, the Soviet Union had been an atheistic country. No religions were allowed. Before then, the Russian people were mainly Orthodox Christians. In Soviet Russia, religion was repudiated as though it was a poison, an evil and dangerous thing.

Brainwashing began from kindergarten. Children were supposed to convert their grandparents to atheism, but the older people were the hardest to convince: they still believed in going to church. The churches, however, became non-functional. The only services allowed were funerals and Easter services.

Russian churches were beautiful. My school overlooked one of these great churches. The environment around the school was exciting. On one side there was a stadium called "Lokomotiv," and on the other side there was a church with the cemetery behind it. The cemetery looked mysterious, but it was the church that really fascinated me. Because I could go to the cemetery any time I wanted (although at times I did find the silence quite scary), it didn't seem as mysterious as the church did.

As pupils we were told that to go inside a church would be as bad as committing a serious crime. Because of this edict, I was sorely tempted to see the inside of them.

Of course, I didn't want to go by myself. I wanted some of my friends to go with me. I asked my classmates if anybody wanted to join me, and eventually I got a group of five girls and boys. We made a secret plan to sneak into the church.

That day, after our last class, we crossed the schoolyard, took off our red ties, and hid our school bags under a bush. The plan was that we would all wear coats on top of our uniforms. Naively we thought that this way we wouldn't be recognized as pupils of the nearby school.

Our expedition began successfully. No one stopped us—no one even paid the slightest attention to us—and as we entered, I found myself inside a grand hall with very high ceilings and then inside an endlessly large room with pictures painted all over the walls and ceilings. The faces were painted in gold and someone said they were the faces of God and all his brothers and sisters.

Whatever they were, they were magnificent. I stood there with my mouth open. Then I heard singing. It seemed to be very different from any singing I had ever heard before. This was an entirely different world. I had no idea what it was all about; I just stood there in awe.

When I finally realized that I'd been there a long time, I started to look for my school friends. I couldn't find them amongst the old people, who were continuously whispering something with their eyes closed. Now I really had to go or my father would kill me! I left the church, and that night when I realized my father had not found out I happily fell sound asleep.

The next morning, however, during my first class, an announcement came blazing from our school sound system.

"Attention! Attention! We are calling an emergency meeting in the schoolyard. Every pupil must attend immediately, and, every teacher, please listen for your turn to lead your class out!"

These orders sounded ominous to me. I had never heard of such a thing happening before.

When our class came out I saw all eight hundred pupils from seven to seventeen standing quietly, waiting for the meeting to begin.

No one knew what it was all about, but everyone sensed that it was very important. Finally, the principal came out while all the administrators seated themselves behind a long table covered with a red cloth.

It was so quiet that all I heard was one little bird singing her song. It sounded nice and peaceful. Then the principal, Nina Anatolievna, began to speak.

"The reason we have called this very important meeting is that last night one of our pupils committed a crime. In spite of all the rules known to everyone from grade one to grade ten, this pupil broke the most important rule. The worst part is that this pupil did not do it alone. This person went through the entire class trying to persuade everyone to do wrong. Fortunately enough, the majority of those loyal to the Communist Party refused to join her. But four pupils, who were not as strong, followed her. We cannot afford agitators in our school. We have a reputation for high moral standards.

"Therefore, this person is very dangerous to our organisation! This person must be punished for committing this crime! Our school administration will not tolerate any actions of this kind!"

With that, she gave the microphone to one of the heads of the Pioneer Organisation, who said, "To my great regret, I must admit my own fault in this case. The Pioneer Organisation has to improve its efforts to explain to each and every member how harmful religion is! The damage it does to people's morality can be irreparable! Realizing our weakness, we have to ask our people to join us in helping to educate each and every person so that crimes of this nature will not take place in the future! Let us hope that this will be the first and only crime in the history of our school! And now I will announce the name of this person."

Everyone stopped breathing as they waited to hear who this person could be. There was total silence for several minutes. It seemed to me that even the bird had stopped singing to listen.

Finally she said, "The name is Janna Laidman! Please come to the table!"

I couldn't believe I had heard my name. I felt as though I were dreaming. Then I heard it pronounced again, this time very clearly.

"Janna Laidman! Come to the table!" It was I. I was the one who had to go to the red table. I was the one who had committed some terrible crime, and I was the one who would be punished for it. I started to move forward. The walk to the red table seemed unbearably long. The hardest part was that I could feel all eight hundred pairs of eyes piercing my body like eight hundred needles. It felt as though my body were bleeding. My walk seemed to take an eternity.

Finally I was there, in front of the table, facing many threatening looks from the adults, whose stares were now burning through my face.

Breaking the silence, the president of Pioneer Organisation said, "Janna Laidman committed a crime by going into a church yesterday. The worst part of it is she led a group of four other pioneers who were forced to follow her. The administration of our school cannot afford to ignore this very alarming incident. Therefore, the decision was made this morning that Janna Laidman is to be expelled from the Pioneer Organisation as of this moment!

"Now, Janna, take off your red tie!"

There was complete silence again. Then the president of the Pioneer Organisation came up to me and removed my red tie.

While she was doing this, someone played a drum roll and one of the older pioneers came up to me holding a black cushion. The president placed my red tie on the cushion, and then the drumming stopped. The principal gave me an envelope and told me not to come back to school without my father's signature.

That awful day I stood outside our house, waiting for my father to appear.

When he read the letter, his lips began to tremble violently, a sight I had now become familiar with. He became totally enraged to the point of madness.

He struck me again and shouted, "You see? Nobody wants you! You are hopeless, hopeless!" And then he went on beating me until he was exhausted.

From that time I became an outcast at school too.

I knew I was useless. I knew nobody wanted me. The woman who had thrown me on to the wooden logs—she didn't want me! Anna Ivanovna, who I loved so much, had let me go! Why hadn't she wanted me? My father…at least I knew why he didn't want me. If it hadn't been for me, his wife would still have been alive. Perhaps if I had been a boy he wouldn't have hated me so much. My stepmother Polia…I wanted her to be my mama, but she loved her niece, Lusia. She also seemed to like Sema more than she liked me for some reason. Perhaps it was because I was so ugly. I wanted my hair to grow, but how could it when she kept cutting it? She didn't touch Sema or Tania's hair, so they had nice, long hair.

Where could I go, seeing that no one wanted me? There had to be somebody who could like me. After all, I wasn't so useless.

I could wash dishes. I knew how to iron. Even Mama said so. My Baba was nice to me. Once she gave me three cubes of sugar she had been hiding and said, "Here! These are good for your brain!" But she had many grandchildren and I was basically a stranger. Besides, she and Aunt Rita kept saying that Polia was a monster and that my poor father suffered because of her. That was not true! It was the other way around, but they wouldn't listen.

If I stayed where I was a little longer and learned more about cooking and cleaning, somebody might need my skills one day. Maybe it was my fault that Mama suffered so much. If I hadn't called her "Mama" that day, she probably wouldn't have stayed with us. If so, I was responsible for her and I had to stay and protect her, even though she didn't recognize my endless efforts.

On the other hand, maybe Mama and I would leave my father's house together some day!

CHAPTER 9

My Eleventh Birthday

One day I asked Mama, "How come I'm nearly eleven years old and I've never had my birthday celebrated? I've been invited to my friends' birthdays and I've never invited them back."

Mama said, "Janna! It's not right! This time we'll invite your friends. One way or another I'll get the money and we'll celebrate it."

The truth was that my father paid for everything himself, even the milkman, because he didn't trust Mama with his money. After he finished his dinner that evening, which went peacefully because of Mama's concerted effort, she said to him, "Boris! You have three daughters. We always celebrate Tania's and Sema's birthdays and we've never celebrated Janna's. She is going to be eleven in a couple of days and she is your child too. You shouldn't deprive her of a party!"

My father, who had been quietly reading his paper, became instantly enraged.

"What? What are you talking about? This 'thing' here? You ask me why I don't celebrate her birthday? It's simple! Because she doesn't deserve it! Do you hear me? Now that's the end of it!"

Mama dared to keep trying. "But she was invited to her friends' homes and she's never had them over. Please try to understand this!"

My father's face turned deep red and he began to shout. "Look who's talking! Her great defender! You two had better learn never to talk back to me and that's all I can say!" And he went back to his paper.

After a while she tried again. "Please, give me just a few rubles, and I'll do everything! It will make her so happy! Please, Boris!"

Now my father started to shout at the top of his lungs how rotten I was! That I didn't deserve anything! That I should be thankful he kept me under his roof! If it hadn't been for him, I'd be on the street like a stray dog.

Mama tried to defend me, saying that I was a good child. That if it weren't for me she could never have handled all the work around the house. They went on screaming and arguing, neither listening to the other.

By now I was sobbing in the next room. Finally I couldn't take it. I ran to the dining room and pulled at Mama's skirt. "Please! Please! Mama!"

I managed to drag her away. And then she put me on her lap and in a soothing voice talked me out of crying.

In the next couple of days she got busy. She borrowed money from our neighbour and did some shopping. She had to be very careful preparing everything so that father wouldn't discover her little plan for my birthday. She told me to invite all my friends for midday on July 1, knowing that my father worked all day and never came home before seven o'clock at night.

July the first arrived. Mama and I made the table look beautiful with a crispy white tablecloth, our best crystal glasses for lemonade, and our fine china plates. She made a few delicious salads, including my favourite potato salad. For the main course she prepared meat patties with mashed potatoes. She also baked her best cake, which was made with twelve eggs. I helped her by stirring the sugar into the egg yolks until the mixture turned from yellow to almost white. Then I beat the whites with a fork until it looked like whipped cream and my arm was aching.

By noon I was dressed in my best pants and a fresh white shirt, clothes that still remained from the ones my father had brought from Berlin when he hoped for a son. It seemed as though he had brought enough to last this "boy" for his entire life.

As I grew older he never bought me anything new. My first-grade uniform was the only new outfit I ever had. The rest of my uniforms were hand-me-downs from my sisters who had new uniforms every year. Mama promised me that one day I would have something new too.

She now put on one of her two best dresses for the occasion and wore some lipstick, which I hadn't seen on her for a long time. Her two dresses were from the first time she had ever come to our house. Since that time, she also had gotten nothing new to wear.

We both worked happily as we prepared everything. It was quiet and peaceful because my sisters were away.

My two girlfriends arrived first, and then a little later eight boys arrived.

Everyone was dressed in their best, and some of them brought me flowers. I thought to myself how sad it was that we wouldn't be able to keep the flowers after my guests left. They were all overcome with shyness, and it was a bit strange to see this usually rambunctious bunch of boys and girls suddenly being so polite and quiet.

Mama asked them all to the table and poured everyone lemonade for a toast. In the meantime, they helped themselves to salad. As she stood up to make a speech about me, my father walked in.

I had never seen him so pale. His lips were trembling and turning blue. I knew immediately what I was in for; I just hoped he wouldn't strike me in front of my friends.

He stood in the middle of the room for a few seconds, then pointed to the table, then to the door, and in a deadly whisper said, "Get out!"

He didn't move. He just stood there. After a few seconds of silence, my friends got up and left, one after the other, until I was the only one at the table. He was waiting for me to leave too, but I didn't have the strength to move. I felt weak. How long it took me, I don't know, but somehow I managed to walk out too. Finally I was outside, where in the meantime Mama was organizing some kind of game for my friends, to get their attention away from the incident. I felt dizzy. I couldn't stand up anymore. Mama noticed and gave me a bench to sit down on.

That was the last thing I remembered.

"Janna, do you recognize me?" The voice sounded far away. I had difficulty opening my eyes. My eyelids were very heavy. Finally, I opened them and saw the woman who lived next door to us. Her name was Frida Rotman, and she was a doctor.

I whispered, "Aunty Frida, it's you."

"She's back," Frida said.

I didn't know what she meant. When I got my bearings, I was lying in bed, my pillow all wet and with towels all around me. I could see the large bowl that Mama used to make dough in. There were more wet towels in the bowl. And that was how my eleventh birthday celebration ended. I had fainted outside the house. I had simply slipped off the little bench.

Mama had brought me inside and put me to bed and a little later realized that something serious had happened to me. My body was shaking violently and something white and foamy like toothpaste was coming out of my mouth. It was then that she ran for Doctor Frida next door.

During that whole time my father just kept reading his newspaper.

CHAPTER 10

Summer Camp

After my birthday trauma, my father and I ceased to speak. At the same time Mama began to worry about my health. She took me to see doctors with a strange name: neuropathologists. They asked me many questions and used a tiny hammer on my knees, which made my legs jump. I didn't know what it all meant. Sometimes they sent me outside and then talked to Mama for long periods of time.

The visits to the doctors began to bore me, but one good thing came of it: I didn't have to go to school and Mama always bought an ice cream for me at the end of every visit.

All that time, I felt unusually tired and strange things happened to me. I would walk along the street and all of a sudden hit an electrical post and bruise my forehead. Or I would sit in the classroom and my pen would fall from my hand. It always felt as though I had lost consciousness for a moment or two. Finally I overheard Mama's conversation with one of the doctors.

"Epilepsy is incurable. She will just have to learn to live with it. Nothing can be done..." It sounded scary to me, but Mama wouldn't give up.

She kept on taking me to see other doctors until one day we had an appointment with a very old medical professor, who said, "There is only one thing you can hope for. Perhaps when she starts her period the attacks may cease. If she doesn't have one for a year, there is a good chance they may never come back."

My period started when I was eleven and a half and was very painful. But that was the end of it. No attacks ever happened again. In fact, I was very lucky that the trauma happened before my period started.

One good thing my father did for me between my ninth and thirteenth year was to send me to summer camp, usually for the month of August. Every time I went, I had a good time. It was far from home, and I was happy to be there. I would spend some time in the kitchen, which felt like being at the orphanage. They liked me there because I was so quick with my work. I also got involved in all kinds of sports and was quite successful because I'd had plenty of competition with the neighbourhood boys back home.

I was good on a bicycle even though I'd never had my own. Boys always shared theirs with me because I'd become one of them. I wasn't a bad gymnast either. It was such a precise sport and taught me balance. I also liked short-distance running competitions. So, in that sense, I was superior to girls my age.

I could climb the tallest tree faster than anybody else, as I had no fear of heights. I would climb up, sit on top of the tree, and whistle with two fingers like a real boy.

When I was thirteen for some reason I was put in a group of fifteen- and sixteen-year-olds. The girls in this group weren't part of my circle because they had no interest in sports. They were more interested in the evening dance, and every day before going dancing they would spend a long time making themselves beautiful.

One day I watched the whole group of them getting ready to go out. I sat there mesmerized by the process.

It was so interesting to see them change their hair from straight to curly. They used aluminum tubes with aluminum sticks tightened by elastic, wrapping them around with thin pieces of wet hair. I counted fifty rollers on one girl, which made her head look like a giant ball.

While their hair was drying, they would do all kinds of things to their faces. They looked very serious, while they did this. It was very quiet in the room because everyone had to concentrate.

I sat there in my wrinkled shirt and my three-quarter-length pants, which I'd had cut because it had been so hot, and watched them, completely fascinated.

Finally their faces were finished and their clothes for the evening selected. They had nothing more to do except wait for their hair to dry, and they began to talk. They talked about the boys, about the night before, about who'd danced with whom, and who wanted to dance with whom.

Suddenly one girl turned her attention to me. They called me "Jandi." She said, "Hey you! Jandi! I'm talking to you! How come you look like shit? Why? Don't you want to look nice?"

"I don't know how," I said. "Let me fix you."

"Why?"

"Look at you! You look like hell! In fact, you don't even look like a girl."

"I know. But I was supposed to be a boy."

The girl kept after me. "Listen, let me show you something."

I didn't know what to say anymore, and before I could, she was already working on me. She put my head in the tub and washed my hair, or whatever it was that was supposed to be hair. The water was cold, and it shocked me for a moment. She soaped it and washed it and soaped it again and washed it again. After drying it with a rough towel I was a little dizzy because she treated my head as though it were a cooking pot.

"The first thing is," she said. "Your hair has to be clean."

Then she put in a few of the aluminum curlers. I didn't have much hair, so it was finished fast: one, two, three.

After that, a few of the others got involved in working on my face, while the rest of them gave all kinds of advice and lent their own makeup. It was very difficult to keep my eyelids open while they worked on them. I sat like a dummy as they went on and on with their brushes and fingers, enjoying themselves.

By the time they finished my face, my hair was dry. They took the rollers out, pulling at my few bits of hair. Then they brushed it and teased it and brushed it again, looked at the result, and then brushed again! They spent as much time working on my few strands of hair as if I had a full mop of hair. When I ran my fingers through it, it felt pleasant and very different!

Then there was a commotion about what I was going to wear. Everybody offered their clothes, and, again, nobody asked me if I liked them, they just asked each other. After some arguing, they made their decisions. They all agreed on this tiny little white skirt and a silky blouse and then a belt. The big problem was the belt because they said it was very important to make the skirt look right and the shoes were supposed to be the same colour as the belt.

"Oh! Please, let go of me already! I really don't care!"

What I really wanted was to go and wash off the makeup now that they'd had their fun. The only problem was how to get to the shower cabins without anybody seeing me looking like a clown.

But they wouldn't leave me alone. Now all twenty-five girls grouped around me and started to praise each other for what they had done, wondering aloud what could be done differently. Now I was being taken apart. My hair. My eyelids.

They talked so much about my eyelids! It was as though they were the most important area of my face and I hadn't even known I had them before this! Then came my skin, my nose, my neck, even my breasts and the rest of me. It seemed to me that I should be wearing at least two or three different outfits at the same time.

Finally, somebody mentioned a mirror. Now they started to look for one that was full-length because we only had a small one. One of the girls ran to the counselor's room and came back with a long mirror and put it in front of me.

And there I sat, looking at someone who looked absolutely stunning. There was silence in the room. I really couldn't understand why, so I turned around and saw all twenty-five girls and two of our counselors who came to check on what was going on. All of them were looking at me with different expressions on their faces and nobody was laughing. Then I turned to the mirror again and realized that I was looking at myself.

From that moment, everything changed in me—my posture, my movements, my voice, and even my thoughts. I knew I could not go back to being a tomboy, nor did I want to.

That was all behind me.

CHAPTER 11

My Sister's Coat

Sema ended up becoming a university student studying transport engineering. I think the reason she chose that field was because once a year, all the students within that program were allowed to travel by train to any location within the Soviet Union for free.

At that point, Sema was number one with my father. She knew that while Tania had been in that position my father had showered her with all kinds of material benefits. Sema had kept her neutral position, and only once in a while would she side with Father and Tania, but those were exceptions. Normally she would just sit there and read during the stormy sessions. She was more or less on peaceful terms with Mama, who was hoping that in the future, with Tania married, life would be better.

Tania was married at eighteen and moved to Nikolaev near Odessa. Her husband was our Baba's sister's son, which made him a third cousin. He was a ship's engineer and worked in a huge shipbuilding plant. Of course, Father blamed Mama for Tania's early marriage, claiming that the poor girl wanted to be out of the house. He gave a big wedding for her, to which Mama and I were not invited.

Shortly after that, Sema realized the only way to win Father's pocket was to become "Polia's victim." It seemed the war was to continue. She made her choice quickly, and all of a sudden Polia did everything wrong and all the good things had been forgotten.

Now she accused Mama of exploiting her for domestic purposes when Sema had more important things to do. The collisions grew bigger and louder while Sema slowly but surely pursued her plan of action. She would run out of the house when she had an argument with Mama and go right to Father's workplace, crying and telling him all kinds of bad things about "Polia, the witch."

Father comforted her. "See? I told you! She wants to get rid of *you* now. I'll show her!"

And, of course, he would come home in a fury. Sema got results right away by getting money for all her needs. She had an appetite for fine things, especially clothes, and within a short time she had her own beautiful redwood dresser full of sweaters, silk lingerie, and elegant high-heeled shoes.

She was very neat and tidy with her own things. Everything was nicely folded, arranged by colour, and she kept her dresser locked at all times. She had luxurious leather and fur coats, good winter boots, and so on. These things never bothered me until she had a coat custom made for spring and fall. She talked about it to her friends all the time while it was being sewn. In my imagination, this coat was magnificent. I couldn't wait to see it. Finally it was ready, and she brought it home.

Indeed, it was magnificent. It was made of cashmere. The colour was off-white with a touch of coffee. She described it as "café au lait." The style was also very elegant, especially the collar and sleeves. The shoulders were padded and the sleeves were very wide at the shoulder, gradually narrowing down to the perfect fit at the wrist. The collar was large and shaped softly around the neck, fastened in front with an unusual button made of pearl and natural bone, like a brooch. At the back there were three soft folds coming out from underneath the collar.

The coat was beautiful. I was dying to try it on just once, but Sema, of course, made sure I would not. It was always locked up.

By the time the coat was ready, spring was in full bloom and it was too warm to wear it.

That year after her exams, Sema was going to Sochi on the Black Sea. Her train was scheduled for eight in the evening. Summer evenings in Moscow were quite cool, even chilly, up until the end of June, which was the month she was going away. Naturally, she decided to wear her coat on the way to the railway station, which was in one of the central parts of Moscow. She put on her sweetest smile and asked me to go with her to the station for the obvious reason that I could then take her coat back home.

She made me swear that I would hand it over to Father who had the key to her dresser where she kept all her coats and other things. I agreed. After all, this would be my only opportunity to try it on and actually wear it on the way home. I was very excited and looked forward to this chance.

At last the day arrived—and, of course, part of the deal was that I carry her suitcase. I didn't mind that at all. She was very pleasant to me on the way there and even kissed me before she stepped on the train. I almost felt like crying, but it was only for the moment.

As soon as the train started to move, I thought of putting on the coat and how everybody would look at me the way they looked at Sema when she wore it. The train seemed to take forever while everybody waved to one another, blowing kisses. Finally it was gone!

I carefully unfolded the coat and looked at it for some time, trying to visualise how it would look on me. I knew I wouldn't have a chance to see myself in a mirror, as there were none in the railway station washrooms. Even if there were, I wouldn't put on Sema's coat there because of the stench in there.

The coat was light and cozy, and it instantly made me feel like a million dollars! It was too big for me, but thank goodness it wasn't too long. I was a little taller than Sema, so I could wrap it and hold it with one hand so it would appear to fit me. Oh God! It felt great! I thought about how wonderful it was to wear beautiful clothes, and this was my one opportunity to show it off.

But how could I go home straight away? If I did, my joy would end too quickly. I would have to hand the coat over to my father as soon as I arrived and that would be the end of it. Why not go some place where I could walk along and enjoy it just for a little longer? Anyway, my father would be asleep by the time I got home. It was already eight thirty and he usually went to bed at nine. This would be my only chance!

I went to the recreation park called "Sokolniki" in central Moscow. Going by subway convinced me more and more that I had made the right decision. Not one person passed me without looking at the coat. Some even stopped for a second and smiled at me, and I smiled back. In Russia, people always noticed what you were wearing.

When I entered the park I felt even better because everybody was there to just enjoy the evening, strolling and looking at one another. So I walked along feeling exhilarated. Soon I heard music—dance music. I walked toward the sound, and it got louder and louder, first a waltz and then a tango. I saw that the music was coming from a dance veranda, and without the slightest hesitation I bought a ticket and went in. I felt so high, as though nothing could stop me!

I waited until the dance stopped to make an entrance, and I did. Somehow I felt more comfortable entering from the left side of the place. Perhaps it was because I was left-handed—although I actually wrote with my right hand. My left was my strong side in everything other than writing. And I had to feel strength walking into this unfamiliar place by myself.

I stationed myself in a spot where I could watch everybody dancing—this time a beautiful tango. Quite a few couples were dancing, and a few men were asking girls next to them to dance. All of a sudden, I noticed this handsome man walking across the dance floor. He seemed to know where he was going. As I watched him, I looked around and there was group of girls next to me whispering to each other with some of them looking at him. I felt a touch on my elbow. It seemed to mean that this handsome man was inviting me to dance!

I followed him, and we started to move. Yes, that's what we did, we moved. I tried to stay as far from his body as possible, so I wouldn't touch this stranger. He was wearing a soft beige coat and a beige hat. I didn't look at his face.

After the dance ended, they played a tango again. The same thing happened. He walked towards me and I knew he was coming to invite me. So, we began to move again. He didn't say a word, and I didn't speak either. The next dance was a waltz, and again he came up to me. By now I was even more afraid to look at his face. I just kept trying to concentrate on the steps. Actually, I simply followed what he was doing, which wasn't that easy. His moves were unpredictable. It took a lot of concentration, but I didn't even once step on his feet.

The next dance, the emcee announced, was the last dance: "And now, it's the last dance of the evening, and it's our famous 'Moscow evenings.'"

Yes, indeed, it was wonderful. The song went, "We will never forget you. Those Moscow evenings…" and then the words went on about "a boat moving slowly, hardly moving on those quiet evenings." It was very romantic. I saw a few couples kissing each other, and I couldn't believe my eyes at the sight.

During the dance my dance partner asked me where I lived, and I told him.

He said, "Can I escort you home?"

I said okay.

After the last dance we made our way towards the exit. Everyone, perhaps three hundred people, were moving towards the exit at the same time. We were practically on top of each other. We moved so slowly, and I was afraid my sister's coat would get wrinkled. Finally, we were out of there and walking towards the subway.

On the train we sat next to each other and hardly spoke a word. At my station I got up, and he got up with me. We had to cross the railway bridge, and as we went up the stairs he put his arm around my shoulders. I got really scared. What if this guy was after my sister's coat? What could I do? She would kill me! We walked through the entire long bridge and then down the stairway. There were no big buildings on that side of the bridge, only houses. It was very dark with hardly any lights.

I thought to myself, "That's it. He is going to stop any minute and take my sister's coat from me!" Of course, I wasn't going to be so stupid as to give it up just like that. I would fight. I'd kick him right between his legs like I had with my father that time. What if he hit me on the head? He might even have a knife! How could I know? I was saying goodbye to my life.

One thing I knew: It would be better to die fighting for the coat than go home without it. I thought of stopping somewhere close by the bridge and saying, "This is my house." While all these thoughts went through my mind, we moved at a faster and faster pace. The closer we got to my house the more quickly we walked. By now he had taken his hand from my shoulder, so I could have run, but I didn't. At last, I was just a few steps from my house!

"What's your name?" he asked.

"Janna."

"I am Valentin, but you can call me Valia. Would you like us to meet next Saturday?"

I said yes without hesitation. All I wanted was for this strange evening to end and get my sister's coat back safely. He told me where and what time on Saturday, and I said yes to everything. I just wanted to get away.

Then he asked me, "Would you like me to sing you a song?"

I said, "Okay," and thought, "What a strange guy! Well, at least he isn't attacking me. Let him sing!"

His voice was very touching, and the lyrics were about the snow falling slowly on the rooftops, making them look like white sheets. When he finished singing, he said goodnight, and I slowly opened my door. It was dark, and I didn't turn on the lights. I just got undressed and went right to bed.

My head felt dizzy. I couldn't fall asleep. I lay there with my eyes wide open and counted the days until Saturday.

CHAPTER 12

Enough! I'm Leaving

At this point, life at home continued as it had been, with my father and I hating each other. I could never understand why he had wanted a boy so much. He wouldn't have done things with him anyway. After all, he had eight brothers and he wasn't close to them. He saw them when they got together at their mother's place once in a while, but when she died at seventy-two, four years after I came from the orphanage, they hardly got together.

Mama, of course, was not invited to any of the family gatherings. After "the milk episode" she was no longer welcome.

Every one of my father's brothers thought they had a great sense of humor. They liked telling jokes, most of them about Jews and Gentiles and their different mentalities. Their attitude seemed to split the world into two colours, black and white. There were the good ones and there were the bad ones. I couldn't understand it. I thought if they were so good, how was it that when my father went to war leaving my mother alone with three small children, none of them helped her? After all, most of them, except Uncle Uri who didn't have children, had stayed in Moscow during the war and nothing happened to their families. These questions bothered me.

Before my father married my stepmother, I never saw any of them, but afterwards every last one of them made a point of criticizing her. Listening to my father's complaints, none of them ever said, "Look, Boris, you are not the easiest person to live with. This woman is trying her best to look after you and your three daughters. You should thank God that you're so lucky enough to have found a woman to put up with this whole package!"

No, no one ever said anything to him. They just sat and listened to my father's stories. It made them feel sorry for him as he went on about this incredible monster of a woman, Polia. Naturally I hated these lies and distortions.

On the other hand, my uncles were good fathers and husbands. They were close to their children too and were all good providers, living comfortable lives. Their children had everything they needed. All of them had university educations and stayed at home until they married.

In the end, I came to the conclusion that my father's obsession with having a son was simply his male ego. He was the kind of man who couldn't feel like a real man unless he produced a boy. I also think he had a Napoleon complex. He wasn't a tall man nor was he handsome, and men like him had a need to have power. They liked their women to be tall, and my birth mother was apparently much taller than he was.

To describe my father's image is a difficult task for me because of the pain he caused me in my life. In spite of trying for years to forget him completely, his cruelty has stayed in my mind. Many things I did in my life I did to prove to him that I wasn't a "good for nothing."

I had this problem even after his death. I simply couldn't let go—until one day the penny dropped. After that moment, whatever I worked hard to achieve was for me, not for my father, and this realization happened on my fortieth birthday.

Since that terrible eleventh birthday of mine, I had made up my mind that I was going to celebrate every one of my birthdays. I never looked to anybody else to do it. I was going to do it all myself. I celebrated it elaborately, whether I could afford it or not. I always prepared a lot of food and invited as many people as possible.

So, that day of my fortieth birthday, while I was preparing for my party, a poem formed in my head. At one time I had written poetry, but it had never been about my father. This time it came to me in a matter of seconds. It was so clear and complete that I dropped everything and quickly wrote it down, not even washing my hands so there were grease stains left on the sheet of paper. It was about this angry little man who was locked in his own narrow world and who never knew how to be happy. The poor man wasted his life by being miserable and angry with everybody. He never really knew me, I wrote, and I should forgive him and let the poor bastard rest in peace.

Amazingly, the minute I read the poem to myself, I suddenly felt free from this burden I had carried so many years, and it made me feel peaceful. From that time on, my birthday celebration wasn't as important to me any more.

To describe my father: He was short and bald with small bloodshot blue eyes and lips that were rather bluish as well. I never saw him smile at home—although I sometimes saw him smile at attractive women, and then his whole face changed. He wore glasses and read nothing but the paper *Pravda*.

It was one of two newspapers in the USSR during those years of Soviet dictatorship. Both were the main sources of political propaganda. Most of the articles praised the Communist Party achievements and their plans for even greater strides in the world. Only Communists knew it all and how to do things right. They went on building this image of a perfect society that no country in the world had ever achieved and other such nonsense.

My father believed everything that was written in *Pravda*. He read it carefully, taking in every word. After Stalin's death when Khrushchev revealed Stalin's wrongdoing to the Soviet people, many Soviet citizens stopped believing in the printed word; they were looking for outside publications. Although they weren't easily obtained, a lot of people found ways to get them. My father ignored it all and continued to believe in the Soviet regime.

After the war, he had a hearing problem but wouldn't admit it. I never understood how it worked because although we had to repeat things to him to hear, how was it he could hear Mama and me whisper? We were constantly in trouble over this, and he would look at us from underneath his glasses with such anger and hatred that we wished we were invisible.

He was always very neat and tidy and wore nothing but starched white shirts and a tie. Of course Mama looked after all that and ironed his shirts religiously. He wore long underwear year round and before he went to bed, he neatly folded his trousers, making sure they would be tidy in the morning. He didn't like to change his trousers. He only had two pairs, and they were very shiny in the back because of wearing them for years.

Speaking of his trousers brings to mind an episode that I'm a bit ashamed to admit. It has to do with stealing money from my father when I was about ten. Mama and I never had a penny of our own. And I had an absolutely obsessive desire to have my own ball to play with. I asked my father if he would buy me one, but he refused, saying I didn't deserve to have one. So I thought up all kinds of ways to earn the money. I made a couple of deals with my sisters, like washing dishes or ironing clothes for them, which they paid me for, and bit by bit I collected enough money to buy a ball for myself.

I was full of anticipation when I got up that day and went to the bridge where there were a few of stores on the either side. Unfortunately, they didn't have the ball I wanted at the store on one side of the bridge, so I went over to the other side. The bridge was built over a large railway, and as I went up the stairs I felt a little weak and somewhat dizzy, but of course that didn't stop me. My money was in my left hand, and I held it tightly as I walked slowly up the open stairway from where you could see the railway tracks and trains below. It was scary to look down, and as I did, I lost my balance and tripped. All of my money scattered onto the tracks below!

The next thing I knew, I was sick in bed and going in and out of sleep. This big blue and red ball with silver stripes bounced back and forth over my poor aching head, but every time I opened my eyes the room was in darkness and there was no ball to be seen.

When I got better, I wept about my lost money. I couldn't think of any way of replacing it, and I wanted a ball more than ever. So I decided to somehow take the money from my father's trousers. I knew he had a lot of change in his pockets because every time he folded his pants I heard the sound of coins jingling. I didn't have the guts to do it while he was asleep because I was afraid he might wake up and catch me.

I decided to sit on the chair where his trousers were folded and talk with him while he was reading in bed. With my hands behind my back I tried searching, but every time I got hold of his pockets he looked over at me as though he knew I was up to something, and so I would stop. After a while, I continued the search but I had to take my time—after all, I couldn't get all the money in one shot. I also couldn't sit down and be with him every evening because we weren't exactly on friendly terms. It took me at least three attempts before I got enough money together to buy myself the ball, but I even had enough left over for an ice cream!

My father never found out that the money was missing. Every time he came back from work I expected him to say something, but he never did. My ball was the only thing in the world that was worth the risk of stealing from his pockets!

Since there was no love or peace in my family, thoughts of finding ways to leave my father's house become more and more constant. This deep longing had started when I was eleven. But where would I go? The night my father was about to hit Mama with a chair and we ran to Aunt Luba's house, Mama cried all night.

Aunt Luba said to her, "Look, Polia. Nothing is going to change in your life unless you leave him. I'm prepared to find a room for you and Janna and pay the rent so the two of you will have a roof over your heads."

"Oh! How can I do it?" Mama cried. "I don't have a job and we won't be able to support ourselves. Janna is too young to work. She still has to go to school." She sighed. "Unfortunately, I have to go on living with this monster and can only hope that when Sema gets married things will ease up."

How many years would that be? I knew I'd end up sick as a dog, taking Mama's side all the time and that there'd be no end to it. Sema was in no hurry to get married. She had all the money she could ever want. Her life was a luxurious one with all kinds of things coming to her from my father.

Mama really had no idea how to end the situation. She had the wrong approach. She tried to justify every argument instead of cutting off her services, such as cleaning, cooking, and catering to all of their needs. She never had the strength to do anything like that. She just continued to slave for my father, but the more she tried to please him, the more he abused her.

On the other hand, I would not sell myself to my father for his money, and I couldn't see myself doing what Sema did. I begged Mama to leave my father's house, but she couldn't do it.

Finally, at the age of fourteen, after my graduation from seventh grade, I said to myself, "That's enough. I'm leaving!"

CHAPTER 13

Moscow Meat Plant

But leaving was easier said than done. I needed a job, and I began to look for one.

According to the Soviet educational system, one had a choice: either continue until grade ten for a high school diploma (allowing one to enter university) or get a seventh-grade certificate with which one could be accepted into trade schools called technicums.

I couldn't afford the ten years of high school education. I had to get training on the job because I determined to move out of the house and start life on my own. I planned to continue my education while I was working and was confident that eventually I would complete university. I felt sure that one day my father would know that I had made it.

There was one problem. In the Soviet Union, no one could get a job without a passport, and you had to be sixteen to get a passport. I prayed for a miracle. I was quite tall, and I looked mature for my age. When I asked for a job, they always said, "No problem. Come in tomorrow morning with your passport, and you can start."

Since I didn't have a passport, I continued my search. To stay another two years at my father's house was out of the question, so I went looking every morning. Jobs were never advertised in Soviet newspapers. You had to resort to legwork or have connections. After a month my search extended further and further away until one day I found myself staring up at this huge meat plant.

I found the place by the smell of it—or rather by the stench! As the bus approached, the smell became almost unbearable. I had to cover my nose, and I felt quite nauseated.

Little did I know that not only would I get used to the smell but I would get used to seeing a lot worse: cows and pigs killed and skinned in front of my eyes, plus many other gory sights.

The sign above the front gates said Miaso Kombinat Imeni Mikoiana ("Mikoyan Meat Plant "). I asked the guards how I could get to the personnel department.

"Inside the plant," they said, "but you'll need a pass. You'll get that without any problem once you tell them you're looking for a job." As I went through the gates, I felt faint not only because of the smell but because of both exhaustion as well as excitement. My determination to get a job took over, however, and I managed to keep on going.

Inside, the plant looked like a small town. There were several huge trucks driving around, some carrying livestock, others loaded with bones or frozen animal parts. The drivers were yelling at each other and using the foulest language I had ever heard. Even my father didn't use such words. Later on I had to use them myself because there it was the accepted language; otherwise, how could I fit in?

The traffic was very heavy, and there were hundreds of people walking about, but they looked quite different from people on the outside. I noticed that the majority of these pedestrians were women. They wore white uniforms covered with horrible bloodstains. Many of them had on rubber aprons with dry pieces of ground meat and bits of natural casings. On their heads they wore starched cotton kosinkas (kerchiefs) tied in a specific way with their foreheads covered as well. The kosinkas were the only part of their uniforms that looked clean. Their shoes were made of rough leather with wooden soles. They were slip-on clogs so that when people walked, they made a thumping sound.

I was in a different world, indeed.

It took me at least an hour to find personnel. I walked on and on and walked through long corridors with no signs or directions and was amazed how gigantic the plant was.

Nobody asked for my passport in personnel. I thought they might have forgotten, but then they asked me to fill out a very simple application form. All they wanted to know was my name, first and last, and what department I was interested in. I had no idea. I knew I didn't want to kill any animals but thought I wouldn't mind making sausages, so I put that down, and then they asked if I needed accommodation or if I would be living at home.

This was the best question of all. They weren't even interested in my age, and that suited me fine. They also wanted to know what sex I was. That was funny! I told them I was a girl. After I filled out the entire application, they told me to come back on September 1 with my suitcase. And that was that.

I had no idea what was going to happen on that date, and I didn't care. I just knew with certainty that I would be out of the house and starting my new life. I would be on my own—where nobody could scream at me, nobody could tell me I didn't deserve a crust of bread. I would earn what I needed and wanted myself from then on. I felt so high. I even bought myself two ice creams on the way back!

In the meantime, I had almost two more months to wait and that Saturday I was going on my first date.

The whole week was full of excitement. First, my sister's coat, then there was Valentin, who instead of attacking me simply sang me a song, which had turned my heart upside down. Then I actually got the job, and, not only that, I was to be given a place to live! The world seemed full of surprises.

CHAPTER 14

My First Date

On Saturday I woke up at five o'clock. Mama was already working in the garden. The minute I came out she immediately found something for me to do. I was to build up the soil around the strawberry plants and then water them. She and I worked along while she sang operatic arias in her beautiful voice.

When Mama first came to our house, she had sung constantly, especially when she was ironing. Gradually, however, she sang less and less except in the mornings when she was outside where she loved nature and nature loved her. When she sang the birds sang with her.

It was a beautiful morning, and I kept remembering how in our first year together Mama had taken me to the Bolshoi Theatre to see the opera—my two older sisters hadn't been interested—and then I recalled something funny.

After the war, for some reason girls had problems keeping their hair clean. In Russia at that time there were no shampoos or conditioners. There was only one kind of soap: large, rough, greyish-brown bars that smelled foul and that weren't soapy. The water had something to do with it too. It was never warm enough, and as a result we were all infested with lice from time to time. It caused me acute embarrassment.

When I was younger Mama treated my hair with kerosene, which helped, but after I was ten I was too bashful to ask her to do it for me and tried to take care of it by myself.

One night I woke up with a terrible itch in my ear canal. I scratched and scratched, but it wouldn't go away. Somehow, I managed to fall asleep eventually and found I had no problem during the day. The next evening, as soon as I began to fall asleep, it happened again. It felt as though something was crawling deep in my ear canal. I knew it must be a bug, but how had it gotten in there? I scratched until it hurt, digging my finger as far inside as I could until sleep took over.

One day that week, Mama took me to the Bolshoi Theatre, and it started again during the performance. I was in agony and anxiously waited for the intermission. I knew it would stop then, and it did.

During the final intermission, I went to the washroom. I rolled up a tiny stick from a page of my theatre program and pushed it deep inside until it really hurt. I didn't care; I was determined to kill the bitch! I pushed it in until I saw blood on the piece of paper. It felt like my ear canal had been split in half. I had to stop my self-surgery because the bell was ringing, indicating the end of intermission. Before the doors closed, I realized I hadn't even gone to the bathroom, but that was the least of my problems. I knew I could survive for another forty-five minutes.

When I got back and the play started, all I could think of was whether or not the thing might start moving again. I waited and waited, but nothing happened, and that night, for the first time in days, I fell asleep peacefully and slept the whole night through!

I realized I could have damaged my hearing, but that morning in the garden with Mama, as I thought of the incident, I started to laugh. Mama asked me what I was laughing about and I told her.

Now both she and I were laughing until tears ran down our faces. She kept trying to tell me something, but I couldn't stop laughing. Finally she said, "You should have told me so we could have done the coal oil treatment for you and that louse would have been dead in five minutes!"

The glorious morning was turning into a most exciting day: the day of my first date. I started to prepare early. First, I washed myself until my skin was bright pink, and I rinsed and rinsed my hair until it squeaked, which felt luxurious. Then I dried it in the sun with my fingers, so that it turned silky and wavy. To my surprise, I seemed to have nice hair! Then came my face, which by now I had almost learned to accept as not that bad. After all, large eyes and full lips were not the worst things one could be born with. As for my large ears, they didn't seem to look as prominent anymore. Nobody ever saw them anyway because they were covered by my hair.

I didn't have a problem selecting an outfit for this special evening since I only had one. Mama had managed to get a blouse and skirt from her niece who had outgrown it, and it was an outfit I adored. The blouse had been made to order by a German dressmaker. I called the style "Natasha Rostova" after my heroine from *War and Peace* by Tolstoy. The blouse had eighteen tiny buttons from the collar down, and the colour was dusty blue. Both pieces fit me perfectly.

I was concerned about my bust, and my bottom stuck out a little too much for my liking, but Mama said there was nothing we could do about it. Anyway, she thought I was too skinny for my height.

My shoes! My first high-heel shoes! I had gotten them from Sema in exchange for two months of dishwashing and ironing. When I finally got them, I practiced walking in them for a whole week, until I knew how to hold myself properly. By six o'clock I was supposed to be at the bottom of the bridge to meet Valentin. Mama said a girl should never be exactly on time for a date, but the boy should wait a little. It was five o'clock when I finished getting ready and I had to wait another whole hour.

The time simply stopped then. The watch hand would not move. I looked at it and looked at it and finally it had moved five minutes. I started to count to sixty to get the feeling of how long one minute was. Endless! What a torture! Did every girl have to suffer like this? I was beginning to regret I wasn't a boy. Then I wouldn't care who arrived first for a date.

I always used to run to the bridge and it would take me five minutes. Today I couldn't run—not on my first date. I had to walk slowly on my high heels, otherwise everyone would laugh at me and I didn't want that. So I took my time walking slowly, trying to look self-assured.

When I could see the bridge I started to look for him. I was afraid I wouldn't recognize him or that he wouldn't recognize me. After all, I looked quite different now without my sister's coat, and I really didn't remember his face. All I could remember was his voice. Then I saw him with some flowers! I didn't know the man was supposed to bring flowers on a date. Never mind, I was learning.

I stopped walking about ten steps before reaching the bridge and had to take a breath. I was much too excited. The second I stopped, he came towards me with a smile and said hello.

He was a different person than I remembered. He was much taller, had light brown almost blondish hair, and had small, bright and smiling brown eyes. He had quite a large nose and small lips, but the thing I liked most about him was his neck. It was quite big, and I noticed it was very pink as though he had really scrubbed himself. He was wearing a dark brown suit and a white shirt and tie and smelled of nice cologne. When he stretched out his arm to give me the flowers I noticed he had very large hands with hair sticking out from under his sleeve.

I said hello back, and he gave me the flowers.

"Thank you," I said we began to walk along. I didn't ask any questions like How are you? Where are we going? None of that. All I knew was that I liked being next to him.

After a while, he said, "We're going to a movie, okay?"

The theatre was full when we arrived, and we took a couple of seats in the last row. It was dark, so he held my hand as we approached them, and once we sat down he didn't let go. I didn't mind at all. Next thing I knew, I felt him put his face very close to mine and I could smell his delicious cologne. I stopped breathing. I pretended I was watching the movie, but in reality, I had no idea what was happening on the screen.

I felt dizzy and very warm and from time to time hot waves kept washing over my entire body. I was afraid he would think I had a fever and would decide to take me home, but he did no such thing. He simply watched the movie. I knew this because his eyelashes kept brushing my cheek from time to time. I closed my own eyes, praying the movie would last forever.

A few times I heard bursts of laughter, but I didn't know what they were laughing at. I was too concerned with the sound of my heartbeat. I covered my heart with my hand so the sound wouldn't be so noticeable.

My right hand was beginning to feel damp from the heat. I thought if he noticed, he'd probably feel uncomfortable, so I very carefully freed my right one and at the same time I had my left hand ready to replace my right so he wouldn't even be aware of the difference. For the moment it was better.

By now, I knew I had no way out. I was trapped by my own emotions, which were overwhelming. It was all very new to me, something I had to go home and think about. I also worried that if he started to discuss the movie with me afterwards, I wouldn't know what to say. I now decided to concentrate on the movie or else he would think I was too stupid for him and would never want to see me again.

I started to watch the screen, but it didn't take more than ten minutes before the sign on the screen said, "The End," and the audience began to get up and leave. It was dark for a while, but the music continued playing softly and romantically.

Finally, Valentin took his cheek away from mine. I felt a little cold on that spot, but he didn't take his hand away as he got up, so I got up with him. He stood looking at the screen, and I did too, trying to read who'd played what, who'd produced the movie, and who'd directed it and so on. Then the lights came on.

When we came out of the theatre it was dark, damp, and chilly. I started to tremble, and it became very obvious. Valentin took off his jacket, not saying anything, and put it over my shoulders. It was unbelievable! I felt his warmth, and now his scent was all around me. Oh God, what was happening? I wanted to say something, but I couldn't. He didn't say anything either. We just walked.

And walking wasn't easy either. I seemed unable to walk in a straight line! All of a sudden he stopped, took my face in his hands, and looked into my eyes for a long time without saying a word. I gazed into his eyes until it became unbearable. In that moment I felt this unbelievable sensation of closeness and touch that I had never felt before in my life. I lost my sense of reality. My heart flew out somewhere, my head seemed disconnected from my body, and I didn't exist as an entity any longer. He wouldn't release me but carried on observing me—my whole being. He took me inside himself, and I didn't hold back. I simply could not. I was his and he was mine.

I hardly remember the rest of the evening. I know we stopped kissing and then walked and then stopped again, holding each other and kissing. We stood for a long time by my house, under those huge maple trees. The skies were moving above my head, and I was moving in tune with them. I was flying somewhere.

We managed to part from each other when our magical night was turning to day. He walked away finally, whispering, "I'll see you next Saturday. Same time. Same place."

I stumbled into the house. Mama was not up yet, thank goodness! After I kicked off my high heels, I quickly washed my face and managed to get out of my blouse, opening only a few buttons. I didn't have the patience to undo all of them. This was the one time I wished Natalia Rostova hadn't come up with so many buttons in her design. The skirt wasn't a problem—only one button—and I slid my body under the blanket and just lay there.

My body felt new. It felt beautiful, so I began to touch it, inch by inch to see how he would feel touching it. I touched my waist, and I could feel his hands making me feel slender and graceful. When he touched my back, I was concerned that my bones stuck out too much. Mama used to say it wasn't feminine to have such a long skinny neck and bony shoulders and that I should eat more potatoes.

One thing he hadn't touched was my breasts. I knew he had an idea how they felt because he'd pressed me against his chest so hard that it hurt. It felt that way when they were growing, so painful, and I wondered why girls had to go through such pain. My period was another painful thing. I thought of what would happen if I got my period the next Saturday. I prayed it would start and end by then. My breasts would be sore too, as always before my period. God help me!

Lying there, I had so many different thoughts. I didn't notice how light it was in the room. Thank goodness Sema was away and I had the bed all to myself. I knew, in a few minutes, Mama would open the windows and sing her usual wake-up song, since it was only she and I.

She'd sing, *"Vstavai, Vstavai druzhok! S posteli na gorshok! Vtsavai, Vstavai! Partochki hadevai!"* ("Get up, get up, my little friend! Get up from your bed and go right to the chamber pot! Get up! Get up! And put your panties on your butt!") Before her morning song I was still in a very blissful state of mind. I was going to make sure nobody knew about it. This would be my own secret. By now, I realized my face was burning and my lips were hurting; they felt much fuller than usual. What if it was noticeable? But I really didn't mind the burning and the pain. They were kind of sweet. I hoped it would feel like this until the next Saturday. Seven days was a long time and perhaps the swelling would go away by then.

CHAPTER 15

Is It Over?

During this time my whole life was Saturdays! I'd count every minute, every hour. I kept myself very busy during the week, helping Mama at home and in the garden. I'd go to the stadium Lokomotiv, where I could go on my favourite short runs, ride somebody's bicycle, or use the parallel bars to work out until I couldn't take it any more. Afterwards, I would fall asleep, dead tired.

But no sooner would I fall asleep than I'd be awakened by some kind of wave, bringing me back to my new reality. The excitement of touching and kissing made my heart pound under the dark skies and stars.

Until I met Valentin, nobody had ever hugged me or kissed me in my entire life. No one. Not even Mama.

As summer went on, the nights became warmer but shorter. Valentin and I spent our dates walking through parks holding hands and noticing no one and nothing. We always ended by my house under the trees, where we said goodnight to each other for hours and hours. We hardly spoke. Our hearts were overflowing with emotions. We couldn't bring ourselves down from those heights into real life. We were above all of that.

I very quickly realized that Valentin was a fully developed man. He was already in his second year of university, studying space aviation. He was twenty-one years old and had been shaving for years. He had hairy arms and chest, but the main thing I noticed after a few passionate explosions was something hard touching me from time to time.

I was afraid to ask him what it was, and there was no way I could ask Mama. There were no books to be found in Russia about such things either. I began to study some of the young men in the stadium, and I found nothing. All of them wore regular baggy tracksuits or shorts. Then I decided to talk to some girls about this. Some of them had brothers. Finally I got an answer.

It so happened that when a boy was growing, his penis was growing too. Then when he touched a girl he liked, his penis got hard and became erect. I also learned that if the penis remained like that for a long time and nothing happened, it was very painful. But what ought to happen? Men had to make love to release the pressure so the penis could go back to normal again.

Once I found this out, it scared the hell out of me because I knew something else very well. A girl was not allowed to make love until she was married. The girl had to be a virgin. What could I do? I decided that only answer was to not allow him to touch me, so he wouldn't suffer.

The next Saturday when we met, the first couple of hours were okay. We walked along holding hands and as usual quietly enjoyed this. The hard part began when we got to the park and were walking along the riverside. It was beautiful. It was almost the middle of August by then, and the leaves had just started to turn their colours, with touches of orange and yellow here and there. The view was magnificent. The river flowed quietly, and it looked like a big mirror, reflecting the trees and lights. From time to time a bird would sing out a short, sweet tune. It felt so peaceful I wished it could continue forever.

Suddenly Valentin stopped, and I stopped too. He was facing me with this very dangerous look, and I knew what it was going to lead to. What should I do? On one hand I knew it wasn't good to let him hold me and kiss me, but on the other hand, I knew it would be impossible not to allow him to do it. I couldn't stand the temptation! I decided I'd let him go on as usual and later I'd tell him that I knew about his agony and let him decide what to do. Maybe he'd stop seeing me, but I didn't think it was fair for him to suffer such a pain any longer. Perhaps he'd find someone else who was older and ready to marry.

Oh my God! Those kisses that seemed to go on forever! They made my heart feel ready to explode and my body turn into fire! Those waves that came and went made me feel dizzy until it was impossible to go on—until after a short while when I'd want it again and again! Then we would return to my front door and he would say, "Goodnight. See you next Saturday," and I was right back to the beginning of the cycle all over again. Oh, the unbelievable sweetness and excitement! It was crazy.

I wanted to say something, but I couldn't. I didn't want to spoil this miracle. I kept trying not to let my body lean in too close to his so his penis would barely touch me. It felt awkward because he was trying to do the opposite! Finally I had to give up, and immediately I felt this hard part of him again.

In the end I said, "Valia! I don't want you to go through such pain. Maybe you shouldn't touch me."

He whispered, "It's okay," and kept on touching me. Finally we parted.

As usual, I couldn't fall asleep. I was up all night until Mama asked me to get up and fetch the water for cooking. It was Sunday. My father stayed in bed until ten o'clock while Mama and I prepared a huge breakfast of mashed potatoes and herring with lots of onions, cheese blintzes, and tea. I was her constant helper, although by then we were just a family of four with Tania married and no longer living at home.

During the summer we didn't use the stove. We used a kerosene burner and a small electric element, so it took us longer to prepare meals. My job was to bring the water, peel the potatoes, clean the herring, and cut the onions. In the meantime, Mama would prepare butter and cottage cheese for the blintzes while I watched the crepes and made sure to flip them onto the wooden board as soon as they were firm enough, and then she would fold the stuffing into the crepes. It was an art, and Mama taught me how to do them step by step.

When we were finished, we would go to work on the garden. There was a lot to do. We dug potatoes and picked the ripe tomatoes and cucumbers and strawberries and raspberries. Afterwards, we pulled weeds and the grass growing between the potatoes and strawberries and then watered the tomatoes and other vegetables. The potatoes we wouldn't water until after sunset.

Mama loved her gardening, but for me it was a duty. It was too hard for Mama to handle alone.

Every Sunday we had to get up at five o'clock and work until Father got up. Sema didn't get out of bed until ten thirty or so either. Everything had to be ready by the time Father was up. He would wash, get dressed, and sit at the garden table under two huge trees and read his newspaper from A to Z.

I never saw my father in casual clothes, even on Sundays. He wore trousers and a blue shirt instead of white but no tie. It was as casual as he ever got. He looked slightly more peaceful on Sunday mornings, but God forbid something didn't go his way or he'd pick a fight. It could be a mild one, and I would beg Mama not to react—which didn't help much, as Father would then pick on me saying it was all my fault for supporting her behavior. I knew better not to answer, so the fight would die.

We served breakfast on the patio table with a freshly ironed white linen tablecloth and the fine china. Everything looked beautiful, but not a word was spoken at the table. Mama almost never sat with us. She would keep running back and forth bringing or taking away things, while my father would gaze at her with contempt.

Sema always stayed at the table longer than I in order to ask him for money to buy something she needed. When he'd finished eating and I had cleared everything away, she would start. Father would ask her why she needed this or that. She would give him such a story that it sounded as if her life would be impossible without it.

In the end of course, Father would give her the money, and the minute she got it, she would leave the table, make herself pretty, and be on her way to visit someone. Father would then throw a pillow on the folding bed and read until he fell asleep, his face covered by his newspaper, where he'd remain for hours.

During his nap he snored loudly. In the house, his snoring would often wake us up in the middle of the night. It sounded like the walls were caving in, but no matter how disturbing it was we were forbidden to wake him up. I did one time when I couldn't take it any longer, and I got such hell for it I thought he'd kill me! After that no one said a word.

But when he slept outside, it didn't bother us as much because we were free to move around and we weren't so aware of it. No doubt about it, my father was a very odd human being. I even wondered at times if he were human. He never did anything that was positive or friendly in all the time that I knew him! There was only one episode where he showed an emotional side. It had to do with a dog and cat.

One day my father brought a full-grown German shepherd home. "This dog is for security!" he said.

We called the dog Stanley. He was very friendly, never barked, and I trained him to give me his left paw to say hello. I was around nine years old at the time and was very happy to have a friend.

A couple of months later someone gave us a cat, and my father agreed to keep it because we had mice in the house. We never thought about the cat's gender, and we called him Basil. We found out, however, that Basil was a female, as the cat gave birth one day to a litter of kittens! At the same time, Stanley had puppies. We were shocked to find that out, but we had enough space outside to house the bunch of them.

Mama made mats for them, which were soft and clean. Our Basil settled on an old quilted blanket folded in four and Stanley on a thick flannel blanket that we didn't use anymore. I went out every morning to look at the two bundles, Stanley and Basil surrounded by all their little kittens and puppies. They both looked tired because their babies were hungry all the time and sucked the milk from these poor mothers nonstop! Stanley was a more patient and responsible parent than Basil. She rarely left her puppies alone. Even when she was very tired of constantly being there with them, she would just get up and walk away for a short time to a spot where she could keep an eye on her puppies.

It was different with Basil. She got restless very quickly. She felt restricted by her role as a mother and was not willing to give all to her kittens. She would go out in the middle of the day and happily leave them alone as she went on her rounds of the neighbourhood. She visited everybody and checked everything that was important for her to check. These visits would take three or four hours, during which Stanley would begin to look worried seeing the little kittens lonely and lost without their mother's big warm body next to them. At this point, the kittens were blind and the only way for them to survive was through their mother. Stanley fretted until eventually Basil would return to fulfill her motherly duty. Only then would Stanley relax and go to sleep.

One day, at the end of the first week, Basil left her kittens for too long. It was getting dark and she still hadn't come back. I was very upset and went looking for her, but she was nowhere to be found. I didn't know what to do with the little creatures. I tried to get them to feed from a saucer, but they weren't able to. Then I tried feeding them from a spoon, but that didn't work either. They simply did not understand any of it; they needed their mother and she wasn't there for them.

Stanley watched it all and by now looked positively beside herself with worry as well. When it got really late we knew something had happened to Basil or else she would have returned by then. Finally Stanley made a decision. She was not going to let those poor little creatures die because of their mother's stupidity. She got up and moved herself onto the kitten's blanket, and the next thing I knew Stanley was lying there with twelve tiny kittens fighting over their own spot for milk. This big German shepherd was letting them suckle her!

At first the kittens looked a little confused, probably because of the different smell. Something was not quite the same—but then, who cared, they were getting what they needed! Soon the puppies started feeling lost. They were spoiled with their mother always being available to them, but they weren't lost for long. They smelled their mother's body and crawled towards it. Now the seven of them started fighting for a spot. Eventually everybody was satisfied, and then they all happily fell asleep in such a funny mixed bunch that you couldn't help but feel great love and admiration for our generous, kind German shepherd, Stanley.

All our neighbours came over to look at the scene, and even my father had a smile on his face. His eyes were moist too, which was a shocking sight to see. From that moment, Stanley made a rule: the kittens were to be fed first and only after that would she allow her own puppies to be fed. All of them learned the rule and stopped fighting. It was incredible to watch.

Basil never came back. Later we learned that she had been hit by a car and had died. We never found her. Mama and I decided that cats were too irresponsible and that we were not going to keep any of the kittens. We also decided to give all the puppies away. We only wanted our beautiful Stanley. Everybody wanted our puppies and kittens—they had became so famous, and, of course, everybody adored Stanley. I loved her more than anyone—she was my real pal. I could picture her being my lifelong friend; she was so close to me.

Everything went as planned. Each kitten was placed as soon as it learned to eat from the saucer. They were so funny to watch, playing together with the puppies until the last one was gone. As much as I loved them all I was glad to see them go because of the extra work with them. Yet when they left one by one, I felt a little sad. However, I knew I could see them from time to time and I was happy to concentrate on Stanley. Unfortunately, my happiness didn't last long.

One day Stanley went for her usual walk. We never worried about her because everybody knew her. She was never on a leash and never went out for more than an hour or so, but his time she was out longer than usual and I went looking for her. Not seeing her around, I became worried and went from street to street, calling her name. Finally I saw her in the distance. I called her, but my voice didn't reach her; she was too far away. I ran to her when suddenly I saw a huge, unusual-looking truck pulling some kind of equipment, and at that very moment I saw my best friend disappear into the truck. My dog was gone! I couldn't believe it.

"Stanley! Stanley!" I screamed helplessly, but the truck was gone. Not able to believe what had happened, I ran and ran until I reached the spot where she'd been taken, but except for tire tracks there was no trace of her.

Later that day I found out there was a municipal campaign to pick up and kill homeless dogs and cats, a legislation that none of the local citizens were aware of. Nothing could be done about it. I didn't go home for some time. I couldn't face anyone, especially my father. I was sure he'd blame me for Stanley's disappearance. But this time I was wrong. For the first time in my life I saw his tears in his eyes, and he said nothing.

The last Saturday of that August was to be my last date with Valentin before I left home. The next time we met I'd be on my own, a working girl! I was excited and looking forward to both: meeting with Valentin and moving out on Monday. By six o'clock I was at the bridge, but Valentin wasn't there. I thought, "Okay, once in a while a girl could arrive before her date. It would make him feel good." At quarter past six he still wasn't there.

I started to feel uncomfortable. Too many people passed by me and saw me waiting. It didn't look proper—a girl alone staying by the bridge. I decided to move closer to the trains. This way I couldn't miss him. I went all the way down to the platform. The trains arrived every ten minutes from where he would be coming.

Every time a train approached my heart was in my mouth, but he didn't appear. By a quarter to seven I was losing hope. I knew he wasn't coming to meet me. The trains were coming half-empty by now. At eight o'clock it began to rain, and I allowed myself to cry. Nobody would see me anyway as there were so few around at this hour.

As the rain got heavier and heavier, my hair became soaking wet. My eyes stung from my mascara, and my handkerchief was black and red from my running makeup. I knew I should go home, but I just couldn't bring myself to believe it was over.

I made a decision. The next morning I'd get up early, take the train, and look for him. I would do anything to find him, to look in his eyes one last time and hear his voice. Now that I had decided what I was going to do, I felt so much better.

Once home, I undressed quickly, hung up my wet clothes, and put my shoes under the stove. Mama had started lighting it now that the nights were getting cooler. It wasn't easy falling asleep with so much in my head. I tried to stop thinking about what had happened, but my thoughts were too stubborn. They wouldn't go away. I counted to fifty…It didn't help. I counted one, one, one…

When I woke up it was still dark and my eyes were swollen. If I had been on a date with him I would be just getting home then and feeling great. But it was terrible now. It was over. No more dates. No more excitement—only pain. One thing I was determined to do: find him and at least say goodbye.

I would go as soon as Mama got up. I'd tell her that I needed to go and see the place where I was going to be living. I definitely wouldn't tell her the truth.

I walked quickly to the station, got myself a ticket, and waited for the first train going out of town. It came in twenty minutes and was almost empty because it was early Sunday morning. The few on the train were sleeping; I sat there, glad they were asleep and not looking at me. I felt completely resolved to find Valia, even if it took me until midnight.

I actually knew very little about him, except that he was twenty-one and that his last name was Ribakov. His father's name was Filip which was very important to know and his birthdate was December 31, 1933. He never told me they had moved from Mytischi, where they presentlyHe'd told me he lived in Mytischi and was a student at the Moscow University of Aviation. His father had been killed in the war and he lived with his mother who was a nurse, but at which hospital I didn't know.

Mytischi was about an hour away by train. I thought it would be a small town and that I could knock on every door until I found him, but I was wrong. It was a huge industrial city with a bridge that was much bigger than ours.

The day was wet and grey with just a few people around, but it was still early. I crossed the bridge and went straight to the information kiosk, but it was still closed. I would have to wait another hour and then I'd get his address and wait a little before going to his place.

The woman in the kiosk looked at me strangely when I asked her to give me Valentin's address.

She said, "Unless you know the place of birth, I cannot do anything for you. There are many Valentin Alekseevich Ribakovs in Mytischi."

"Could you give me all of them?" I asked. "I'll find the one I'm looking for."

"No," she said. "I couldn't do that!"

I had told myself it wouldn't be easy to find him, and now I had to do the job. First, I was going to search street by street for Valia's house. The bridge divided the city, and I decided to search on the right side first, going door to door. By four o'clock I was completely exhausted, hungry, and soaked to the skin. Worst than that was the fact that I didn't know where to look! The streets seemed endless, and I didn't have the money to buy a map. I was lost—but far from giving up. I needed to warm up, so I went over to the train station. A group of people was there, which made me less conspicuous hanging around until I got warmed up.

As I sat there shivering, I noticed three guys who were sixteen or seventeen years old with musical instruments. One of them said, "Let's wait fifteen minutes more and then leave."

Something came to my mind. Valentin had told me that he and his mother lived in the same apartment as his younger cousin, Ura, who played the saxophone. I looked at these boys and wondered if by some chance they might be waiting for Ura.

But how could I ask them? On the other hand, what did I have to lose? But a girl talking to strangers? "Come on!" I told myself. "Don't chicken out! You said you'd do anything to find Valentin. Do it now! Grow up!" But I went on waiting until I heard them say, "Let's go!" Then I spoke up.

"Hello!" I said.

"Hello!" they answered.

"Are you waiting for a guy with a saxophone?"

They nodded. "Yes, we are."

"By any chance is his name Ura?"

"No."

I apologized and started to leave, but one of them must have seen the disappointment in my eyes and said, "Is his last name Ribakov?"

I almost screamed, "Yes! It is!"

"I don't think you're looking for Ura," he said. "You're probably looking for Valentin."

"Yes! I am!" I couldn't believe I had heard Valia's name!

"I don't know the exact address, but it's not here in Mytischi. It's out of town. You have to cross the bridge and get bus eighty-six that goes north. Get off right at the end, and after that you can ask."

How could I thank this fellow? I almost felt like hugging him.

I ran across the bridge, not caring that my shoes were soaking wet! I skipped through the puddles, and the water splashed on my stockings. I got to the bus as it was loading, but the line was long and the bus was already full. I had to catch this one! I couldn't wait another minute! The driver began to close the doors, but I saw one little spot on the step and took a chance.

On his loudspeaker he said, "Please everyone move to close the door!" But there was nowhere to move to. Everybody leaned towards one another but there was no space—no room to move, none. Half my body was almost hanging outside the doors. Little by little, I managed to squeeze in, and the doors closed. I was on my way!

It took about half an hour to get to the end of the line. When we came to the last stop I was the only passenger left. I got off and just stood there. My heart was pounding. To think that this was the place where Valia had grown up and gone to school! I now realized how far he had to come every time he met me. I couldn't imagine how he had managed to get home after our dates when most of the time we parted at around three o'clock in the morning! I would have been sound asleep and he would have been still sitting in the station. I would never allow myself to get him stay that late again!

But what was I thinking about? He had quit on me—and actually he was right. What business did he have with me? He needed a woman, not a fourteen-year-old girl! I needed to wake up! Even so, I couldn't let my first love end just like that! I only wanted to look in his eyes again, to hold him tightly, and thank him for letting me feel such beautiful emotions. He was in my heart. Oh, so deeply! And he would stay there for as long as I lived! Somehow I felt much better now and walked along with renewed courage.

As I did so, I found myself facing a huge field with lights in the distance. It was dark, but the rain had stopped. I didn't know what time it was. The first thing I would buy when I got paid would be a watch! After a while, I saw a man coming towards me and I took a chance and spoke to him.

"Excuse me. By any chance do you know the Ribakov family?" I asked.

"No," he said. "No one by that name lives in this area. They could be on the other side, in the military part of town."

I thanked him and picked up my pace to avoid getting there too late.

I came to the first house. It was a four-story stucco building with two entrances. I knew I was close to finding him, but I was scared to face him. What was a fourteen-year-old girl doing looking for a guy who had no time for her? Should I turn around and go back before it was too late and I made a complete fool of myself? I may have thought this, but I did the absolute opposite! I knocked, and the door opened. It was Valentin, who smiled and said, "Hi," like nothing had happened! He invited me in, and he introduced me to his mother and stepfather, who were just starting dinner.

His mother smiled at me in exactly the same way as Valentin. He looked just like her, and I loved her instantly. They invited me to have dinner with them, and until that moment I hadn't realized how hungry I was.

Oh, how I enjoyed that food! There were lots of boiled potatoes and a large piece of pork, which we never had in our house, and there was homemade pickled cabbage. It was so crispy and juicy. I could have eaten it nonstop. They also gave me a shot of homemade Vodka, which I had never tasted before. I swallowed it quickly and hoped that Valentin's mother didn't realize how young I was. I was beginning to feel much better!

We ate and talked, and his mother asked me where I lived and who my parents were and which university I was going to. I told the truth. After dinner, she and her husband got up and went to the kitchen to wash the dishes.

The room was very small. There were two beds and a couch in it with the dining table in the centre and a little desk and a dresser as well. It was very clean and cozy.

Valentin got up, took my hand, and led me to the couch. He hugged me for a long time and looking in my eyes, said, "Thank you for looking for me, Jandi!"

CHAPTER 16

You Don't Belong with Workers Like Us!

September 1, 1955. That day I opened the first page of my adult life. I had to grow up overnight. At five o'clock I got up, and in ten minutes I had packed a small bag. All I had to my name was one skirt, two blouses, a warm jacket, and two pairs of shoes. I said goodbye to Mama. I never said a word to my father and Sema who weren't interested whether I stayed at home or went all the way to Siberia—and left.

It took me two hours to get to the meat plant. I had to check in with the personnel department by eight, and as I walked in, I saw a large group of girls and a few boys, all of them approximately between fourteen and sixteen. I was the only one from Moscow, and I noticed many curious looks when the instructor called it out.

The girls were divided into two groups of forty-five each, and the boys formed a separate group. Each group had its own instructor. Mine was Nastasia Vasilievna. She was about sixty, very short and fat with a huge stomach, which she seemed to carry with pride. She was quite funny. She looked to me like a hen with her chickens, especially when everyone changed into their uniforms and we all looked absolutely identical!

The first thing Nastasia Vasilievna did was to take us for a tour of the meat plant. To go through each division, one had to have a pass. We started from the transportation division, which had 2,000 trucks of all kinds, mainly used to transport animals from the various farms. The trucks had open cages, and most of them held animals that had just made their final journey. They were baaing and mooing nonstop. There were other open trucks as well, full of frozen meat, and then there were refrigerated trucks, which held the finished products, and finally there were delivery trucks.

The head of the transportation division proudly showed us these gigantic freezers, inside of which were thousands of frozen animals hanging from hooks. As the man walked past them, the hanging animals moved as though they could have still been alive! Most of us turned pale and were close to fainting. We couldn't wait to get out of there, but this man seemed to have all the time in the world and carried on telling us about the plant.

He told us the place was never closed, even on holidays. They employed thirty thousand workers, and he named off all the other divisions, which would be shown to us in their correct order. When he had completed his tour, he led us to a division called *uboinaia*, which means "killing."

I couldn't sleep or eat after what I saw there. Some of the girls threw up, and one of them fainted.

How do I describe this "killing" process? First, the animal was put on a platform, which moved along on a conveyer belt. It stopped periodically for exactly thirty seconds, during which an electrical plug with a high voltage was connected to the animal's brain and activated. After this, a giant-sized hook picked up the animal and skinned it. Another conveyer belt then took away the skin, which traveled in the opposite direction. We were shocked to see that even after the animals were skinned, they were still half-alive!

It was unbearable to watch. I don't think fourteen- and sixteen-year-old kids were ready for such a grim sight, and to show us this wasn't very smart, in my opinion. Unfortunately that was part of the training program and nobody could say or do anything about it. I won't go into details of the other procedures, such as taking all the insides of the animal out and separating the meat from the bones, or what they did with the animals' heads. It was all completely horrible.

We were also taken to a division called *kishechnaya*, "casing," where there were mountains of natural casings. After seeing the "killing division" we all knew where they came from. The smell was terrible, and, thank God, we didn't stay in that area for too long.

Next came the sausage-making division. All the girls would be trained to work in this division, and the boys would be trained for the killing division. The hires for all the other divisions were those being transferred from other positions. Those with particular disabilities brought about by accidents on some job at the plant were placed here, in the sausage-making division..

After what we had seen already, the sausage-making division didn't seem so bad. The working area was very large, and the area was divided in two parts by a concrete platform with a railing on both sides. On the ceilings above were automated trolleys, where the ground meat for stuffing the sausages was delivered to the workstations. Below the platform, there were twenty-five huge marble tables on either side. These were the workstations for the sausage makers.

Every table had a team of ten women. At the end of each table, close to the platform side, there was a machine called *shpritz*, which had to be filled with the stuffing. Its capacity was two hundred kilograms, and after the stuffing was put into it, it was shut tightly with a cast-iron lid with a handle like a ship's wheel.

In front of the shpritz there were two holes into which fifteen-inch-long steel pipes of different diameters were screwed. To release the stuffing—to push it through—there were pedals on both sides of the shpritz. To form the sausage, the casing had to be held firmly over the pipe. The stuffing emerged under high pressure and would often break the casing. The women who worked on this machine had to be highly skilled and were the team leaders of each worktable. Two machine operators supplied the rest of the team with strips of sausage to be tightened and hung on cast-iron frames. After this procedure, the raw product would be taken away for cooking or smoking treatments, depending on the kind of sausages they were to become.

The tying up of strips of sausage was the lowest paid position in the plant and the most tedious job of all. This operation had to be done perfectly because the look of the finished product depended on it. The pay for doing one strip was so low that the workers had to make thousands per shift to earn their wages. As well, every so often during a shift, the quality controllers watched from the platform above and took points off for the accumulation of raw products (waste was frowned upon) or for air bubbles in the sausage, which in time would create green spots, making them unsalable items.

Most of the time, overloads were inevitable because of the shortage of frames, but the administration still penalized the teams as though it was their fault. Due to this, all the workers fought to find ways to secure the frames for their teams when they were delivered to the floor. When the frames arrived from the terminal and became available, workers from each team had to be resourceful, grabbing several of them as quickly as possible. If they didn't their team would be without frames until more were delivered.

The fines, which cut earnings, were always on every worker's mind, and at times there would be fights among the teams, who accused one another of stealing their frames or grabbing more than their share when they arrived on the floor.

Nastasia Vasilievna warned us of the many accidents that had disabled some of the workers for the rest of their lives. The hazards were part of the operation, she said, which was why they always needed new workers and why they didn't care what age the workers were. This was the reason apprentices were provided with room and board for several months, so that the factory would always have a ongoing flow of workers.

After the sausage-making division we came to the last area, the thermal rooms where the sausages were cooked or smoked, and saw the finished product. This was the only place that smelled all right, but even so, nobody wanted to taste anything that was offered. Everyone simply felt sick, and most of us were beginning to realize what lay ahead. We still didn't have any idea what it would be like after our graduation from training, and even if I knew, I didn't have much choice.

Of course I did have a choice. I could go back home and either continue to be the "black sheep" or prostitute myself by telling my father lies about Mama, which was what he wanted to hear. I couldn't see myself doing either. I actually had only one choice, and that was to take a deep breath and go through what I had to in the meat plant. This was my single opportunity, but when I turned sixteen, my opportunities would increase.

The next day we were told that the first few months wouldn't be so bad; we would be treated as students. We'd go to theory classes every day at seven o'clock in the morning until eleven thirty and then have lunch. After that, we'd have a workshop right in the sausage-making department and learn how to make different varieties: baloney, martabella, wieners, and all kinds of salamis, and so on.

During these classes, we were taught about animal parts, and we took some basic mechanical subjects pertaining to the machinery in the plant. After classes, Nastasia Vasilievna took over, and after lunch she would take us to the changing room, where we put our uniforms on and proceeded to the workshop.

The first part of the day was kind of interesting, and during the second part, we were taught the tricks of the trade. In just a month's time we were learning how to speed the work up, which was enjoyable, because we had all started from zero, and it was fun to compete.

During this six-month apprenticeship I felt good. I became very popular and organized all kinds of concerts, even a little play. At one point we were invited to give a concert for the soldiers, and I read from Maxim Gorky's novel *Mati*, which was about a mother's hands. It was something I loved, and I noticed tears in some of the soldiers' eyes.

We all slept in one room at the back of the school, and at moments it felt like being back in the orphanage. It was a carefree time, and we were all happy. All the girls were from villages outside of Moscow, while I was the only one from the city. As well, I had my orphanage experience so I wasn't as shy as most of them, and I quickly realized that the majority of them needed to be led. I didn't mind that at all. Most of the time I knew what I wanted for myself and for them, and I spoke up on their behalf, which they liked. They used to say I was different from the others because I was from Moscow, but I had no idea what that meant.

The six months passed quickly with laughter and some tears. We teased Nastasia Vasilievna, who would sometimes go to the thermo division and steal some kolbassa for us! She would return with this very innocent look on her face, and we knew she had something hidden in her apron. Sometimes she hid the sausage in her bra! Most of the girls didn't mind eating sausage, but I couldn't do it after I found out how it was made.

At the end of six months we had exams in theory and practice, and during our graduation party, we were given contracts to sign, after which we received our certificates. Becoming the proud owner of a professional certificate meant I was going forward!

None of us knew that we had signed a three-year contract, of course—a contract that couldn't be broken. So the "free of charge" school wasn't free at all. This was the way the meat plant secured its labour force, otherwise they would have had real problems to keeping it in operation.

After graduation, I had to find a place to live. Nastasia Vasilievna suggested I see Auntie Grusha, who lived fairly near the plant. I needed a place close by so I wouldn't waste my time traveling, as I was planning to go to school after work. Auntie Grusha lived in a six-story brick building ten minutes from the plant, and I went to meet with her.

She lived on the sixth floor with no elevator, and when I knocked, a tiny, old lady who was less than five feet tall opened the door. She wore a big smile in spite of having only one tooth! She invited me in without even asking who I was or why I was there but immediately opened a door on the right and showed me into a quite large almost empty space with two windows. There were only three pieces of furniture: an old couch facing the windows, a small table with two chairs, and a single bed. The floors were bare, and the walls were empty of pictures except for one icon in a corner next to the window.

Still smiling her toothless grin, she said, "You must be looking for a room. Here's the bed. I charge twenty-five rubles a month."

"Where would you sleep?" I asked.

"Here," she said. "On the couch."

"I need to move in tomorrow," I said.

"That's fine," she answered. "Come any time, and if I'm not at home, just knock and my neighbour will let you in the apartment."

On the way out she showed me the rest of the place. She had a small kitchen with two tables and a gas stove, a washroom, a small room with a toilet, and a shower, which was separate. Her neighbour's room was opposite the washroom. After this quick tour, we said goodbye, and I left.

Now I had a roof over my head, and I was going to work hard to pay for my own little corner in Auntie Grusha's room!

At around four o'clock on Sunday I was there with my bag, and Grusha's neighbour opened the door for me. There was no smile on her face. In fact, she didn't even answer when I said, "Hello, my name is Janna." She was already on the way back to her room. I closed the door behind me and walked into Grusha's room. She wasn't there, so I put down my bag and sat in one of the chairs. Two minutes later, the neighbour walked in, which scared me for a moment. Without the slightest hint of a smile she began to speak.

"You must be Grusha's tenant," she said. "Grusha has three sons and a husband. All four of them are in jail. The two older sons were in and out for ten years—stealing, of course. Thank goodness, now they're locked in for twenty-five years. Her youngest seemed not that bad, and her husband was a decent man, but the youngest son began to have problems when he turned sixteen. He started drinking and going girl-crazy.

"The father kept warning him," she went on, without waiting for a response from me. "He told him that if he turned out like the other ones, he'd kill him with his own hands. Well, one day, this boy goes to a restaurant with a girl and when the girl went to the washroom, he took money from her purse, but she reported him to the militia and they caught him! When they came to arrest him, his father took a knife and stabbed the boy in the stomach! Split it right open! So the militia took both of them!"

She paused for a moment while I sat there, frozen by this horrible story.

"So!" she continued, "Now all Grusha does is pack food, whatever she can get, and waits for visits with her poor husband. She can't see her older sons at all. They're too far away. The youngest is still in a jail hospital, and he's in bad condition. She doesn't know if he'll live, and her poor husband is very sick too. He was never a healthy man." She whispered confidentially, "After all, he worked in the plant for twenty-five years, you know, and after that nobody can be healthy. He worked all his life in the killing division. He's really an invalid, and Grusha gets his pension now. Her own old-age pension is only fifteen rubles, and she spends all her money on parcels, poor woman. She even sold everything she had until there was nothing left to sell. That's why she has you now for a tenant."

She took a breath and told me not to wait for Grusha. "She always stays out late on Sundays, visiting her daughter-in-law. She has one grandson from the oldest son, and it won't be too long before this one will end up in jail too. It's in their blood, you know. So, you'd better go and unpack and go to bed early. You have to be at the plant by six, and you must never be late for work!"

With this she turned on her heel and was gone.

After she left, I sat there feeling sick. It was getting dark, and I began to imagine all kinds of horrible things happening to me. I imagined thieves were walking in and grabbing me, putting a gag over my mouth and tying me up. I pictured the young boy's stomach with blood pouring out, and it all seemed so real. Oh my God! What was I to do?

I don't know how long I sat there. Finally I got up and went to bed in my clothes. I don't know how I talked myself into sleep, but somehow I did. A strange noise woke me up, and for a moment I couldn't even breathe. Where was this sound coming from? Then I realized it was a whisper. Somebody was whispering.

I looked around, trying to see in the dark. I made out a tiny figure on her knees. It could be no one but Grusha, and, of course, I'd forgotten about the icon. The poor woman was praying—and no wonder, with whole her family in jail. Again I imagined all kinds of crimes that might have happened within these walls. My heart was racing, and no sooner did I fall asleep than I was awake again. This time, the lights were on. Grusha was on her couch, doing something and whispering to herself. I thought to myself, "That's it, she's a mental case!" Suddenly she noticed me looking at her and whispered with a sweet smile, "I seem to have been bitten by some fleas! I haven't slept on the couch for a long time, and I think they must have gotten excited and bit me!"

She tried to reassure me. "It's okay. Go back to sleep. I'll do something about it tomorrow. Don't worry. They won't be in your bed. I sprayed it before you came. Goodnight, sleep tight."

Easy for her to say, "Sleep tight!" I hoped five o'clock would come soon and that my first night there would finally be over!

The sausage factory was a whole new world of discoveries. All the young workers were mixed in together with the experienced team workers. The earnings were to be based on total team production and would be split amongst all ten in the team. The leader of the team was paid 10 percent more and an assistant 5 percent, which was taken from the top of the total team earnings. The first problem was that experienced workers didn't want to have these beginners training at their expense, and rightly so. Why would they be interested in giving up part of their hard-earned money?

The result was that we were treated badly, kicked from team to team, and nobody had the time to deal with us. We felt rejected, which didn't help anybody progress, and yet we wanted to learn as quickly as possible. We were too uptight as a result of our treatment to really grasp what we needed to know for the job.

Many girls wanted to quit and simply not show up for work. But the administration would hunt them down and bring them back. They weren't going to waste the time and money they had spent on their schooling! The administration had promised all kinds of things to these girls, but the bottom line was this:

"You signed a three-year contract, so back to work you go. No arguments!"

In reality, nobody ever stopped to consider how put down and frightened these young kids were. One day, one of the workers on the team splashed a bucket of freezing cold water all over me. It was full of slippery natural casings, and she screamed at me, "You stupid spoiled Moscow brat! Get out of here! You don't belong with workers like us!"

I thought, "Oh? Is that right? I'll show you all! I can work even better than you! You'll see!" But the unbearable thought was that there was no way out. I was trapped by that contract just like everybody else and was forced to work there for three bloody years!

I began to try and figure out how to solve the problem for the young workers. I figured out a few ways to do so, and it surprised me that it hadn't been done before. The solution was simple—much less painful for everyone, a lot more profitable, and I intended to do something about it as soon as possible.

The solution, as I saw it, was to organize the teams of beginners and start them all at the same level. The obstacle to this plan was the established quota, which had been set down and always expected. It wasn't possible for the beginners to fulfill these expectations established by the administration.

I came to the conclusion that if the administration would allow us to reduce the quota for at least the first three months, it would to allow us to gain psychological and physical confidence and the quota could be increased gradually. I was positive that the beginners would catch up with the rest of the workers in those three months. It was a simple solution, and I was determined to make my team a winner!

I began to talk to the shift supervisors, none of whom were interested in my view. Consequently, I decided to go right to the top. Nothing was going to stop me! To get an appointment with the director was as difficult as it was to see the minister of industry. It took me some time. Meanwhile, we had to cope. We worked three shifts, which changed weekly. I also enrolled in the school, which had a rotating schedule. I would go to evening classes or morning, depending on which shift I worked. The most difficult part was going to day classes after the night shift.

My budget was very tight, too. After I paid for my corner in Grusha's room and paid for my books, I had very little money left for food or anything else. Ironically, working in a sausage factory, I was literally starving. My budget allowed me to buy six meat patties, three loaves of bread, half a kilo of sugar, three or four jars of soup and some potatoes and cabbage each month.

The meat patties were 30 percent meat and 70 percent bread. To have some sausage during work hours one had to steal, and in order to steal, you had to be a real pro. Of course, there were workers, who did steal, but I was not up to learning this trade. I simply had to cope with my ongoing hunger.

In the beginning the hunger was difficult, but gradually I got used to it. When I came home, instead of thinking "food" I would think "sleep," and it worked. I would drift off immediately, as soon as I put my head on the pillow.

At the beginning of the second month, I began to work on my plan. I learned the whole bureaucratic apparatus from top to bottom. I knew my plan would take time—and that nobody would want to take the responsibility for it. If I didn't inform some of the more senior people about it I would probably make enemies. However, I realized I wasn't going to please everybody, as that would take too long. So, I went ahead with trying to make an appointment to see the director of the meat plant. It took me a month to achieve this.

The appointment was in the morning and fortunately I happened to be working the evening shift that day. I prepared myself for the meeting as carefully as I possibly could. I wore my Natasha Rostova outfit. Both the blouse and skirt were a little loose on me because of hunger and hard work. The real problem was my high-heeled shoes that wouldn't stay on my feet! Well, there was nothing to be done about it; I just had to keep them on somehow. I made sure to walk very slowly, and thankfully I didn't have to walk too far.

The secretary was an older woman. Without a smile she told me to wait and that I would only have fifteen minutes with the director. She looked very important. I sat down, and for the first time I became unsure whether I was doing the right thing. What if the director got angry because I hadn't gone through the appropriate channels? What if he were to call my immediate boss? What would happen then? Maybe I should leave before it was too late! But no—I couldn't go back. I knew one thing for certain, that if I gave up then I'd only have to face the same situation later on. This was my opportunity! It had to be. The secretary interrupted my deliberations.

"Comrade Laidman!" she said. "Follow me!"

The man behind the huge desk was on the phone. As I walked across the soft carpet I thought, "Thank goodness! I can walk slowly, and my shoes won't fall off. And I can give him time to finish his conversation."

He glanced at me while talking on the phone, and as I approached his desk, he motioned to me to sit down. I only wished he would continue the conversation a little longer, so I could collect my thoughts. Then again, I only had fifteen minutes of his important time, and the clock was ticking. I had to make my point quickly and clearly.

"What seems to be the problem, Comrade Laidman?" he asked me as he hung up the phone.

I told him my story as quickly as I could, and when I finished, he called the secretary and told her to put the director of the meat plant on the phone immediately. The conversation was very short. The director simply ordered the manager to organize the youth team and cut the quota by 40 percent for two months, and then he gave him my name as a team leader. After this he asked me if I needed anything else, and when I said no, he got up and so did I.

The meeting was over. He shook my hand, and I was on my way out. Once outside his door my heart was beating so hard I thought it would jump out of my body! I had to sit down for a moment. I couldn't believe how easy it had gone! Why nobody had done it before, especially with so many beginners going through such hell, was totally baffling!

Back in Grusha's room I felt like a winner. I knew I could do it! This triumph called for a celebration, which meant a feast. Two whole meat patties, potatoes, and tea, and Grusha was to be my guest. I told her the whole story. She was very pleased about it and brought out a jar of homemade plum jam, which was delicious.

She and I had a great time! She enjoyed the feast and told me a couple of stories about her and her husband. We both cried a little and then laughed again and again. I felt so good! I could hardly wait for the venture to begin!

It didn't take long to organize a new team. My manager was quite pleasant about it, although we had to wait for the beginning of the next month, which was in another ten days. It made sense to start on the first of the month, although the ten days seemed an eternity—as it always does when you can't wait for something to happen. Finally the first of the month arrived, and my team and I arrived an hour before everyone else.

We planned our strategy well to make sure we'd never have a shortage. Each team member would take turns watching for the frames, and when they arrived on the floor, two or three of us would collect them instead of just one.

Meantime, those at the table would concentrate on the operation. They wouldn't be intimidated by anyone because we were all in the same boat. I would make sure that the delivery of stuffing and the filling of the shpritz would be synchronized too so that we wouldn't lose time, and everything else would be coordinated as well. And that's how it went from day one.

We met our norm daily with no points taken off. At the end of the second week, our daily quota was met by two o'clock, and so we had a whole hour to make money for our team. Two more weeks later we had even more time to produce over the quota. Everybody was beginning to feel confident, and by the end of the second month we easily met the allotment established for the factory workers.

By the middle of the third month we were making the regular required amount by one o'clock. By the end of the third month we felt comfortable with 15 percent over the quota. At the end of each shift we were completely exhausted but proud of ourselves. We had done it! And no one looked down on us anymore. We felt like real people now.

We also took care of each other, which brought us closer to each other. Our team became known around the whole factory and nobody ever said to me, "You don't belong with workers like us!" When we were given the standard quota officially, everyone wanted us to be named the number one team. Normally, the top team produced an average of 6 to 7 percent over the quota, but our team was far ahead of that.

As soon as this fact was established, it became public knowledge. My picture was taken as leader of the winning team. I dressed for the occasion in a brand new uniform. My photo appeared on the board of winning team leaders for the entire plant. Then a full-page article appeared in the local newspaper, and I was asked to attend all kinds of meetings to share my experience.

At this point I said, "Hold on!" If I had to attend all kinds of meetings and carry my workload as team leader, I couldn't do it! I had enough on my hands, and at the moment I could not take on any more! After I told them how it was, they left me alone.

My school was taking up a lot of my time, and doing my homework at Grusha's was often difficult. I lacked sleep and food, and my budget was still very tight because I had to buy a watch as well as a winter coat and boots. I needed some other winter clothes too, but the watch was my first purchase and it was the only thing I could buy through the layaway plan. Everything else had to be cash, so I had to hurry up and save!

Valentin and I saw each other once in a while, but we lived too far away from each other, and I was very busy and tired. A few times he took me to his house, and I stayed overnight. The funny part about it was that every time it happened, his mother took a night shift at the hospital and his stepfather was never there. Before leaving home for her shift she would say, "I need to earn more money to see my son become a professional engineer of aviation!" It was her dream, her goal. Even though we slept together, every time things heated up, we simply stopped, I couldn't allow it, and Valentin would never force me either. Each time I left him I thought I'd never see him again, but then I would receive a letter from him asking me for a date.

CHAPTER 17

My Accident

Almost a year after I became, so to speak, "a star," the manager of the sausage factory came to me and said that I had been chosen to perform on a new improved shpritz machine. The capacity of it would now be 300 kilos of stuffing instead of 250. He said it was a great honor to be chosen and also that there would be many important people there for the first demonstration so that I should get myself a brand new uniform. I agreed to this because, after all, I was interested in any production improvements.

The morning of the big event was very special. I felt so excited I didn't sleep the night before because I kept thinking about how it would go. Everyone was excited looking forward to it. The new shpritz had been installed the day before and was sitting there with a red ribbon tied to it, looking bright and cheerful. I was the first to arrive on the floor. I wanted to be perfectly prepared. My team was ready to go by six thirty. Normally, the shift started at seven, but by six forty-five most of the important people had arrived.

There were many faces I had never seen before. Photographers stood at the ready with their cameras, and at 7:00 a.m. the director arrived. He made a nice speech, even mentioning our little meeting. He then cut the ribbon, and the first portion of stuffing was inserted into the shpritz. I closed the lid, which was now fifty kilograms heavier. In other words, the weight of the lid was now 300 kilograms, not 250, which was equal to the amount of the stuffing. I double-checked to make sure the lid was closed tightly and that everything was ready for production to begin. I pulled the casing and pressed the pedal to make the first loaf…

It happened in a split second. All I remember was that the giant lid flew off, hit my head, and I went flying and hit the ceramic floor.

When I opened my eyes I saw two beds and white walls. I realized where I was. I needed to throw up, and I wanted to use my hand to stop myself from vomiting, but I became aware that the upper part of my body was strapped down, including my arms. There was no way I could move. I felt so sick I couldn't hold it any longer. The bitter liquid came out through the tube that was in my mouth, and even though I felt better after that, it left me with an unbearable headache.

Gradually, the picture of the accident came to my mind.

Oh my God! My head had been crushed. What was going to happen to me? Was I going to be an invalid? The headache was terrible. I closed my eyes. It was dark, and I felt dizzy and scared. Sleep, sleep, sleep. It was the only way. "Don't think—just sleep," I told myself.

The next time I opened my eyes it was still dark. I moved my legs; though they felt numb, I could move them. That was good! Something was bothering me between my legs, and I guessed it was another tube, but I definitely could move my legs. What a relief! At least I knew I could walk.

My head seemed to be flying, and it also felt hot. And why were my arms still strapped down? I was worried that they were paralysed! I tried to move my fingers. They moved. Oh, thank goodness! If I could move my hands, things weren't so bad. It was my head. I could think and remember what had happened, which meant my head wasn't so bad. It hurt, but I was thinking, even if it were bad, it could all be worse.

On the other hand, maybe I was paralysed from the waist down, which was why they'd strapped me to the bed! "Oh God, let me move!" I pleaded. My head was on fire, I couldn't think anymore…Sleep sleep…that was the only way. "Close your eyes and sleep," I told myself. "That's all you can do. Sleep, sleep, sleep."

The sun was shining, and I heard some voices, then laughter. Two women were talking and laughing. They talked about food, how bad it was. How could they complain? They could eat or not. If they gave me something to eat I wouldn't complain. I would eat anything.

People were funny. They took food for granted. Not only food—everything. Their legs, hands, heads...They had no idea how lucky they were. If I could only move! But at least I was hungry now, which meant my brain was working. Yes, I was in agony, but it wasn't so bad. That meant I still had everything it took to be a human being. Maybe I wasn't an invalid.

"Close your eyes and sleep, sleep..." I heard some voices say near my bed. They talked about me, but I couldn't open my eyes. I didn't know how to concentrate. Let them talk, I was sleeping...

It was dark again and very quiet. No voices this time...I felt sick, but I couldn't throw up. Something stopped me. "It's okay," I thought. Almost bearable. The only thing that was unbearable was my headache, but I had to try and sleep through it. At least I could talk myself into sleep.

"You can do it. Count. Don't think—it's too painful. It hurts to think. Don't think. Sleep, sleep..."

It was sunny again, and again I heard voices. The same two women were talking and laughing and smelled of food. Oh, it smelled so good! Were these women going to complain again? They were saying something about eggs. They said the eggs were the only edible food around there. But even a single egg would have done for me. I loved eggs.

My head. It was still in agony. Was it going to hurt forever? "Stop thinking, just sleep." It didn't hurt as much when I slept. I was lucky that I could sleep, so I just said to myself, "One, one, one..." It was hard to count, so I just repeated, "One, one, one." It was easier. It was dark again and quiet, except for somebody snoring. That was okay. It meant I could hear. It was a quiet snore, but I could hear it clearly. I didn't feel sick then, but my stupid head...it hurt. How long would it be so painful? No use guessing. It hurt like hell, and that was a fact. But as long as I could feel I would live..."Just sleep for now."

It wasn't as sunny the next time I woke up; it was better this way. I could keep my eyes open at least for a while. It seemed that breakfast was finished. The women weren't talking about food anymore and I didn't feel hungry. I suppose one could get used to not eating. How I wished I could move my arm to find out what was on my head that hurt so much!

I suppose I fell asleep again because when I woke up, two doctors were trying to open my eyelids. When they realized that I could open them myself, they said, "That's good. You're doing fine! You're going to be all right!"

I tried to say something, but no sound came out from my throat. Oh, my God, had I lost my speech? How would I be able to live without it? Nobody would ever hear me. This was ridiculous! Why had I opened my mouth at the meat plant? Why couldn't I be like everyone else? All I did was get myself in trouble, and now I couldn't speak! "Good, Janna," I said to myself. "Next time, keep your mouth shut! But there won't be a next time!"

The doctors were still there. They kept saying, "You are doing fantastically!"

I fell asleep again.

The next time there was a woman doctor standing right in front of my bed. She pulled at my eyelids again. Why? If they wanted me to wake up, they could say so. "Why are you pulling my eyelids?" I tried to ask, but no voice came out. "Oh, please give me my voice back! I'll be very quiet from now on. Just give me my voice back!"

Tears started flowing from my eyes, and I couldn't even wipe them! They were running down my cheeks, meeting at my chin, and burning my skin, and this stupid doctor didn't care! She was writing something. She looked at me and wrote. Couldn't she see I needed someone to wipe away my tears? They were burning like hell. What was she writing about? She didn't seem to see how I was in pain! How could I trust her? And then she was gone!

Oh, God, now what? She was back with a nurse. Both of them were doing something to me. Whatever it was, it didn't hurt. Then they talked to each other as though I weren't there, but I could hear them. They were saying that maybe the next day they would free my hands, if everything was okay. "What should be okay?" I wanted to ask. But my voice refused to speak. I didn't think my lips were moving either. All I wanted was to be able to speak again. I had to! "I must and I will!"

"Just sleep your time away until tomorrow...Sleep, sleep, sleep."

Then there were three doctors: one woman and two men. Again, each one of them pulled at my eyelids.

The two male doctors said, "She's doing fantastically!"

But I wanted to say back to him, "Then why don't you take these stupid straps off so I can move a little? My bum is hurting…my back is hurting…Move!"

I thought I heard myself say "Move," and it seemed the doctors heard me say it too because they started to laugh and shake each other's hands. But they were too much into themselves and nobody rushed to do anything for me.

I gathered all my strength and tried to say, "Please!" There was hardly any volume, but I knew they heard it because one of them said, "Okay, let's try it for two hours today." That was the one who kept saying I was doing fantastically.

They called the nurse, and in a second my arms were set free. I didn't move them at once; I just tried to deal with the sensation of freedom. That moment, which as long as I live, I will remember. I would never again take my body for granted.

What happiness to be in control of your own body! From that day on, they freed my arms each day with only my chest and head strapped down. My headaches were still excruciating and I now felt pain throughout my entire body. I couldn't speak yet, but I knew I would, in time.

The day finally came when they unstrapped my arms during the night. The doctor explained to me that my body and head had to be held in place for at least another two months because they'd been crushed and my forehead had been split open so that I'd had to have surgery. She told me I needed complete peace and rest, and, as I was connected to tubes, I would get all the nourishment I needed. Sleep was essential.

She said, "You are extremely lucky. We didn't think you'd pull through." She told me they didn't know what the side effects might be, so I was to stay completely still for the next two or three more months or so. One morning, someone I never expected to see walked into my room. It was my father. He even brought something with him, which he quickly put in a drawer next to me, and sat down on the edge of my bed. He really didn't know what to talk to me about. In fact, he looked rather uncomfortable because he could see that for the first time I couldn't talk back.

His conversation consisted of lines such as, "Your stepmother is hopeless, you know…what a stupid woman! She always, you know, does these things. Like—I don't know—she—" he couldn't find the right words to describe this terrible woman. I knew then what he was trying to do. He was hoping I would finally take his side. I began to feel sick; he was so impossible and I couldn't bear his presence any longer. I tried to hold back my tears, but they streamed down my face uncontrollably and my head started to pound more then ever. What a relief to see the nurse walk in and escort him out!

It took me a while to settle down again, but I finally fell asleep and slept for some time. When I opened my eyes it seemed to be late afternoon. Suddenly my stepmother came into the room. Apparently, it was parents' day! She burst into tears when she saw me and said how lucky I was to be out of the dreadful family atmosphere, that I was better off with my head crushed than living there! And then she told me of the latest episode in which my father had gotten himself into his usual rage. He raised his hand to strike my stepmother and Sema, who was sitting on the couch, yelled, "Hit her! Hit her!"

"Can you imagine?" my stepmother said.

By now my head was in agony and I lay there thinking how selfish these people were. Neither of them gave two hoots about me. They had no idea what I had been going through. All they cared about were their own problems. So I agreed: I was indeed very lucky to be out of there!

At this point, (thank God), the nurse walked in and said to her, "Please. You'll have to leave! I told you to stay with her just fifteen minutes and now look what you've done to her!"

Mama looked at me and seeing the tears running down my face said, "Don't worry, Janna. I'll be okay. As soon as Sema gets married I think your father will treat me better."

I closed my eyes.

Eventually my head began to improve and the headaches became bearable. But my whole body was in unbelievable pain. The doctor said it couldn't be helped. My body had to be completely still until my head and the bones in my neck had healed. She estimated it would take no longer than two or three months, as they didn't want to take any chances. Little by little I was able to speak a couple of words, but I couldn't concentrate on anything for more than a few seconds and I still couldn't move my eyes. It was too painful.

I was being given liquid food now, a bit at a time. I was told that my stomach would have to get used to food again. Because I was lying flat on my back, I couldn't drink (they didn't have plastic straws in Russia). Once in a while a nurse would come and give me a few spoons of tea or milk. They didn't have juice. Once in a while, they would connect the tubes again.

By now I had come to know who those the women were. One of them was a young woman, of about twenty-seven, whose leg had been amputated about five months before. By the time I was out of my comatose state, she was up and about on her crutches. She was happy they hadn't amputated both legs and that they had left her part of her leg below her knee. She had had the beginning stages of gangrene. I was happy that they hadn't amputated anything from me, and seeing her made me feel that life wasn't so bad. The other woman was in her sixties and had broken her right arm and leg. She looked bizarre. Her bed was now closer to mine on the opposite wall, and I began to make out a little at a time. She lay in bed just like I had, on her back. Her stomach looked like a hill, and they had her arm in a cast that had her arms pointing to the ceiling.

Every time I saw the hill shaking I knew she was laughing. She seldom laughed with her voice, but I never saw her face either, until much later. All I wanted was to be able to turn my head a little bit. I was still getting sleeping pills, so I was knocked out most of the time, which was the whole idea.

I had a visitor from the plant eventually who said I shouldn't worry. They intended to pay me a 100 percent of my average earnings and they would finance some holiday trips for as long as I wanted. He said they were going to buy me a holiday package at one of the most popular Black Sea resorts, plus some other good things. I said nothing because I could barely speak or think.

The following day I had a visit from my shift captain, who warned me not to fall for any of the promises. He explained that the accident had been the administration's fault, not mine at all. The engineers and the administration hadn't organized the safety protection properly and that I should sue them.

"All they worry about is that if you sign an accident report, they'll be in big trouble," he said. "That's why they're trying to sweeten you up, so you won't sign the paper."

"Let me tell you, my dear girl, no matter what they offer you, sign this bloody paper. If you don't, you won't be able to lay any claims later and if in a year's time you find yourself an invalid, nobody would do anything for you. You can forget it! Without this report signed, you are lost. Those bastards only worry about themselves."

When he left I thought, "Oh my God. What a good man! It all happened in his shift, so he was just as responsible as the others and he'd be at the same risk of being charged as them. No doubt it took a lot of the best of human qualities—a big heart and real honesty—to come and tell me how to deal with that heartless bunch." So there were some good people around, which I had always felt.

At the end of the third month, the doctor took off the rest of the straps and left the cast on my head and neck. It covered my entire head, neck, and shoulders. It was heavy, but without the straps it was much easier. They told me I could start turning my head now, and if everything went well, in two weeks' time they would take off the cast and I'd be walking. In the meantime, they taught me how to exercise my legs and arms while I was in bed. I felt better every day. The only problem was the headaches.

At last, the big day arrived! I was wheeled into the operating room for removal of the cast. They gave me a shot and put me out, and when they brought me back, the nurse told me to wait until she had the time to help me walk. This was the moment I'd been waiting for. She returned and helped me get up very slowly and then sit down. I felt dizzy and saw all sorts of colours in front of me, nothing but colours.

"It's okay," she said. "You'll be able to see. You have to sit for a while." When I stood up again, the colours were still there. Eventually I got past it while the nurse helped me take a couple of steps close to my bed. My head was pounding. I needed to go back into bed, but I asked her to take me to the mirror first.

"Not now," she said. "In a couple of days we'll do that. You still have a light bandage on your head, so we'll put you back in bed for the moment."

I had to wait. I lay back feeling dizzy and nauseated, but things settled down after a while, and, for the first time in four months, I fell asleep on my side. My head hurt, and my whole body was sore, but I felt great! I'd soon be on my feet again. I knew it! At the end of that week they took my last bandage off and gave me my first real food.

If I live to a hundred I will never forget that first piece of bread and butter: that egg and that hot chocolate! Oh, what bliss! Life was good, and I was going to stay with it! It was a gift and I would treasure every moment of it!

Right after that first real breakfast, I asked the girl on crutches to help me get to the mirror. What I saw there was a nightmare! I was so ugly! My head was shaved, although the hair had started to grow back just a little. There were huge stitches right across my forehead, and my face looked as if it were painted yellow.

I broke down. "No! I don't want to live like this!" I cried. "Nobody will ever love me again! No! No!"

As I sobbed uncontrollably, I noticed the "hill" was shaking. It went on and on and was making all kinds of waves—slower, then faster, stopping for a second and then starting again. I couldn't take my eyes off it and suddenly I saw how funny the whole thing was and I found myself laughing too. The girl on crutches looked at me and the "hill," and she joined in the laughter too.

CHAPTER 18

How I Fooled Them

In spite of the fact that I had signed the accident report, I was still provided with a few benefits. One of them was that the plant administration was going to send me on a two-month paid holiday to one of the Black Sea resorts in Abkhazia near Georgia, a place called Gagra.

By the time I was discharged from the hospital, the front of my hair had grown in and my face was no longer yellow. I could eat normally now, and my friends from the meat plant brought fruit and chocolates, which helped bring colour to my face. When I was ready to leave on my trip I had a new hairstyle, which was designed to cover my scar. With a little makeup I looked almost back to normal. In fact, anybody who didn't know what had happened to me would never have been able to tell.

When I arrived at the resort, my period started. I had had a rough day travelling, ending with a crazy taxi driver speeding up the mountains for a couple of hours, and I felt completely exhausted. Everyone was going to a dance at the resort next door, but I refused to go. All I wanted was to go to bed and rest. Unfortunately, there was a girl who had arrived with me that day and who was one of those who could survive only by sticking to someone like glue, and I was the chosen one. She wasn't going to the dance without me. In the end, when everyone else had already left and I had taken a little rest, I agreed to go with her.

The minute we walked onto the dance floor an absolutely gorgeous young man invited me to dance and didn't leave my side for the rest of the evening. I couldn't understand why this incredibly handsome man wanted to spend the whole evening dancing only with me when there were so many beautiful girls around. If he only knew that the bangs on my forehead were covering a huge scar. If he had known, he would have quickly disappeared!

He was a great dancer too, the best I'd ever been with! This guy could win anybody's heart in five minutes, and I wondered why was he was wearing shorts when everyone else was dressed up. And his hands and his shoulders! I had never really fallen for looks before, but Sasha had everything. One of the charming things about him was that he spoke Russian with a Georgian accent, yet he couldn't have been Georgian because he had blonde curly hair and blue eyes. No Georgian ever looked like he did.

He told me that he was Russian and that his grandfather had been one of Stalin's favourite chefs, who had been brought many years ago to work on Stalin's huge estate in Gagra. Since then, his whole family had established themselves there.

Interestingly, after the Revolution, every Republic in the USSR kept its mother tongue as their first language, and most of them strongly objected to Russian. Georgians took the strongest stand. Many of them hardly spoke any Russian, in spite of the fact that the Russian language had become mandatory in all schools in the USSR.

At the end of the evening Sasha asked me if he could escort me to my place. I told him that this girl from the resort was counting on me and that I had to go back with her. He offered to accompany us both, as he knew the place where we were staying without my ever telling him! He also offered to take me out on his boat the next day and that if I wanted to bring this girl along, it was fine with him.

I thought it was pretty decent of him, and I found out that his parents' villa was immediately adjacent to our resort. He had seen this girl and myself going down the hill while he was up in a tree picking oranges.

My first thought was, "Oh, no! He must have seen me when I pulled my dress to adjust my underwear!" I knew I'd done that when we were going down the hill! I asked him if he had seen me doing something funny, and, smiling, he said he had. He said he was sitting in the tree when he saw me stop and pull up my dress to fix something. He thought it was rather cute and decided he had to meet me before anyone else could ask me to dance. He apologized for not being dressed appropriately, but he hadn't had time to change because he wanted to arrive at the dance floor before we did.

I thought it was crazy, that he must be blind! Tomorrow on the boat he'd find out. I wished I had some kind of cap, but even if I had one, it would be windy on the boat and there'd be no way I could cover up my scar. Oh, well! Let him discover it. Let him discover it and be turned off. I didn't need anyone to fall in love with me anyway. I loved Valentin. And even if I didn't, there was no way I could have a long-distance romance. I'd come to this place to rest and recuperate after my disastrous accident. After this holiday I'd have to go back and continue slaving for one more year in the meat plant.

Right then, I was in a different world, a dream world. The resort wasn't reality. Reality was at the Moscow meat plant.

Surprisingly, Sasha didn't quit on me the next day or the day after. He was at my place early in the morning, right after breakfast, and took me everywhere. The clinging vine came alone the whole time, but she hardly ever spoke and most of the time we even forgot she was there.

He talked about all kinds of personal things and also how much he liked me. "I'm falling in love with you," he said. "You're so different. You don't pretend! And I love your poetry and your sense of humour. I think you have a very interesting face, and your eyes are so alive! They express so many different emotions and they even change colour, depending on your mood!"

I had the best three weeks of my life. We went on his boat every morning after breakfast, and he taught me how to row. I loved it! He was a great swimmer and wasn't afraid to dive, even though we were often a long way from the beach. He would swim for a long time while I rowed. Then he would catch up and jump right back in, without rocking the boat at all, and sit across until he dried off.

Unfortunately I couldn't even try to swim. I was terribly scared to, ever since I'd almost drowned once at summer camp. He understood my fear and didn't push me. "One day you will discover the beauty of swimming again," he said.

After the boat, he took us to one of the hidden places in the mountains, where we had our lunch. Everybody knew him wherever we went. And he was totally at home no matter where we were. Almost every day at five o'clock in the afternoon he played volleyball and insisted I go there with him. He looked like a prince when he played. I was sure all the girls went there to watch him play and to admire his figure. His legs were absolutely stunning! I still couldn't understand what he saw in me. Truly, I wasn't myself during that time. I couldn't do many of things I normally did, and I still had my headaches. I definitely was not at my best.

One day, Sasha invited me to meet his family. He told me that it was going to be a formal dinner. I really didn't know what that meant, but I knew because it was a seven-o'clock dinner on a Saturday, I would have to look my best. The problem was, I didn't have anything special to wear. I had the dress that I'd worn the first night we met, but I'd worn it more than half a dozen times since. My Natasha Rostov blouse was a little out of place and wasn't appropriate for this climate. All the girls in my room offered me their clothes, but most of them were too loose on me and didn't look right. We settled on a silk blouse and a skirt from two different girls, although the skirt needed a safety pin to fit me better.

To hide the scar on my forehead I needed bangs. I pulled my hair up using fancy hairpins from one of the girls. My high-heeled sandals were still the best shoes I owned. Finally I was dressed and ready to go.

"You look like a princess!" they all said.

"But don't you think this skirt is a little too short for me?"

"No, no! Your legs look great, and with the high heels you look nice and tall!"

One of them said, "Tall girls are in style now, did you know?"

"Oh," I said. "But now what about lipstick? My lips are so big. I don't think I should wear any."

"Full lips are the fashion now!" the same girl announced.

"Yes!" all of them chimed in. "They are! You should be happy to have full lips and large eyes!"

It all sounded extremely strange to my ears. The accident had obviously taken away my confidence. I mean, I couldn't so quickly forget how I looked when I first saw myself in that hospital mirror!

Sasha came to pick me up at a quarter to seven. He wore a silky off-white suit with a shirt and tie of the same colour. Even his shoes were a cream colour. I liked the way he looked, so comfortable and casual. In fact,

I liked everything about him, except his last name. It reminded me of my father's name. I told him so and that I had a bad vibe about the name.

"Well!" he said, smiling down at me, "there's nothing I can do about my last name, unfortunately. If we got married, you'd have to take my last name! It's the law."

I thought he was joking. I soon found out he wasn't. When we walked through the gates of his family estate, I realized that their place was as big as our resort, which was huge. We had to go up a very long set of steps leading to the main house. There were all kinds of fruit trees on either side. Trees and more trees of oranges, mandarins, lemons, grapefruit, apricots, peaches. I'd never seen such a sight! And there were vineyards with different-coloured grapes everywhere as far as the eye could see. By the time we got to the house, I was out of breath. His mother met us at the entrance; she was a beautiful woman in her mid-forties. Sasha looked exactly like her. She had natural blond hair and blue eyes, and her smile was very soft. She looked so relaxed that I immediately felt at ease.

Before we entered the dining room we passed at least ten other rooms. They were all beautifully decorated, yet they had a certain warmth and simplicity to them. In one of the rooms we met Sasha's younger sister, Tonia, who was about ten years old. She didn't resemble her brother or mother at all. Their mother, whose name was Nina, told Tonia to join us in the dining room in ten minutes.

The dining room had an enormous table, which was set for five. I now understood what Sasha meant about a formal dinner. Two waiters in black tuxedos and white gloves stood on each side of the table, which was set with the most exquisite china and crystal I had ever seen. Beautiful white flowers were not only on the table but also everywhere in the room. The waiter on my side helped me with my chair, and Sasha was seated right next to me.

I felt comfortable in spite of all the luxury surrounding me. There was something warm and natural about everything and everybody, including Sasha's father, who came into the room just as I sat down. He introduced himself in a very simple manner and told me his name was Nikolai and that I should call him by first name.

This was very unusual. Normally the first name would be given along with the person's father's name. He and his wife were seated across from us, with Tonia at her father's side. I could see she resembled her young-looking father, who was tall and slim like Sasha, with brownish hair and grey eyes. He wore exactly the same colour suit, shirt, and tie as Sasha.

The whole environment was like a beautiful fairy tale. Dinner began with delicious appetizers, which were brought in by two more waiters also dressed in black tuxedos and white gloves. The other two looked after our wine, and all of them had white towels over their right arms. I was completely stunned. I couldn't believe that the whole affair was in my honour. Yet this was exactly what Nikolai was saying at that very moment. He welcomed me and said that he hoped I'd find myself happy being part of the family. He said that their family was huge and that I was going to meet everybody next Saturday. I couldn't understand why, but I soon found out.

After the first glass of wine, our glasses were filled again, and Sasha got up to say that he was in love with me, and then he asked me to marry him!

"You don't have to answer right now," he said, with a charming smile, "but it's our custom to propose marriage in front of our parents!"

There was no such custom in Russia, but, apparently, although these people were Russians, they had adopted Georgian traditions.

When Sasha asked me to marry him, I turned red all over. My head started to hurt, and I felt weak. Then Nikolai told us his love story. Apparently, exactly the same thing had happened when he met Nina, with this difference—that Nina had come to Gagra with her parents for a holiday and they had stayed at the same resort where I was staying. She was a young graduate of the Moscow medical school at the time, and they fell head over heels in love with each other and were married in a couple of months. Both of them were twenty-one years old and were still in love now.

Nikolai looked at us. "It's amazing how history repeats itself, isn't it?"

After dinner we all walked out onto the beautiful veranda off the dining room, which was covered in grape vines. I'd never seen so many grapes. Nikolai said that they had another custom. When a son was born into the family they put aside a barrel of the best wine and kept it underground until the day the boy got married. Today they'd decided to take out Sasha's barrel for us to have the first taste of the wine.

We all went down to the wine cellar, which had an enormous collection of wines. Nikolai told me about the different kinds, some of which were a hundred years old! His father, the famous gourmet chef, had been a collector of wines, and he showed me an empty barrel that had been there since his wedding day. The fairy tale continued, as we tasted the wine from Sasha's barrel.

My head was killing me, however, and I was afraid I'd be sick. Sasha took me back to my place a few minutes before midnight—just before the doors were locked at exactly twelve, which was a rule for the "guests' protection." Georgians were known to be hot-blooded and were always after Russian girls. When we got to my place, he wanted to kiss me, but I excused myself until the next day. Once in bed, I lay with my eyes wide open, thinking of how it had all happened so fast.

He was at my place the following morning, both of us feeling somewhat awkward as we went to his boat. We said nothing about the night before, and he went swimming as usual. Only when he returned to the boat did we feel more at ease, especially after he splashed water on me and then kissed me on cheek. Then he held me in his wet arms, and we kissed for a long time. Suddenly, everything felt all right, with the boat the only witness to our new intimacy. It was wonderful! That evening we went for a long walk on the beach, holding hands, talking, and kissing. Later that night, Sasha again talked to me about marriage.

At the end of the week we applied for a marriage certificate, and on Saturday we had a big dinner with the entire family and their close friends. I found out that Nikolai was the number one surgeon in Gagra and that Nina worked as the head of the health department of the Gagra resorts. There were many speeches that evening and endless toasts while the family story unraveled clearly through all of it.

It was a remarkably loving family. Nikolai's father, the celebrated chef, told me a few interesting stories about Stalin's elaborate dinners, which he had conducted in his younger years. He said that although Stalin had huge estates all over the country, the Gagra estate was his favourite.

That night Nikolai rang my resort and asked permission for me to arrive home late, which was granted with no problem. Sasha and I didn't have to rush to get me back in time, and we walked slowly, enjoying the beauty of the night. He wanted me to stay in Gagra until our wedding at the end of September, but I couldn't do such a thing. I wanted to go back to Moscow and arrange everything properly. Although he suggested going with me, I told him it wouldn't be necessary. I was capable of doing everything by myself.

The time of my holiday was coming to an end, and Sasha and I were busy going places and doing things—we even ordered a wedding dress for me. I wrote a letter to my friend at the meat plant and told her all about my marriage plans. The last couple of nights before my departure, Sasha didn't want to be away from me for more than a few minutes. On our long walks along the beach, he still tried to convince me that we should go to Moscow together. I wanted him to move there after our wedding, but it was out of the question, which bothered me a lot.

At the railway station both of us wept. I think somehow we had a feeling we weren't going to see each other again.

I felt both relieved and confused when the train left. I was dying to be alone, and my first question to myself was, "Am I really in love with Sasha?" If so, why I wasn't looking forward to moving to Gagra? Something was bothering me. In fact I felt a sense of panic. How was I to live in Gagra? I still had to complete high school and only then could I go to university.

We had talked a lot about it with his family, and all of them kept telling me it would be no problem. After I graduated from high school, I could study in Tbilisi and we would commute; it was only a two-hour drive. In fact, Sasha's parents said it would give them a reason to go the Georgian capital more often.

All of it sounded so ideal but how much reality was there in all these plans? What if I got pregnant? What would happen then? Would my plans then be delayed? Probably, but every time I brought the subject up, Sasha had an answer. His parents and grandparents would be happy to take care of our baby while I was in school. As a matter of fact, both Nikolai and Nina confirmed that they would have really liked to have had one more child, but it hadn't worked out.

Since Tonia's birth, Nina had been unable to get pregnant, and so they were looking forward to having Sasha's children while they were still young and while their own parents were still around. It all sounded great, but I still wasn't sure about my own career under these circumstances.

Another thing was the Georgian language. I had decided to become a lawyer, and to practice law in Georgia without real knowledge of the language was a big problem. These things weren't a problem for Sasha of course, only for me. Deep down I knew I would find myself trapped with no choices of my own.

Suddenly the whole thing appeared totally unrealistic. Sasha was already a doctor, and his career was all lined up for him in Gagra. He had the support of his whole family. He had no worries about his future. But what about me? I was not going to have a career as a housewife no matter what! On the other hand, it was very tempting to become part of such a happy family as this one.

My thoughts raced back and forth, and the more I thought, the more impossible it all appeared to be. When I had asked Sasha to live in Moscow, he said he would never do such a thing.

"I prefer to be a king in a small place," he said, "than a nobody in a big place." And I couldn't blame him for that. I'd grown up in a big city, and life in a place like Gagra didn't appeal to me that much. In actual fact, it seemed clear I shouldn't marry Sasha, or at least not right then.

So, what was I to do? How could I have agreed? Where was my head? And all of it had been so nicely planned and organized; it was too late to back off. Or was it? Maybe not! Perhaps it could still be corrected. I felt terrible, but the truth of the matter was that it would be a big mistake on my part if I went ahead and married Sasha. I knew I couldn't go through with it. What was I going to do?

I was supposed to take care of everything on my own, and then Sasha was to come to Moscow for some shopping. We were going to stay in a hotel for a couple of weeks, after which we would both travel to Gagra in September. I didn't think it was fair for me to carry on another day without telling him.

I had to let him know so he wouldn't come to Moscow. I figured the right thing to do was to write him a letter and tell him the truth. It was the hardest letter I had ever written. When at last I finished writing it, I felt much better. I decided to post my letter in the train station during a long stopover, after which I returned to my seat and fell into a deep sleep and stayed that way for the remainder of my journey.

The train arrived in Moscow in the early morning, and I went straight to Grusha's place. She was up already, and I noticed something was wrong as soon as I walked in. Her smile wasn't the same.

"Grusha!" I said. "You look so sad! What is the matter?"

She sighed heavily and tears came to her eyes. "Janna," she said, "we have a big problem!"

"With what? Tell me!"

"Somebody wrote an anonymous letter to the militia that I was doing something illegal renting my place to somebody. And then a militia officer came and told me I had to get rid of my tenant in fifteen days or they'd take away my own room and give me a smaller one."

"Grusha! That's terrible!"

"Well, I don't need this place, and I can't afford it anyway now that I'm alone."

Now tears were falling in big droplets down her cheeks. "Some families of three or four live in much smaller rooms. I know that!" she sobbed.

Her tears poured down and her nose began to run. As she picked up her skirt to wipe her face, I noticed she had no underwear on and I began to laugh. She was startled.

"What's so funny?" she asked.

I told her, and she said that all her life she hated wearing underwear, even during the winter. I couldn't believe it! For some reason, I found it excruciatingly funny, and I couldn't stop laughing!

I had always laughed nonstop for some silly reason every now and then, which my father hated. He'd yell at me to stop, but the more he shouted at me, the more I laughed. It came from deep down in my gut, and I couldn't breathe in for a while. When I did, I made this ridiculous sound, and then my father would slap my face.

Later in life I found out that Cancers were known for their wild laughter, which was exactly how I found myself at seeing Grusha's bare bottom. Finally, Grusha too broke into peals of laughter. Then, at the sight of Grusha's toothlessness, I became so hysterical I nearly had an accident!

The next day I went to the militia and explained to the officer that Grusha hadn't charged me any money to stay in her place but had invited me there for company. I told him about her husband, who was very sick in jail, and that she was the last person who deserved any kind of punishment. In the end the officer had tears in his eyes as I pleaded with him not to take Grusha's place away from her. It was enough that she'd lost everything, I told him.

The officer dialed a number and spoke to someone. In an informal manner, he simply told the person on the other end of the line to leave Grusha alone, that she wasn't doing anything illegal. She had just had someone there to keep her company and that this person was going to be gone within a week.

I returned to Grusha's and told her not to worry, that her room was safe but I would have to move out. She hugged me over and over.

"Thank you, thank you, Janna! But oh how I will miss you! Come have tea with me. I won't cry." She looked at me slyly. "But it would be nice to hear you laugh like that again!"

The following morning I received a long telegram from Sasha who said he was coming to Moscow to get me. He wasn't going to take no for an answer.

How I was to deal with this? I had to go to work. When I walked into my supervisor's office to report, he got up from his chair and greeted me as though he were my father! "Congratulations, Janna, I am very happy for you! Are you going to invite me to your wedding? I love Gagra. I was there many times, especially when I was young. Oh, those were the times...The wine we drank, the songs we sang...Anyway, you must invite me to your wedding! It will give me a reason to go back there again!"

I listened to what he was saying, and I couldn't understand where all this had come from. Then I remembered the letter that I had written to my girlfriend about Sasha and me. It looked like she had spread the news!

This was my chance! I wasn't going to tell the truth to my supervisor since this was my one ticket to freedom. This way I could break my contract. I intended to use it, and I did.

After that, everything was easy. I had a list of all the divisions to obtain clearance signatures, and by the afternoon my workbook was ready. Actually, every step I made that day was smooth and easy. Everybody smiled at me and wished me luck and happiness, but I felt sorry for the girls on my team. They had to stay one more year—and some of them probably for life.

At three o'clock in the afternoon I found myself outside the meat plant's gigantic gates, holding my first workbook (a record mandatory for future jobs) in my hands.

Sasha never found me. I was free!

CHAPTER 19

At the Top

Now I had to make a decision as to what I wanted to do. I had a passport, which meant I had a choice. I could choose anything I wanted. That made the whole difference, and it felt great!

My head still bothered me and was affecting my ability to memorize to a degree. Before my accident, I had an almost photographic memory. I would sit in a classroom, listening to the teacher, and the next day I could repeat everything word for word. I seldom had to read things over and over to memorize. Now I had to work really hard at learning by heart.

I wanted to be a lawyer and could have used that ability to memorize so easily. I also loved poetry and could remember so many poems. When I left the orphanage, my father's brothers used to get me to tell them what I knew, and I was happy to demonstrate. I would stand in the middle of the room and recite poem after poem until nobody listened anymore!

They also used to tease me about my love of cooking. They would ask me how I made borscht. I would tell them everything in detail. "What if it was too salty?" they would ask.

And I would answer, "Put in lots of sugar!"

My answer made them laugh. "And if there was too much sugar in something?"

"I'd put in lots of salt!"

Anyway, my memory had changed, but I wasn't an "invalid," and that was what counted. "Remember," I told myself, "take nothing for granted." The decision about my next job was a simple one. I knew I wanted to work in the most important firm in the entire Soviet Union. It was near the Kremlin, the Central Planning Institution for the entire country, called Gosplan USSR. That was where I wanted to work! It was the top place in Moscow, and nobody could stop me! What would I do there? It didn't matter—even if I had to scrub the floors. That was where I had to be. I wanted to learn everything I needed to know to prepare myself to be a lawyer. I would go to night school, but after graduation I would continue working in the Gosplan as a lawyer. It was an ideal plan!

The next morning I dressed in my Natasha Rostova outfit; I had dyed it black and it looked even better than before. I walked into the building at the Prospect of Karl Marx, Number 12, right at the corner of Gorki Street and the Ohotny Riad Subway. The Hotel National was on the opposite side of Gorki, and the Metropol Hotel was right across from it. You could see the Kremlin from any window of the Gosplan offices. I thought about the meat plant and what a contrast it would be to work here.

As I walked in, the security guards looked at me a little suspiciously, but I showed them my passport immediately and told them I had to see the head of the personnel department, that it was very important.

"Have you got a pass?" they asked me.

"No," I said, "but it doesn't matter! I have to see the head of personnel!"

"No, no!" they said. "You must make an appointment! Then a pass will be issued. Then you have to show it and your passport too!"

"Well," I said, "I don't have any of these things, but it's a matter of life and death, and I'm not going to leave until I see the head of personnel."

I must have said something right because they called and spoke with this one and that one and then they told me to wait.

In a short time, a woman in a black suit came down and introduced herself as Akimovna. She said that the head of personnel wasn't available, but I could talk to her. She had a pass made up then and there in the security office and invited me to follow her.

We passed a number of enormous doors, some of which were open, where I caught a glimpse of people behind their desks. Nobody gave me the slightest glance. They were all too busy. We went into a large office with two secretaries, which had beautiful mahogany double-doors that led into a big office where Akimovna then seated herself behind a massive mahogany desk. Pointing to one of the most beautiful antique chairs I had ever seen, she asked me to sit down.

I told her my story from the beginning up to my accident and about my decision to work at the Gosplan. "I'll do anything!" I said. "I could start by washing floors and you don't have to pay me until I learn to do it perfectly!"

She listened carefully, and at the end of my story she told me to come back the next morning, not saying what I was going to do. I couldn't believe it! It had worked! I thanked her several times and she asked the secretary to have me fill out some forms. After I did, the secretary, who was a very pleasant older woman, gave me a temporary pass and told me to bring in two pictures of myself for the next day.

I danced all the way to a photography studio to have the photographs taken, but when the photographer said they would be ready in three days, I nearly cried.

"I can't wait three days!" I said. "I need them now!"

"Okay!" he said. "Come back tomorrow morning at eight o'clock, and I'll have them ready for you."

The next morning I was up at five, unable to sleep. My new place was so small I could hardly move. There was only enough space for my bed, which was the couch, and there was another bed in the room for my landlady. The couch and bed were separated by the dining table, which doubled as my desk, and there was only one chair.

If my landlady and I wanted to eat at the same time, I would have to sit on the narrow hard arm of the couch so that she could have the chair. The dresser containing all our clothes was next to the door, and if I sat at the table, and my landlady wanted to get into it, I would have to move out of my chair!

My new landlady was a retired widow with no children. She had worked at the plant for thirty-five years. Her pension was only forty rubles a month, fifteen of which went to the government, for her apartment. Her medication cost her ten rubles a month, and whatever was left had to go for food and other things. She took me in as a tenant to help her out, and in actual fact the fifteen rubles I paid only covered her medication, with very little left over.

With a heart condition and high blood pressure, she needed as much rest as possible, and I had to be careful not to disturb her. I had to prepare everything the night before and go out to a little corridor to change. Her apartment was shared with another single woman. The tiny bathroom and washroom were opposite our room. The kitchen was as tiny as everything else. It was only big enough for a stove, some shelving, and two tables.

The best part of the kitchen was the marble shelf under the window, which was about a metre wide and a half metre deep. Half the shelf space was shared by each neighbour and since our half was empty, I used it as my makeup table, where I would take my time to make myself beautiful!

This particular morning I felt like an actress getting ready for her premiere performance! Before I got into my bath I made myself a facial mask from an egg yolk and then the whites with a few drops of lemon from my landlady, who I knew would never notice. After all, this was going to be my big day. I was going to work at the top place in Moscow and I had to look glamorous!

By eight o'clock I was at the photographer's. My pictures were ready and luckily I didn't look too bad because they reflected my excitement. I had three quarters of an hour to kill, but I decided to go straight to the Gosplan building and wait until it opened. To my surprise, the security guards were at their posts. My three-month temporary pass was ready, so all they had to do was check my passport, compare my photos, and put one on the pass. The other photo was to go to the personnel department.

I couldn't believe I was actually allowed to enter the most important building in Moscow other than the Kremlin! This was the place where the most important people in Russia were working, controlling the whole USSR economy! Could this really be me walking along and soon to become part of this organisation?

While waiting, I decided to get myself acquainted with the building directory, which was on the main floor. Reading it, I was overwhelmed with the number of services provided for these civil servants. It looked to me as though all the workers, like the meat plant people and other industries, were catering to the civil servants of the Gosplan USSR. I didn't understand why they were called "servants." They weren't servants. Everyone else was!

They had five restaurants, two cafeterias, a cleaning service, repair services of all kinds, a shoe-making store, separate women's and men's clothing stores, a food store called "special foods," and other services. All of it was open from nine to five, so the people who worked in the Gosplan could buy everything they needed during working hours. They didn't have to stand in line like the rest of the people, which meant they could spend quality time with their families. Also on the third floor they had a travel office, cultural office (entertainment box office), jewelry office, and stores. After that, the directory listed the real planning-related departments along with personnel, which was on the fourth floor.

I went straight there, but the doors were still closed. However, in the hallway I studied the offices of the department. Personnel occupied the entire floor and every office had double doors, beautifully hand crafted in perfect detail, which looked very grand.

On the right of each door was a glass-plated sign stating the name of the department head and with long titles of everyone's rank. They all sounded very important. I didn't know how there could be such a variety and number of such high executive positions and titles—then again, what did I know?

My only experience was the structure of the meat plant, where I figured they had more than enough high-ranking titles, but at least there they had thirty thousand workers and were making tons of meat products. On the other hand Gosplan, this huge organisation, planned all kinds of industries for the whole country! And I knew that every republic had the same Gosplan setup. I didn't understand at this point, however, why they needed to have everything duplicated in Moscow.

All of this I had to study and find out about.

By now, the elevator was stopping every two minutes letting out at least twenty people. Most of them were young, well-dressed women, all of whom had keys to their particular doors. They all looked like very important secretaries.

The next couple of loads were mainly men, most of whom were middle aged and dressed in very elegant three-piece suits and carrying leather briefcases. Later on, the elevators let out only one or two people at a time. All of these were men, who came out of the elevators at a very leisurely pace. They carried nothing—not even newspapers.

They were all tall and on the heavy side, except for one who was tall and slim. He stopped when he saw me and said, "Hello. Are you waiting for me?"

"No, I don't think so," I replied. "I'm waiting for Akimovna and she's supposed to have me start my job."

"Oh yes," he said. "That's what she told me, that she hired a secretary for me yesterday. Come with me."

He opened the door with his own key and then I realized he didn't have a secretary. The room was huge and nicely decorated with a large mahogany desk and another table with a typewriter. A third table had several telephones on it, one of which was ringing and which he ignored as we walked in.

I didn't know what to say. I was shocked, and my hands were trembling. I couldn't believe what was happening to me. Then I told him there was some mistake. I wasn't a secretary and didn't even know how to type. "But I could work as a courier between the offices," I said.

"Come to my office, Janna," he answered.

He knew my name!

"This is not a mistake. From now on you are my executive secretary. I don't need a typist. My department has a separate typing bureau, so you will be giving them whatever needs to be done. You may have to type a few short memos from time to time, but your responsibilities will be quite different and you'll learn them as you go along. Let me explain what we do," he said, "and after that I'll introduce you to the members of my Glavek."

I knew what that term meant because I'd read the directory. It was *Glavnoye Upravlenie* ("main supervision"). He explained that he was the head of the Civil Building Industry of the USSR. His Glavek dealt with this industry by planning and controlling it in every republic of the USSR. It was a very high-pressure job.

"You are going to be a very important part of this Glavek as my personal executive secretary," he said, with a smile. "The communication between myself, members of my staff, and many other organisations will be through you, so there you are!"

He then explained the telephone system and how to communicate with him. After that he took me around to the other offices on the floor.

And that is how I started to work in Gosplan! At the end of the first week I knew everyone on the floor by their last names and had memorized the first and last name of the head of every department within the Glavek. My biggest problem was not communication; it was typing, which I was painfully slow at. It was fascinating to watch an expert typist who never had to look at the keyboard. The typists used "the blind system." As for me, I would have been happy to learn to type with four fingers. I practiced every free moment and would arrive at least an hour and a half before work and stay an hour after. My school didn't start until seven, so I used my time to improve my skills.

At the end of the month, I received a phone call to go to personnel and get my pay at the cashier's window. I told them it was a mistake. I wasn't supposed to be paid yet because I was only learning. They called me again closer to five o'clock and reprimanded me for holding them back.

"The cashier won't sit there forever waiting for you! She has to close her window!"

I told them again that it was a mistake—but oh how I needed the money! I had been hungry for weeks now. All I could afford was some bread with tea and no sugar, although I still had a little bit of money for my transportation. My landlady had agreed to wait for her rent, which was a blessing, and nobody except her knew how strapped I was for food and money. Even she thought I ate at the Gosplan.

Anyway, the people in charge of pay wouldn't leave me alone. They kept calling, infuriated, until finally at ten after five, Akimovna herself called me and told me to go to the cashier's window. She said that my boss was very pleased with my work and that typing was the last skill required for my position. In fact, he had called her personally and thanked her for hiring me.

Now I knew that I had a right to take the money! When the cashier saw me, she looked at me as though I were a mental case!

She counted the money out in front of me and had me sign for it. I didn't even know how much I was being paid. I put my signature in the only blank area and then she firmly shut the window down with a bang. I think she wouldn't have minded slapping me if she could have! When I counted the money, I found it was more than triple what I had made at the meat plant and I hadn't even felt that any of it had been work!

I enjoyed myself most of the time. I was on the phone with lots of people, requesting that they call my boss or connecting him with whomever he wanted to talk to. I arranged meetings with the heads of different departments with my boss and other things of that nature. It wasn't work; it was fun! And everybody treated me with respect and called me by my first and second name, Janna Borisovna. I kept visualising those hard-working, tired faces at the meat plant and felt almost guilty until I began to realize that there wasn't much justice in the USSR.

As time went by, I became accustomed to the many privileges the job provided for its people, and my boss was very good to me. He never made me feel that I was a simple secretary but somebody important. He would call me into his office at the end of every day and talk with me about his business problems or ideas. He discussed politics with me and diplomacy in the business world, and he called certain people "idiots." These were important people, some of them even ministers.

Quite often he asked for my advice and praised me for being smart and mature for my age.

I certainly felt mature. After all, in seven months I was going to be eighteen. I had looked after myself for over three years then, and as far as I was concerned, I was doing a good job. I dressed well and by now had a few good things, like woolen sweaters: three of them! I had a pair of expensive leather boots, which somebody had brought from Italy. I paid two months' salary for them, but it was worth it. I planned my buying ahead of time, and I never bought anything because it was cheap.

Good things weren't sold in the state stores, and even if they occasionally were, the lineups were too long. Some people specialized in buying these things and then reselling them for profit. I was able to order through the company stores, but to me they were old-fashioned. The best clothes were brought in from Italy or France and were sold only through speculators for a large sum of money.

Every time I made a purchase of this kind I would take out a short-term, interest-free loan, which was available for Gosplan employees. I was very careful in every other area of spending, such as food and social activities, but my number one priority was to be well dressed for my job. I also didn't want anyone to know that I had financial difficulties.

The majority of executive secretaries were daughters, nieces, or close friends of those who were big shots. The girls were snobbish. Their families had cars, some of them with personal chauffeurs. They all had winterized dachas (cottages), but for some reason they hadn't gone to university. Their conversations consisted of nothing but marriage or boyfriends or about sons of this or that important person.

The only person who knew a lot about me was Akimovna. She became my true friend, although she was more than twice my age and had a very important position in personnel. Sometimes she would even invite me to her home for dinner. She had a nice husband and a daughter who was eleven years old, and I felt very comfortable with all of them. It felt wonderful to be with a normal family.

As for my family, there had been some changes. Sema had graduated from university and still lived at home, but Mama had a very hard time with her. She catered to her and my father, which I could never understand. She constantly complained to me about their treatment of her, yet when I offered to have her move in with me, she wouldn't consider it. "Well, when Sema gets married and moves perhaps I'll have some peace!" She was hopeless!

Mama told me that when Sema had graduated from high school and written the entrance exam to get into university, there were at least seven applicants for the one opening. Professors and administrators made a lot of money by accepting bribes from those who didn't stand a chance.

Sema got father to pay a large sum of money for her because she was sure she wouldn't get in. She didn't make it, but the person who had received the money suggested she go to a branch of the same university near Minsk. Perhaps after the first semester, a seat might be available in Moscow and she would then be transferred. Sema was miserable about this, but she went.

Not even a month after she left, father received a phone call telling him that Sema had attempted suicide and was in bad shape. Her parents were advised to come immediately.

It was Mama who went. She found Sema in bed, staring at the ceiling and refusing to even turn her head when she walked in. The administration told her that Sema had fallen in love with one of the students in her group. After a couple of weeks of going out together, the young man lost interest in her and started going with another girl from the group. Sema couldn't take it and decided to end her life, waiting by the train tracks until someone saw her, took her by the hand, and brought her back to her residence. To this day, I don't believe Sema intended to actually kill herself.

In a matter of hours, Mama made all the arrangements with Moscow University to accept Sema there and then she brought her back home. She looked after her and made her the best food and did all kinds of things for her until Sema felt better. As soon as she got back to normal, Mama couldn't do anything right. Sema started to bitch and complain to father about her. I could never understand why she continued to take this horrible abuse.

There was something else that happened between my father and me over this three-and-a-half-year period. It happened while he was on vacation in Georgia. My landlady had died, and her room was given to a couple of pensioners, so I had to move out. I had only two days to find another place, but there was nothing available. In fact, most people didn't have enough room for their own families.

Mama told me that Father had gone on his holidays and so had Sema, which meant I could stay with her for a few weeks until I found a place for myself.

"Even though I have no place to go, I don't feel like going home, Mama," I said. "Even for a short time."

"Why not?" Mama asked. "It will be just us!"

It felt strange to be there, however. It brought back all sorts of negative feelings. Yet, I had no choice. I was preparing for my university exams and had taken my holiday time to concentrate on doing just that.

The first week went peacefully, but one day we had an unexpected visitor. It was my father's daughter from his first marriage. Apparently, he had been married once before and had left his wife when his daughter Lora wasn't even three years old. He hadn't kept in touch and she found out about her long-lost father at the age of twenty. She also learned that her father had lost his second wife during the war and had ended up raising the three children on his own. She thought it might have softened him, and she was hoping for the possibility of a reunion.

Her mother advised her not to pursue it. She was sure nothing could ever change the man. She wanted to protect her daughter from more pain. I knew none of this and was completely surprised when she showed up.

Lora was thirty-two years old when she came by the house. She had never married and worked as an x-ray technician. She felt very bitter about her father, who had never bothered to find out what had happened to her. She wasn't beautiful, but she had blonde curly hair and a good figure and was well dressed. I was very happy to get to know her, and I thought we could become friends. But my father returned two days later ruined everything.

That morning, he had his Sunday breakfast in the company of his sister Rita, who'd come to meet Lora. I didn't have my breakfast with them; I had to study. My father and I, of course, were not on speaking terms. When he first saw me in the house he hadn't even said hello.

After she finished eating, Lora came to my room and began to talk to me. She liked my taste and was dying to see my wardrobe. Naturally everything I owned was in my suitcase since I was going out any day, but I let her see what I had. One of the things that attracted her more than anything was my silver fox collar, which could be worn on a coat or dress. It was in fashion at the time and was an expensive piece.

I had bought it several months earlier and my plan was to have a new winter coat made. Then I changed my mind because our Gosplan fur store received the first imitation fur fabric, which looked like sheepskin. It was light at the roots and brownish on the ends and it was a practical material, both light and warm.

When I saw it in our store, I decided that if I could get this material, I could sell my silver fox and that money would pay for the whole coat. The store had a limited amount of this new material and a lot of people wanted it. Consequently it was bought out by the big executives, who purchased it for their wives or daughters. Anything that was a hot item went to them rather than on a "first come, first served basis."

Akimovna, however, my friend, had the status to buy this material, and she offered to use her privilege to get it for me. I needed a little time to arrange the money, although she even offered to buy it with her own money. "It's important for you to have a practical coat, Janna," she said. "Your other idea was too fancy, in my opinion."

I agreed with her and arranged a loan in our loan department, paid her back, and we went together and ordered a coat to be made.

It was going to take four months to have it made but by then, I would have the money from my silver fox, my loan would be paid off, and I would have enough money by then for the coat. Everything seemed to be working out perfectly...until my father wrecked everything.

Lora fell in love with my silver fox. She would love to have bought it, but even if she'd had the money, one of my girlfriends had already put a fifty-ruble deposit on it and was intending to pay me the rest when my coat was ready.

Lora became very emotional and talked obsessively about the fur piece. "It's exactly what I need! And it's impossible to buy anything like it where I live!" she said.

It brought up a lot of talk about our father, and on this subject we had a lot in common. By now she was crying, talking about how he'd never bothered to find out anything about her since he left them in 1931. Her mother, who had had nothing but struggles, had never remarried because she was hurt for so many years, and after the war men simply became a rare commodity.

Half the women in Moscow were widows and many of the others had invalids for husbands, and so it was a hopeless situation. But in spite of the financial difficulties, her mother had taken good care of her and helped her get a reasonably good education. Lora had become a radiology technician, making good money and supporting her mother who had a very little pension.

"Get married?" Lora said, when I brought the subject up. "No! It's out of the question! I could never trust any man after what my father did to my mother and me! Besides, I'm in love with a married man. He's a doctor and works in the same clinic as I do, but of course he would never leave his wife and children and it makes me love him even more!" she sobbed.

Aunt Rita must have heard her and came into the room and listened to what Lora was weeping about. She told Lora that she would go and speak to her brother and make him buy my silver fox for her.

"After all," she said, "you're his daughter and he never did anything for you. He owes this much you this much! I'm sure he'll do it."

"But Aunt Rive," I said, "I've already promised my silver fox to a friend of mine! She has even given me a deposit!"

"It's more important for Lora to have it!" she said and marched out as though she were on an important mission!

In a few minutes she reappeared, looking victorious. "That's it, Lora! The fur is yours! Take it now and your father will give the money to Janna in September!"

In the end, I was happy that Lora got something she loved so much and that finally Father had done something for her. I would explain the situation to my friend and return her deposit.

At the end of September, my coat was almost ready and I was told I could pick it up in two weeks. I called my father's office and asked him for my money.

He said, "What money?"

I said, "For my silver fox, that you bought for Lora." I was beginning to understand what was coming.

He said, "I know of no such a thing, and I'm busy!" He hung up.

I sat by the phone in my office feeling like an idiot.

Then I went to see Aunt Rita. "Don't worry. I'll talk with him tonight," she said. "Call him back tomorrow. You'll get your money. There won't be any problem."

I called him the next day, and he said, "Look, I told you, I know nothing about your dealings!" and hung up again.

I never got my money back. It wasn't a small amount of money, either. It was almost a year's salary! Why had I gotten involved with this? Hadn't I known enough about my father? But it wasn't the money. It was his way of basically saying, "Either beg me and do everything my way or go to hell!"

He also didn't want me to be friendly with Lora. He hadn't liked her showing up at his door and reminding him of his past. He wanted her out of his life, and he knew this episode would do it.

I became so desperate I called Lora and told her. She was very upset and of course had already cut the fur and had had a hat, collar, and cuffs made out from it, and it was all attached to her winter coat!

I had to borrow more money to buy my winter coat, and it took me several years to pay off the loan. Often, when I was wearing it, I felt as though it were made of gold.

CHAPTER 20

My Boss

My love for Valentin still possessed me, although I was very busy and rarely saw him because of working full-time and going to school at night. That summer after I graduated from grade ten, I was preparing myself for my entrance exams into law school. I was pretty sure I wouldn't pass the first time, as there were at least fifteen applicants for every spot. If I didn't pass that year, I thought, I would take some preparatory courses and do it the next. I knew I'd pass eventually. It was just a matter of time.

Valentin by then was in his last year of university and had a little more time on his hands, yet he had his reason for not seeing me more often—which was money. He was a proud young man and generous too. Every time we met, he wanted us to go somewhere, which cost him more than he could afford, and he would never allow me to pay for anything. He had that old-school mentality that only the gentleman bought tickets and flowers and so on.

The only money he had was from his scholarship, which was only enough for books and a few other expenses. His mother was the breadwinner in the family and had very little money to spare. Valentin used to save his lunch money until he had enough for our date. Every time I wanted to buy the tickets for a play or a film, he found a reason to turn my offer down.

He never actually expressed this to me. He was too shy to admit the money issue. I learned this a few years after his graduation, once he was working and could afford to be the gentleman he wanted to be.

Yet, not knowing at the time the real reason for seeing him so seldom made me wonder if it was this sexual problem. I figured our passionate encounters caused him such physical discomfort that he had decided it was better not meet too often. Every time we were together, we had this burning desire to be close to each other. But I knew I couldn't actually make love and Valentin would never force me to do something I wasn't ready for.

Often I tried to talk myself into making love, but when we came close to it, I would feel scared. I would pull myself together and my body would simply freeze. He knew I wasn't ready to take this step and he knew and he wasn't going to push me. I was thankful to him for this. I also knew that not too many men would put up with this kind of relationship, but he did for years, and I loved him for it even more.

Many years later, he told me that he wanted to see me much more often so that sometimes he would come to the building where I worked and watch me coming out after work. He stayed far enough away so I couldn't see him, of course.

My secretarial position became more than just traditional secretarial tasks. My boss, Igor Karpovich, literally made me his assistant and even advisor, to some extent. He would ask me to stay a bit later on the days I didn't have to be at school. This would happen about two days a week, during which we would talk—or rather he talked most of the time and I would listen. He shared a lot of things with me, things that secretaries weren't supposed to know. He asked for my opinion and even advice and often praised me, saying I had a real talent for handling people.

"You have all the necessary qualities to achieve anything you want, Janna," he said. "And I'll help. All you have to do is ask."

My boss was a person who had a short temper, and a lot of people had a hard time dealing with him. I often smoothed things out for him, and there were people who asked me to speak to him for them. Many had trouble dealing with him directly.

I made sure to never to ask him for favours. I wasn't cut out to use anybody, and even though my way was the tougher one, I was prepared for it.

Once in a while, after our long conversations in his office he would give me a lift to my place in his car. He never showed any signs that he had any designs on me. It was strictly boss and secretary working hand in hand, and I trusted him.

How little I knew! It took him close to two years during which he made sure I felt very relaxed in his company as he patiently waited for his moment. He also knew about my relationship with Valentin. He assured me I was doing the right thing, keeping myself pure until I married him, and many times he told me he was proud of me. So I had no reason to think it was anything other than what it seemed: a good working relationship with my boss.

One Friday he asked me to take some important material home to be typed over the weekend. He said he'd take my office typewriter over to my place. He didn't demand this; he politely asked me if I could do this favour for him and of course I said I would.

It was a beautiful spring evening. I loved April and May. They were my favourite months of the year! I enjoyed watching nature gradually changing from winter to spring. Every day, starting from the end of March, it began to take place. It seemed to me that life was slowly waking up from a long winter's sleep to eventually a most exciting time—the spring.

You could see the snow-covered trees shaking off their coverlets and freeing themselves from this heavy load on their shoulders as they prepared to change their clothing to a happy green. The snow melting everywhere created its own pathways—narrow in the beginning and then becoming wider and wider until the entire area had opened up. In the reflecting sun the water gradually evaporated while steam rose up out of the ground.

And the air! The delicious air in early spring smelled of life, future, and happiness! The first blades of grass and the first leaves, so fresh, so pure and innocent!

Spring! Such a magnificent time of the year, and everything and everybody was affected by it; everyone wanted to love and to be loved. My heart was full to the brim with love for Valia, and even if we didn't see each other much, we wrote poems to each other expressing our feelings. His words were good; although, most of his poetry was either about snow or rain. His lyrics were melancholy and mine were dramatic. He also sang his poems, which I never did. I didn't have a talent for singing, yet I loved his music and absolutely adored listening.

That Friday evening changed my life drastically.

After work, my boss loaded his car with the typewriter and paper, and he also brought some wine and chocolates. As he started his car, he turned on his stereo and put on romantic music, which we listened to with enjoyment. His car moved along slowly as we went through the avenue of Central Prospect, passing by hotels, museums, and theatres. All these buildings were in old Moscow, representing power and art.

We passed by churches—architecturally astonishing buildings with their golden crosses stretched so high up that it seemed as though they were connected to a different life we knew nothing about. These churches had been built centuries and centuries before, crafted by human hands and talents now inaccessible to our present way of life. Probably for this reason they appeared to be magic.

And then the car was taking us to the outskirts of the city toward the north, along the edge of the forest. We breathed in the fresh air, and the music slowly played, adding to the harmony of the magnificent spring environment. I was lost in my thoughts.

At one point, my boss suggested we turn off the road for a short time to admire the sunset. His words were, "We should allow ourselves time to experience the pleasure of these rare, peaceful moments. We live such busy, high-pressured lives, always trying to achieve more. In the meantime, only moments like these are what real life and happiness is about."

I couldn't argue with that. Ever since I'd started working at age fourteen, I was at school most of the evenings and didn't have time to enjoy my favourite season of spring.

As the car proceeded along the narrow road, sounds of nature surrounded us. The birds were singing; even the frogs were tuning in with their funny little short quacking sounds, and the car music only enhanced nature's chorus. The whole environment became a complete peaceful symphony.

Finally we stopped. It was beginning to feel a little chilly, and my boss closed the windows and locked the car doors, saying, "You never know what might happen. We must never forget to take care of ourselves!"

He opened a bottle of wine, poured out two glasses, and we sat, sipping the wine and listening to the music. He put his seat down so he could stretch his legs, but even then I had no reason not to trust him. After all, we had worked together for two whole years and he was my boss who shared all his problems with me. I felt comfortable and relaxed.

He offered to put my seat back and then suddenly I felt his lips on mine, and before I could react, his entire body was pressing down on me, trapping me, with no space to move or breathe. I struggled to free myself, but his mouth was pressing on mine so hard that I felt powerless. I was choking, my arms were locked in by his, and his legs were fighting against every bit of resistance I had in my power! I was fighting for my life, which he was beginning to realize, yet his urge to win absolutely controlled him, and he came up with the most diabolical way of getting what he wanted.

The minute I freed myself, he managed to pin my arms behind my back with one hand and rip off my panties with the other. With one quick unmistakable move he simply shoved his fingers into me. I experienced the sharpest pain, which caused me to jump so quickly that I freed myself from his body in a matter of seconds. Without the slightest hesitation, I broke the window with my head and fell out of his car.

Once outside, I picked myself up from the ground and ran. I don't remember how I found my way home, but I did. I was hurting badly. I was bleeding. My entire body was aching and my head was splitting. I was one tingling mass of pain.

CHAPTER 21

In Hiding

I washed myself as best I could and went right to bed, pretending I had a headache. I lay there hour after hour with my eyes wide open while hundreds of images flashed before my eyes: romantic moments with Valentin, holding hands and dying of sexual desire for each other, our feelings so overwhelming, we couldn't talk about anything. We were above it all, totally connected with one another. We were one.

Then there were the memories of that day when I was looking for him, just to look into his smiling eyes and hear him call me Jandi one more time.

He would never forgive me for being with someone after all he had been through. How could I go back to him after what had happened today? No. I simply could not, and I would not. I would disappear, cease to exist for him.

The following morning I was still in bed, pretending I was sick with the flu. I got up only once to write a letter to Akimovna, and I asked my landlady to mail it for me immediately. It was very short. It was a letter of resignation. The only thing I asked her to do for me was to mail my book of employment to me when she had the time. The workbook was a very important document in Russia.

I longed to have a mother to talk to! I could never talk to my stepmother about a thing like this. She would probably blame me for what had happened. She had only one opinion on this matter: that a good girl had to wait until she was married, and now she would think of me as no good anymore.

A couple of weeks later I received an envelope from Akimovna. In it was my book of employment with almost a whole month's salary and money for unused holidays for that year. In her letter she asked me to please call. I wasn't ready to talk with her, but for some reason I had a feeling she realized that something terrible had happened between my boss and me.

One week later, I received another letter from her in which she asked me to go to a certain address and ask for Comrade Artzinovich, that I would have a job there waiting for me. She said nothing else in her letter. I pulled myself together, got dressed for the first time in weeks, and went looking for Dzerzhinsky Street, Number 13. It was a few minutes' walk from the subway, and as I approached the building, I saw it was the Central Club of Culture of Gosplan, USSR.

I didn't understand what it had to do with me. There had to be some kind of mistake. Perhaps Akimovna had sent somebody else's letter to me. I almost turned around to leave, but curiosity got the better of me.

I went into an enormous marble foyer hung with several crystal chandeliers. It was so quiet I could hear my own footsteps. I looked for the offices, which I figured must be somewhere on the upper floors. The stairway leading to the second floor took me to the balcony of a magnificent theatre with hundreds of mahogany seats, thick carpets, and a gigantic stage hung with burgundy velvet curtains. The place looked totally luxurious!

But how to find the offices with no signs and nobody around? There had to be someone in the place, but, then again, I really didn't want to have anything to do with Gosplan.

As I turned to leave, someone came out from behind the velvet curtains. I called out, "Hello!" and heard my own echo at the far end of the theatre.

The person emerging from the curtains stopped and called, "Hello!" back to me, and said, "Please, come down."

"I'll meet you in the hall."

The man was already there when I arrived. He was tall, skinny, and absolutely bald. He wore black pants and shirt. "How can I help you?"

"Well," I said, "I think I may have gotten somebody else's letter by mistake, about some kind of job. Here's the letter."

And I gave him the letter, which had the name Comrade Artinovich in it. The bald man said to me, "Oh, that's our director. Come with me!"

He led me through the foyer and down a long narrow corridor up the stairs and through more hallways until we arrived on a floor that had row on row of impressive huge doors. One of them had a sign on it that said "Director." We walked in to where a secretary sat behind a typewriter. One thing I had decided: I would rather go back to the meat plant than be somebody's secretary again.

"Can I help you?" she asked. I explained to her about my being given the wrong letter.

She asked me my name, and when I told her, she said, "No, it's not a mistake. You are going to be our general manager of public relations."

"What?"

"That's what I was told this morning," she answered. "The general manager has been hired as of today. Come with me." And she led me to the director's office.

As we walked in, the man who was talking on the phone hung up and then greeted me as though I were his best friend!

"Hello, hello! And how are you?" he said with great enthusiasm. Come in and sit down. I've heard a lot about you. Come and sit down. Akimovna recommended you to me highly, and I am sure you are going to be very happy working here. Let me show you your office."

He took me to the office next door, where he introduced me to a young girl. "This is Alla," he said. "She'll assist you with anything you need. We don't have many people working in the administration, but we're a happy group. We love our club, and you'll enjoy working with us! We're like a family and most of our staff have been working here for twenty-five years. For example, Michael Vasilievich Baranov, the man who brought you to my office, has been with the club for thirty years. This is his home! He's a master of the theatre and has designed and built most of our sets. He's a unique person and can help you a lot. Akimovna told me that you love theatre and that you're also a poet!"

"No," I said. "I'm not a poet and I don't intend to become one. I just write poems for myself. I want to be a lawyer. I'm getting ready to enter law school, but the theatre? Yes, I love it," I told him. "And I'd like to learn as much as I can about it. When I was younger, I loved performing in school plays and thought of becoming an actress, but there's no night school for acting, so I dropped the idea. I've had to work for a living since I was fourteen."

He said to me, "You see! You're perfect for the job! And also, Akimovnna said you know how to work with people and that you're familiar with the Gosplan structure. I feel very lucky to have you for the job! You'll see. You'll love it!"

He told me more about the work I was to do, and I liked everything he said. I was beginning to feel challenged, and I knew I could do it. When I left the club, I didn't go directly home but kept on walking throughout the Moscow centre. I knew I had a lot ahead of me, and the best of all—I felt alive again!

When I returned home it was dark, and my landlady handed me a letter from Valentin. She said that he had waited for me a long time. "He asked me to tell you that he would return tomorrow after his classes."

I knew I had to move out immediately, before he came back. I couldn't face him. Once out of this place, he wouldn't know where I lived or where my new job was. I had to find another place to live without delay.

CHAPTER 22

Still a Virgin

The next morning I was lucky enough to find a new place in a couple of hours, and I'd moved in by one o'clock that afternoon. Only when I put my suitcases inside the room was I able to relax, knowing that Valentin would never find me there. My new place was very close to my new job, just a fifteen-minute walk, and my landlady was an interesting personality, although her life story was sad.

She had been a former actress who was also married to an actor, but her husband was arrested in 1937 during Stalin's repression. Neither of them knew why he had been arrested—a typical situation at that time. Although he had been in jail for close to twenty years she still hoped he would return some day, and she had been lucky enough to keep their place right in the centre of Moscow.

Before her husband was arrested, they'd had three rooms and a kitchen all to themselves, but after his arrest, the biggest room was given to another couple and the apartment was turned into a typical communal place. Yet Vilena, my new landlady, was thankful the authorities hadn't thrown her out from her apartment, where she had lived from birth.

Unfortunately, she had been blacklisted because of her husband and had been tossed out of the theatre where she had worked all her life. Her acting career was destroyed, but she couldn't leave the theatre, so she had found jobs within the industry. "These jobs don't pay much," she told me. "I just work for the love of it. Anyway, I'm glad I have an extra room. It's mostly theatre people who rent it, and that makes me happy!"

Actually, for the first time since I had left my father's house I had a room all to myself. I had to go through Vilena's room to get to it, but still it was a huge improvement. By now her neighbours had a newly married son and they shared their room with him and his wife, and so there were six of us in the apartment, which wasn't too bad.

We all shared the kitchen, bathroom, and shower and each tenant had his or her own toilet seat!

At the time I met Vilena, she was working in an old television centre in Shabolovka. She was hardly ever home, and with my busy schedule we didn't have much time together, but when we did, we enjoyed each other. She loved my cooking.

"I am a lousy cook," she laughed, "but I love food!" Once every two weeks I made dinner for both of us, and we would sit at her table with some vodka while she told me amusing stories of her past.

She used to say, "We theatre people are crazy, you know! We love theatre so much that it doesn't matter what role we're playing. All that matters is that we're on stage! As long as you are on the stage. And then when you can't perform, you don't care what job you're doing as long as it's around the theatre. Even the cleaning people in the theatre are special. Theatre is like an addiction. Once you're in it you can never walk away from it."

My new job was exciting. Soon after I started, I discovered that Vilena was right—I quickly got addicted. Now I understood why some of the club service people had worked there for so long—some for over thirty years! It grew on them and became their baby.

Michael Vasilievich Baranov, the stage manager, belonged to the theatre, and the club wouldn't have been the same without him. He was a walking encyclopedia and became a close friend right from the start. In fact, he taught me everything that I needed to know about theatre arts, and he was always there for me.

Everyone who worked there played an important role in the life of the club. There were the doormen, cashiers, cleaning staff, the light and sound technicians, makeup artists, costume people, the couriers, the secretaries.

The administration was composed of a director, art curator, music curator, and my position, the public relations curator.

I was by far the youngest they had ever had in that position. I had Akimovna to thank for giving me this opportunity. It became my home, my family, my life. It represented everything that had to do with culture. It was a theatre, concert hall, conference hall, and an art gallery, and it was everything I loved! I became an important part of it.

I was responsible for securing the entertainment acts, and we worked together as a group searching constantly for talent. The Gosplan was the sponsor, and of course all the workers of Gosplan and their family members had first priority on tickets for all the events. However, it was also open to the public. Whatever was happening in our club, tickets always sold quickly. It turned out to be a rewarding job.

Most of the time I worked during the day with the evening schedule being split amongst the curators. I worked two evenings a week, Wednesdays and Sundays. Whenever we heard of something that sounded like interesting entertainment for the club, we would go and see it for ourselves. Most of the time two or three of us went together, which gave me a sense of protection. My colleagues knew I wasn't interested in getting involved with anyone, and I found being with my group most comforting.

One night we went to the medical school graduation party. It was famous for being a highly successful event and all kinds of young talent came from different universities to be part of the entertainment.

That night I went together with Comrade Konstantinovich, our director. We were hosted by the Initiative Group of the medical school, who were mainly fifth-year students. Throughout the evening we talked about the group's future plans and other things.

One of the students was a very quiet young man named Oleg Kiselev. He didn't say much, but that night my mind was preoccupied anyway. The next day I would be notified whether I was going to be accepted into law school or not. I was beginning to have second thoughts about going into law, but I had taken my entrance exams and had received almost straight A's and only one B.

There were four exams altogether. In Russia, the marking system was numerical: an $A = 5$, $B = 4$, $C = 3, D = 2$, and $E = 1$. The rule for acceptance into law school was straight 5s, although sometimes it was possible to make it with one B. I had a chance with my results.

In the middle of the concert, Comrade Konstantinovich had to go home early because one of his children was sick. I wanted to leave with him, but he asked me to stay until the end, which I promised to do.

There was dancing after the concert, and my hosts suggested I should stay and listen to the musicians, who in their opinion were some the best in Moscow. They were all senior students at the Moscow Central Conservatory, which was the top academy of music in the Soviet Union.

I agreed to stay but soon began to regret it because many of the students were quite drunk and behaving stupidly. They were all asking me to dance with them, which was all too much. I looked for a way to escape, but the place was so packed I couldn't possibly have made my way through the crowd. Oleg read my thoughts and offered his help.

"My peers work hard during the year, but at parties like this one, they drink vodka like fish and end up acting like pigs! Let's go and dance a couple of dances," he said, "and then I'll help you disappear."

I appreciated his offer, and we did exactly that until finally we were out of the noisy, crowded atmosphere. He and I walked from the medical school, which wasn't too near the Red Square, all the way to where I lived, Dzerzhinsky Street.

We had an interesting conversation all the way there about life in general and about his father who was his idol. He was a famous professor-surgeon, and Oleg's goal in life was to be just like him.

"I have a long way to go," he said, "but I'm very lucky to have the best teacher in the world—my father!"

When we reached my building, I thanked him for being so helpful, and we said goodnight to each other.

I found out the next day that I was accepted into law school! I felt so proud, and I wondered what my father would have thought if he knew. Maybe if he did, he'd be forced to recognize that the useless "black sheep," that "thing," was actually worthwhile! Who knows?

After that evening at the medical school, Oleg began to come to the club where we had many conversations. He brought interesting books for me to read, as his father had a large library. Shortly thereafter, he invited me to his house for dinner, and I was most impressed by his family.

How I envied him! Why couldn't I have had a mother and father like his? There was such a healthy environment in their home! They all talked about literature and classical music and they listened to each other's points of view with great respect for one another. Both parents treated Oleg as an equal, without even a touch of superiority in their behaviour. This was my understanding of a normal family. Why couldn't I have had such a family?

But my life was full. I had the club, and I made friends with everyone who worked there. The whole staff accepted me even though I was twenty years younger. I was encouraged to make decisions about hiring the theatre groups; I had the authority to sign contracts and to handle the club budget for plays and other events, poetry and prose readings by famous poets and writers.

I had organized a group of young professional actors who were obsessed with the idea of a new theatre—the contemporary kind—and they were hoping to break through the political bureaucracy of our time.

By the year 1962, the USSR had only one modern theatre group that was allowed to perform. It was called *Sovremennik* of Moscow. People stood in line to buy tickets for months ahead. For that time, Sovremennik was very avant-garde.

Traditional theatre followed the Stanislavsky way of acting, but Sovremennik was the first theatre that didn't follow this system. They didn't have productions that required elaborate sets, and what sets they had were changed by the actors between scenes. Speech and movement was more casual, and the texts were really daring for those times. This theatre landed in our midst like a bomb!

Nobody could understand how the Soviets allowed it to happen, but it gave hope to young producers and their ideas. So the group I was working with was one of those who hoped. At the same time the whole world was enjoying the Beatles, it was illegal to listen to them in the USSR. The Beatles' tapes and records were smuggled from outside the "Iron Curtain" and sold on the black market for a fortune. Many other crazy restrictions were also enforced. In other words, the word "freedom" was something foreign to those of us who lived under the Soviet regime.

In September of 1962 I started law school. By the end of the first semester, I was completely discouraged. Ninety percent of the school program was Marx-Lenin studies, politic economy, and many other subjects that didn't make much sense to me.

As well, I began to learn more about how corrupt the Soviet court system was—and how totally under communist control it really was. The term "justice" was unknown in the Soviet court system, and the real sense of the word "truth" had to be forgotten if I wanted to become a lawyer. The concept simply didn't exist in that context.

Having discovered all of this made me lose interest in becoming an advocate; it didn't make sense to be part of that corruption. I figured I didn't have what it took to be a lawyer in the Soviet system, and I had to make a decision. Where to go from here?

I knew one thing: I had to have a university education. I needed to have a profession, but I had no idea in what area. Of course there was no question of my entrance exams being honoured by another university. Oh no. I had to go through them all over again.

In the meantime, Oleg had fallen in love with me, but not I with him. I was still heartbroken over my lost love for Valentin. My love wasn't lost; I had lost him. But my love for him was very much with me still. It was in me and nothing could be done about it. I was sure. I had to accept this fact and move on.

At the end of October, Oleg proposed marriage, and I wasn't surprised. I knew it would happen sooner or later. I also knew I didn't love him in the way I wanted to love. I liked him a lot, but I knew it wasn't enough for marriage. His family I really loved, and I wanted to be part of it, but it was the wrong reason to marry him. I debated with myself like this for a while until finally I said to Oleg, "Look, I really like you, and I'd love to be a part of your family, but before we both make a final decision I think we should go away for a few days. Just you and me." I knew what I was offering.

Oleg said, "Before we do this, we should tell my parents that we've decided to get married."

Almost any girl at that time would have loved to hear this, but my problem was, I couldn't face telling him that I wasn't a virgin. I simply couldn't. I wanted him to find out, and maybe deep inside I was hoping that after discovering the truth about me, he would change his mind. I knew that most men were brought up that way. To sleep with a woman was one thing, but if you wanted to marry her she had to be a virgin. It was senseless and unfair, but that was how things were then. However, Oleg guessed my reasons for going away and said that it wouldn't make any difference to him. "Our marriage wouldn't depend on that kind of stupid thinking!" he said.

I was thankful to him and felt that I'd better agree to marry him. I was so lucky to have met such an open-minded man, so I agreed to get engaged and then go away with him.

We had a lovely dinner, and Oleg told his parents that we had decided to marry. His father and mother gave us their blessings and said they were very happy to have me as a daughter. When I heard that, I wept. Oh, how I wished I could have truly been their daughter!

We took the train up north the next day to Oleg's family dacha (cottage) near Zagorsk. When the train was passing Mytischi my heart was in my mouth! It was early Saturday morning. There was no one on the platform, but during the five minutes that the train was stationary, I worried about the possibility of Valentin appearing on the train! It was silly to think that way. Why would he? I breathed a huge sigh of relief, however, when the train started up again.

The dacha was about a kilometre away from the Zagorsk station. It was one of those perfect winter days, sunny and crisp. They had a wood-burning stove in the cottage, and Oleg started it as soon as we arrived and suggested that while the room was getting warm we should go skiing. They had three pairs of cross-country skis, and he said I could use his mother's. We had a good time and everything seemed to be working out fine, but I was still nervous. When we returned we warmed up some food his mother had packed for us and we even had a bottle of champagne.

It was so nice to have somebody so thoughtful and caring. I thought of how lucky I was to have a caring, loving family now. I even felt more romantic than I thought I would. We held hands and kissed, yet I was aware that my feelings were very different from those I'd had for Valentin. How could I think about something that was impossible?

"Use your head!" I told myself. "Here is your perfect chance to get out of your mess and have the normal family life you've always wanted!"

Oleg was a shy young man. I felt as if he almost expected me to be the leader. When I took his hand and led him to our bed, I felt like I was about to jump from the tallest mountain to the depth of the ocean—knowing that I could neither fly nor swim! I held my breath and decided to let it happen. As he entered me, I felt unbearable pain. Oh my God. Was this how it was going to be?

In the meantime, Oleg was in his own world, his own hunger, and I didn't matter. He was possessed by his own desire and had no idea what I was going through. Tears were flowing from my eyes. I cried and sobbed... until the race was over and I heard him crying out like a wild animal and his body collapsed on top of mine like a heavy truckload.

His body was wet, and I felt covered with his sweat, which made me feel cold and disgusting. Besides I felt something liquidy coming out of me, and finally I could not stand it anymore and moved away. Oleg was asleep.

I staggered to the bathroom in the dark, bumping into things on the way, and turned the light on. I grabbed a towel and wiped myself to get rid of this horrible wetness and discovered that my blood was all over the towel. Oh my God! What was this? Why now? It had already happened once, that terrible night with my boss—but why again? I was beside myself. I had to leave. I couldn't stand being there one more second!

I decided to go to a hospital right away, even if it took me two hours to get there. It was dark when I arrived at the Zagorsk hospital. The nurse asked me a few questions and told me to wait for the doctor who, I was relieved to see, was a woman. My body was shaking uncontrollably when I told her what had happened. Then she examined me and said, "You needn't worry! It's normal. You just lost your virginity."

"But I had the same thing happen to me already!" And I told her what had happened with my boss.

She said, "Most likely you didn't lose it then. Perhaps your tissue was badly scratched by his fingernails. It's the most sensitive area of a woman's body, you know. But now you've experienced your first normal intercourse, which can be painful for the next couple of times. But then your body will adjust and you'll get used to it.

"Don't worry," she said. "Just remember that you could get pregnant any time, and if you don't want to have a baby, you'll avoid any sperm ending up inside of you. Your future husband, being a doctor, should know that better than most men, so don't worry, you're in good hands. Go back to your fiancé," she said with the smile. "He must be worried by now."

When I walked out of the hospital I stood there for a long time. Why couldn't all this have happened with Valia? Why hadn't I gone to a doctor before? Did I want to be with Oleg if I didn't love him or should I do what millions of other girls did: just get married even if they weren't in love? But what kind of life would that be? I wanted happiness. I wanted to love and be with the man I loved; it made such a difference, I knew.

So many important things were wrong in this country of mine. To begin with, this "girls having to be virgins until they were married" idea! What was it doing to girls? Most of them got married for the wrong reason and much too early in life. Many of them married at sixteen or seventeen. What did they know about life when in reality they were still children?

They knew nothing about themselves or about men. There were no books or any other information about sex. None. The subject was never discussed. The parents of our time wouldn't talk about such things.

Then, the baby problem. There was no birth control whatsoever. The only alternative couples had was to keep the sperm out. What did it do to men? How could they relax and enjoy an intimate life? As a result, the majority of married couples didn't enjoy sex.

For a woman, it was a constant worry, whether she might be pregnant or not, and most of the pregnancies were accidental, which meant most of the babies born were unplanned.

In the very beginning of marriage when couples hardly knew each other, they weren't ready to be parents. To abort one's first pregnancy was highly risky; one could be left childless for the rest of one's life. And what happened after you had a first child and couldn't afford more? With no living space and other problems, abortions were the only alternative available. They weren't really legal, but they were performed in all the hospitals.

A woman had to get to the hospital before eight weeks. After eight weeks, the abortion couldn't and wouldn't be done. This created all kinds of situations, whereby abortions were performed in absolutely unsanitary environments, and no anaesthetic was used for abortions, ever! One can only imagine how treacherous this could be; yet women were having them constantly. There was hardly a woman who hadn't had several.

Five abortions was the average number in a woman's life. There were cases of twelve and up to twenty-five. Unwanted pregnancies made women angry, frustrated, and depressed and left men constantly feeling guilty. In other words, sex between married couples was a burden, and for men, sex outside of marriage was happening all over the place. This was the reality in the Soviet Union and many other countries at that time.

And here I was in the middle of it all, and I didn't want to fall into the trap. Something in my gut was telling me it was wrong! "You cannot marry Oleg just because he wants to marry you! You aren't doing yourself or him any favours. How are you going to deal with it for the rest of your life? Do you want to be miserable? No!" I had been miserable enough throughout my childhood! I had to be in control of my life, but how?

I'd lost the man I loved because of all this ignorance. Yet now I had to step away from this situation I was in and free myself. I didn't want to follow the ridiculous pattern I saw around me. I wanted to make my own decisions about my personal relationships, as I did with my life in general. There was no one to answer to except myself. It was my life and my feelings I had to deal with, and I had to outgrow all this nonsense and do everything in my power to accomplish it. That was it!

CHAPTER 23

Wrong

I had to get rid of this virginity complex! I hated being in the position most girls found themselves. I wanted to be able to make my own choices: who I wanted to be with, why, and when. How was I to do this?

I needed to do what men did: forget the marriage idea and just go with the flow!

That year I went to bed with several men. Under these circumstances, there was never a shortage of them. They were always after your body. Just give them a smile and they knew what to do.

I was in a swinging mood. Most of them I hardly ever dated. I was always aware of the possibility of getting pregnant, so my stipulation was this: no sperm in my body! I hated it anyway. Most of the time I never slept with the same man twice. After that, I had no further interest. Did I enjoy it? I don't think so. It was all poisoned because of my love for Valentin. Also I knew nothing really about sex, and I don't think any of the men I was with knew anything either, so how could I enjoy it?

To begin with, I didn't even like kissing them. On the other hand, I thought it was the right thing for me to do. I suppose I hoped that it would also help me to forget Valentin. Many times I felt terrible about myself because I knew this wasn't my cup of tea either. I knew I wanted much more.

I wanted to meet someone I could care for and who would care for me in return. Was it possible? Or was it impossible because it had already happened to me once and wouldn't happen to me again? Maybe I wouldn't be able to fall in love again!

Yet I knew that being in love, as sweet as it was, at the same time was very painful. Did I want to go through it again? Maybe not...

At some point during that year, one of my admirers was a young man who acted quite differently from everybody else. Rafael wanted to go to the symphony with me, to art galleries, to the theatre, and I was very glad of this development. We'd been seeing each other in this way for a couple of months, and I enjoyed his company. He was tall, handsome, well mannered, and always dressed elegantly. I appreciated the fact that for a change, Rafael didn't rush me into bed.

He was a graduate of one of the top schools in Moscow and was working in one of the best electronic universities. I wasn't in love with Rafael, but I liked him enough to enjoy his company after my "freeing of self" period. I was so glad he wasn't after my body like the rest of them! It was a welcome relief. I didn't know, however, that I was going to end up paying a high price for this very pleasant relationship.

One day Rafael called me at work and invited me to his house. He was having some friends over and thought it would be nice if I joined them to listen to some good music. I accepted his invitation without a second thought. After all, we'd always had great times together.

He lived in one of the most prestigious areas of Moscow—Prospect Lenin—in one of the newer high-rise buildings. When I arrived, he introduced me to two other men, friends of his. They were polite, well-spoken young men in their late twenties or early thirties. After introductions and some laughter and conversation, Rafael offered me a drink. I don't know what kind of drink it was, but it was quite pleasant and I enjoyed sipping it for a while.

The next thing I knew, I woke up and found myself naked in his bed! It was semi-dark in the room, and I seemed to awaken from some kind of deep sleep. My head felt incredibly heavy, like I was coming back from another life or planet into reality. He was lying next to me and suddenly I remembered what had happened. I'd had only that one drink and it had put me to sleep! But why would he do this? If he wanted to take me to bed, all he had to do was to ask. Why had he done it this way? Why?

Something came to me. It appeared in front of my mind like a short flash from a movie: I remembered him saying, "I'm homosexual." The second I realized everything, I grabbed my clothes—they were neatly folded on a chair, which meant he had planned everything methodically! Quietly I crept out.

Only after I'd closed the door of his place behind me did I dress myself and run to the elevator. Waiting for it to arrive felt like an age, and I was ready to run down from the twentieth floor if he should catch me leaving. But why would he do anything? The whole reason he'd drugged me was because he was homosexual and was desperate to change it. He probably was unable to accept what he really was. He'd had to put me to sleep in order to see if he could manage sex with a woman!

What I wasn't aware of at that time was the severity with which homosexuals were punished just for being what they were. The minimum sentence for any homosexual activity was twenty years in prison. I realized later that this was probably why he had resorted to trying out sex with me. It was the desperate act of a very frightened human being.

For the next several weeks I tried to wipe this whole episode out of my memory, but I wasn't to get away from it that easily. I was beginning to feel sick. I couldn't look at food and felt sleepy most of the time. I knew I was pregnant, and the thought of it made my skin crawl. I couldn't even begin to describe how tortured I felt.

From that time on, my entire being was channeled towards only one purpose: to get rid of this drug-induced pregnancy. I did everything I had ever heard of. I jumped, I ran, I sat in the hottest mustard bath for hours—but nothing helped. There was nothing to do but get some money for an abortion. Getting it done before eight weeks were up was getting close to being out of the question. I made it just under eight weeks, and when the day of surgery arrived I braced myself. There was to be no anesthesia, of course, and it would be terribly painful. That didn't matter to me. I just wanted to get rid of this pregnancy as quickly as possible, but I was yet to suffer even more.

I wondered what I was being punished for. What had I done? Was it my fault that my mother had died and I was left to survive? Was it my fault that my father didn't care whether I lived or died? What was wrong with me? Would I ever do anything right? Was I screwed up for the rest of my life? All these questions ran through my mind while the woman, who claimed to be a doctor, butchered my insides, forced my womb open, and then scraped everything out of me.

It made me feel guilty for being born a woman. Pregnant and not married was bad enough, but being pregnant by this homosexual was too much. Perhaps that was why they why they didn't use an anaesthetic. An abortion was considered a shame, which was probably why they talked down to you while scraping you alive? The torture seemed to last forever.

When it was finally over, the woman unstrapped my legs, put a piece of cloth between them, and told me to get off "the prostitution chair."

And where could I go from there? There was no bed for me to have a little rest. "This isn't a hotel!" she said. "Your abortion wasn't scheduled, and I don't want to be caught. You've paid, the job is done. Now get out of here!"

"Can I call a taxi?" I asked.

"Taxi? No, you can't call a taxi! Nobody is supposed to know what you were here for. You can catch a taxi somewhere on the street away from this place," she told me.

Back home I threw my poor aching body on the bed and tried to fall asleep, but that wasn't to be the end. My pain had just begun. For three solid days the pain felt like contractions. One huge pain after another came with only a few minutes' break in between. I tried to catch some rest during those intervals.

From time to time bloody clots would come out, and when that happened, it felt peaceful for a while. In those three days, there were larger and sometimes smaller chunks of these clots coming out. During these attacks, I cried so hard and was so frightened; it felt like I was dying. What could I do? Who could help me? Nobody! So I had to just grit my teeth and get through it.

For months after that, I couldn't get rid of the horrible memories. Job and school were my life from then on. I came home just to sleep, and I got myself so completely involved with my work, I hardly remembered to eat.

I was 5'7" and my weight was 105 pounds or so, which didn't bother me except that all my clothes were hanging on me. I didn't feel like me at all. Usually I wore my clothes fit tightly. Everybody in the club commented on it.

One day our courier, Lidia Vasilievna, who knew how to sew, invited me to her place for a cup of coffee and suggested I bring all my clothes so she could alter them and make me look sexy again.

"No thanks," I said. "I prefer to look like a nun for a while." On the way back to work I kept visualizing only one face.

CHAPTER 24

New Year's Eve

Many times I felt like I should see Valentin again. His image never disappeared from my mind, but what was the point? How would I face him? Although he was history, I still couldn't get rid of my thoughts. No matter how useless I knew it was to think about him, he was still there. I wanted nobody and nothing else.

Poor Oleg Kiselev followed me everywhere. I treated him as I would never allow anybody to treat me. I behaved so badly! I knew perfectly well it wasn't his fault. After all, I had practically taken him to bed with me. I knew it, but that was the way it was—I couldn't help it.

I knew how badly I'd acted that night. I didn't even go back to his dacha after the hospital; I went straight home! Maybe if he'd been more experienced he wouldn't have been so self-involved, falling asleep after our lovemaking. Maybe I wouldn't have done what I did if the poor guy had known how to be with woman. I knew now that it was kind of typical of Russian men at that time. They had the wrong idea about sex. It was considered a "one-way street" for the most part.

They knew how to romance a woman—that was no problem. But when it came to sexual relations, they knew very little. Nevertheless, in my case with Oleg, most of it was my fault; I hadn't really given him a chance.

A few days after I left the dacha, I wrote him a letter apologizing for my disappearance and telling him that I wasn't ready to get married. He was already a doctor, I wrote, but I had a long way to go.

"Nothing is wrong with you," I said. "It was me. And I'm very, very sorry, but it won't work between us."

Oleg acted as though he had never received the letter—as though nothing happened! The more he did this, the more I was turned off. He had no idea how to win my heart. Also, because he acted this way, he exposed himself to the possibility of being hurt even more.

It was a couple of days before New Year's Eve 1964. New Year's was the most celebrated of all holidays in Russia. There was no Christmas in Soviet Russia—although Christmas trees were just as popular there as they were all over the world, only they were just there as part of the New Year's festivities.

It was the ultimate celebration. It was important for absolutely everybody to be part of it. If a person was alone on New Year's Eve it was terrible, so everybody made sure not to be.

There were a few customs we always followed. One of them was that everybody had to wear something that had never been worn. It could even be a bra or in the case of men a new pair of socks or a tie. The majority tried their best to have a new special new dress or a suit and so on. Spirits were always high, yet it could be a sad time if a loved one couldn't be there to celebrate with.

It was a sad time for me. What bothered me was that Valentin's birthday happened to be exactly on December 31, and my thoughts of him were more acute at this time than ever. Why couldn't I meet him at least one more time? I thought about him constantly. I visualized his face, his smile, day and night.

That day, I was on my way to see my girlfriend Alla Agapova. She and I, along with her boyfriend, were organizing our New Year's party at her place. Her parents were away, and they had a separate apartment, not a communal one. Alla was the only friend of that time who knew about Valentin. She lived on the same route where I had lived growing up with my father, only her place was one stop further north. The station was called Lose, and I had to cross a bridge over the railway.

It's hard to believe, but as I got off the train and walked towards the bridge, I felt this unmistakable touch on my shoulder. My heart sank, and I felt almost paralyzed for a moment. It was Valentin.

"You!"

"Hi, Jandi," he said.

"Oh, hi!" I answered as casually as I could. And then we made small talk.

"I know you're working at the Gosplan Club and going to university."

My brain was going a mile a minute in twenty different directions, and I didn't know what to say! Why was I so stupid? How many nights had I dreamed of this moment? And now he was right here in front of me, and I couldn't say anything.

"Did you remember that tomorrow is my birthday?"

"Yes, I did."

"What are you doing on New Year's Eve?"

"Oh, we're getting together at my friend's place. We'll only be six couples." I knew I could invite Oleg to Alla's party even if I called him an hour before. He'd be there in five minutes, and I wanted to protect myself. "Oh yes? Couples? So, you have a boyfriend?"

"No, he's my fiancé. We're getting married."

"My congratulations!" he said as though it were nothing.

Then he said, "How about inviting me too? It would be nice to spend a last New Year's together, before you get married."

I was tempted to say no, but I didn't think quickly enough.

"Don't worry," he said, "I'll bring my girlfriend too."

It was a good solution. At least we could see each other and be at the same place on New Year's Eve.

"Okay, we can do that." We arranged for Oleg and I to meet Valentin with his girlfriend at Lose railway station at nine o'clock the next night. "So, I'll see you tomorrow at nine. Until then!" he said, and we walked away from each other.

As I was walked along the bridge, I saw him jump on the next train going north towards Mytischi. So, he still lived there. I wondered just how coincidental this meeting had been. I went to the first telephone booth I could find and called Oleg who said he'd be happy to be with me on New Year's Eve.

I was very excited! I couldn't wait to share my news with Alla. She and I were looking forward to this party, especially because we had her place all to ourselves. There would be nobody, just us, and I was to stay over for two nights.

First, we were to prepare all kinds of tasty foods and pastries, and then the following night would be New Year's Eve. We were especially looking forward to the first evening together when we didn't have to rush.

Both Alla's parents were living, and they loved her very much. They gave everything to their daughter, who was their only child; yet, I could see that Alla took a lot of things for granted. I often wished that she recognized the fact that she was so fortunate to have such caring parents. They even bought all kinds of delicacies that weren't easy to get for our party and all kinds of other groceries for us. All we had to do was cook, and I was to be the main chef. By now, I'd discovered my passion for gourmet cooking, and I took every opportunity to indulge in it. I hardly ever used recipes; I created a lot of my own, which I enjoyed doing immensely.

In the morning we were up early. We had a lot to do before nine o'clock in the evening; we cooked and baked all day. We had great fun doing it, but I could see how spoiled Alla was. Her mother had put out most of the dishes, such as pots and pans from the cupboards for us to use, but when I needed some other item, Alla didn't even know where to look! It made me wonder if it was better to have been an orphan when you had to learn things.

She had no idea how to make things go further, and when she was peeling potatoes, half of them ended up in the garbage! Alla didn't have to earn money. Her parents took care of everything for her. She was getting married in a couple of months and her parents had everything ready for her future home: furniture, linens, dishes, and all kinds of things.

Anyway, we prepared a lot of traditional Russian food, like a potato salad called "Olivier," and we had many delicacies. There were salamis, cheeses, red and black caviar, liver pâté. Then roasted duck, stewed meat, and fish in garlic sauce.

For desert I baked Russian strudel and apple cake and even homemade truffles. We also had tangerines and oranges, which were extremely hard to get. We displayed the appetizers beautifully on the large table, which was set for fourteen. All the hot courses stayed in the oven.

By six o'clock everything was ready, and we cleaned the kitchen and had plenty of time to take showers and make ourselves look beautiful.

I had a brand new dress, which was the first new one in a couple of years, thanks to Lidia Vasilievna, our club courier and my friend. I bought the fabric and she made it for me and wouldn't charge me a dime! It was a New Year's gift from her, and I had no say in the matter. She simply decided that I had to have a new one—it was made of beautiful coral velour, which looked like silky corduroy. I had new high heels. It felt wonderful to be dressed up like this, especially knowing that Valentin would be at our party. Everything around me seemed more than usually special: the Christmas tree, the music, our table with its crystal glasses, and the delicious smell of the food!

I had never met Alla's fiancé before, but I'd assumed he would be handsome. I was therefore a little let down when I met him. He wasn't even an inch taller then she was—in fact she didn't wear high heels for that reason. He was also a little bald, but it wasn't just the look of him, it was how quiet he was. Too quiet for Alla, I thought. It was obvious from the beginning who would be wearing the pants in the family.

Oleg was at the door at a quarter to nine. By then I was just on my way to the station to meet Valentin and his girlfriend. He had brought me flowers and some nice perfume, which I didn't feel comfortable accepting. I knew I would hurt him again, and I'd warned him when I invited him that nothing had changed—that he shouldn't count on anything. I could see when he came in that he still hoped for things to go right for us. Why had I invited him and not somebody else that evening? It was a pretty selfish reason. I simply felt safer with him than I would have with anybody else.

As he and I went to the station my heart was beating so hard that I thought Oleg could hear it, and I felt so nervous my legs wobbled. I asked myself over and over whether I was doing the right thing. I knew I was making a mistake agreeing to have Valentin and Oleg at the same party. I felt as though I were walking on the edge of a precipice and I could fall at any minute.

When we got there, the train was just coming into the station. There weren't many people on the platform because it was getting close to when everyone would be gathered at the table, drinking and talking about the good things of the past year and the bad and then getting ready for the midnight celebration of the New Year. We still had to celebrate Valentin's birthday and we had a full program ahead of us.

As the train came to a full stop, it was easy to pick out Valentin and his friend coming toward us. I was very aware that both Valentin and I were extremely curious to meet our companions. I heard myself saying hello to them as they approached. I couldn't look at Valentin. The girl introduced herself to us and Valentin and Oleg shook hands while everyone mumbled something about the weather.

It was real New Year's Eve weather. The snow had been falling slowly for the last couple of hours, covering the ground with a brand new coat. It was almost made to order according to the custom of the holiday. Even the ground had put on new clothes. It was quiet—no wind at all and the air felt fresh and crisp. As we walked along, all four of us were silent, each one lost in his or her own thoughts. My own thoughts? I wanted to be walking next to Valentin holding his hand.

By the time we arrived, everyone was there. It was close to eleven o'clock, and we were all beginning to feel excited. We gathered around the table and had a couple of toasts to the old year. There came the usual high point of the evening when it was customary to talk about our lives, "bad" and "good." Each of us had to stop and think about failures and achievements of the past year. It was a very valuable tradition and always part of the New Year's Eve celebration. Everybody wanted to forget about what was negative and concentrate on the good with hope that it would last forever. I had a lot of both. Nevertheless, the whole point was that we were there to celebrate it all.

Finally, food was on our plates and vodka in our crystal shot glasses. All the appropriate words were spoken until all that was left to do was to clink glasses and drink it to the bottom of the glass as the long-standing custom dictated. Valentin and his girlfriend were seated at the other end of the table, almost directly across from Oleg and me. This was the moment when we were all to be tuned in for one single purpose: to have that drink.

Yet, there was a hold-up. Everybody at the other end of the table was trying to talk Valentin's girlfriend into having that one drink. It seemed she wasn't going to do it, and so there appeared to be a delay. This was typical of Russians. There were certain things that were supposed to be done by everybody—no exceptions—and because of this, as silly as it may sound, we all got stuck, and the time was running out.

I felt like stepping in, but then again, I didn't really want to. A few more minutes went by and they were still trying to convince her to join us and have that drink. I finally said, "Look, if she doesn't want to do it, why don't you just let her be! After all, it's her own business and the New Year is almost here. So let's go!"

I sounded very firm, and they all agreed. After that, everything went smoothly. We drank our shots of vodka to the bottom and then sat down and got busy eating. They all said the food was delicious, and it was!

One of the young men suggested we fill our glasses again. "One shot for the whole year isn't enough," he said, "and I want to make a speech!"

"Oh sure!" everyone shouted. "That was all you did last year, making toasts and drinking vodka, as if it was a good thing!"

"Well," he said, "somebody has to do it to support the economy!" After the second shot, we all loosened up, and the atmosphere became warm and comfortable. We almost got carried away joking and laughing until we heard the announcement on the radio, and we hurriedly filled our glasses with champagne. The speechmaker guy, the one who "took care of the Soviet economy," opened the bottles expertly. He was turning out to be our master of ceremonies!

For many years, there was only one radio announcer for all the important events in the country. His name was Yuri Leviton, and he had the deepest voice of anyone and made his name just by that alone. The truth was, he was very short, but his voice made one think it belonged to a very tall man. After he made a short speech, the station began its broadcast of the sounds of the Kremlin bells that were now to tolling the last seconds of the old year.

It was very special. The whole Soviet Union was standing around tables with champagne glasses raised, ready to clink. Soviet champagne was good, and strong too. It had to be drunk from tall-stemmed crystal glasses, which were to be held by the stem so that the crystal produced a lovely tinkling sound like a bell. And that's what went on around the table: clink, clink, clink, and then all draining their glasses to the last drop. Afterwards, the couples were to kiss each other and then everybody else.

I wasn't looking forward to kissing Oleg, but he was! This was his chance. I tried to do it seriously as though I meant it, but I wanted to make it as short as possible and quickly removed myself from him. Most couples were still kissing each other. I made a funny comment, just to break them apart.

I said, "Let me turn off the tree lights so no one will be able to see what you are all doing!"

Everybody laughed and moved away from their partners to kiss the others. When it was my turn to kiss Valentin, I kissed him quickly on his cheek and moved away so that he didn't have a chance to kiss me back.

To be romantic there came the waltz and all the couples joined in the beauty of this wonderful dance. I loved this part of New Year's Eve. People danced when they felt like it or with whom they wanted. I danced a few first dances with Oleg and a few others with someone else, and then I realized that Valentin had danced with everyone else except his girlfriend.

She sat on the couch looking miserable. I couldn't understand what was wrong, and I asked Oleg to ask her to dance but she turned him down. Then I quietly asked Alla's boyfriend to ask her, but she turned him down too. I decided to do something about it and sat down next to her. When she looked at me, I asked her point blank, "What's the problem?"

She burst into tears and told me that she had a boyfriend with whom she was very much in love. Valentin, an old friend of her family, had come to their house yesterday and had asked her to do him a favour, to go with him to this New Year's Eve party because he couldn't go alone. He'd even given her money for agreeing to be his "date," enough for her to buy badly needed new winter boots, and her boyfriend had agreed to it. He was at home with his family, waiting for her to come back. She thought it would all work out fine.

"But when I saw all the couples kissing and having fun, I felt lonely and depressed, and I just wanted to be with my boyfriend. No money is worth doing such a thing!" she sobbed.

I was shocked to hear what she had to say and couldn't believe what Valentin had done to be here! I decided to help her. I asked Oleg to go out and get a taxi so she could go home to her boyfriend as soon as possible, which he did discreetly, and the taxi was soon at the building.

Oleg was freezing outside without his coat and in his new leather shoes and I told him to go in and get warm, that I would go out and see that the girl got into the taxi safely. I also wanted to pay for it. I signaled to her to get her coat, and we left. I didn't bother putting my coat on. It was in the bedroom and I didn't want anyone to see me going out. After she was safely seated inside, I paid the driver and we said goodbye to each other. The girl's face was all smiles now.

I couldn't go upstairs right away. I needed to think for a while, and I had to walk because it was too cold to stay still. What was I to do? It looked as though I'd have to face Valentin and deal with the whole mess. Ever since that terrible episode with my boss I had avoided him because I hadn't known how to handle it. Now, almost three years later, my feelings for him hadn't changed and it looked like his weren't lost either.

But I knew how hurt he must have been, and I wasn't sure I could come up with a logical explanation for my strange behaviour. In the three years that had gone by, we had both been through all kinds of different experiences, good and bad, and had done a lot of growing up. Anyway, I had to deal with it right then, and I still didn't have any idea how I was going to sort it out.

My thoughts were interrupted by the sound of someone's footsteps on the crispy snow. I turned around and saw someone running towards me. Only then did I realize how far I had walked from Alla's building, and I didn't even feel how cold it was. My body was stiff, and my feet were in agony. This was always the situation since the episode with my father when I was a child. Only now did I realize how stupid it was of me to walk in the snow, wearing my beautiful shoes that had cost me almost a month's salary. I wasn't thinking about my feet but about my shoes!

Now I saw that the man running towards me was Valentin! He was right there, before my very eyes. This time there was no escape. I had to face it!

In the next second, without saying anything, I found myself in his arms, with his lips on mine, kissing and holding me tightly me for the longest time. When he finally let go of me, I felt so warm I could have stayed out there in the cold for the rest of my life. Waves of excitement rolled over me! Tears fell from my eyes uncontrollably, and I was speechless. Was my suffering, my pain, pouring out through my tears? Or was it the love I had for this man? And if it was love, then why couldn't I share my thoughts with him?

The truth was he hardly knew me! How strange! Here was the man I had been crazy in love with for nearly ten years, and I couldn't be open with him. One might question the definition of the word "love" in our case and suggest that it probably was "fatal attraction," "obsession," "lust," "first love" or many other such terms. But of course, these thoughts come to my mind twenty-five or thirty years later, but not then.

Then, it was a New Year's Eve 1964 with the fresh new snow and thousands of bright stars in the magic sky and this mysterious man, who was holding me in his arms. My only thought was "Let this moment last forever!"

When we finally drew apart, we stood there gazing at each other for the longest time, unable to speak. What else was new? Were we ever going to be able to speak? Our passionate outbursts controlled us. Then again, he held me. My entire body was pulled into his, as if he were trying to fit me inside him. I felt his every muscle, every pulse, and the heat from his body was overpowering mine. We were connected, and both of us cried like two little children who couldn't yet speak. We never could communicate in words.

We came back to the party holding hands, my lipstick smeared, my hair damp, my eyes looking crazy—spaced out—and, of course, before I could sneak into the bathroom a couple of people saw me. Oleg was gone by then. Apparently Valentin had had a heart-to-heart talk with him while I had been outside.

The rest of the night, Valentin and I were inseparable. The party went on. We all sat down at the table and enjoyed our hot courses, danced again, and then we had tea with desserts. Finally people started to leave around six o'clock in the morning, and I made a decision to go to Valentin's house.

When we arrived, I was prepared to jump in the deep end. I took off my dress and hung it neatly on a chair and then took off my shoes and put them underneath. Valentin watched me as I undressed. I was determined to get it over with; I slipped into bed and softly called him.

"Come here, Valia!" He got up from his chair where he'd been sitting fully dressed, walked over, where I was lying—looking like merchandise, fully available to the buyer—and threw himself on top of me.

He grabbed me by my hair and pulled it so hard that I had to grit my teeth so as not to scream, then he pulled it harder and harder.

"You bitch!" he hissed. "You slept with other men, and like an idiot I was saving you from all that! You bitch! What an idiot I am!" And he collapsed.

I opened my eyes. His face was pale, and his lips were bluish.

I called out, "Valia! Valia!" but he didn't respond. I understood: I had to leave.

I dressed and quietly walked out of the room. As I neared the station I had only one thought: That's it. It's finished. It's over.

I'd waited for our reunion for such a long time, and now it was over. Tears streamed down my face, and I didn't even have a handkerchief! Who cared? My love was gone! Gone! Gone!

Suddenly, I heard Valentin's voice behind me: "Jandi, wait, wait. Forgive me! I don't even know what happened to you!"

Then he saw my tears, and his own began to flow. We both stood there face to face, weeping about our screwed-up love and not knowing what to do.

He unbuttoned my coat, undid my dress, took both my breasts in his hands like two flowers, and kissed them so very gently, just slightly touching them with his lips. Then just as carefully, he fastened me up and said, "Forgive me," and walked away.

I walked away too. We had nothing more to say.

CHAPTER 25

My Father's Divorce

Six months later, July 1, I walked into my office to find the phone ringing. It was Valentin. My temperature rose as I heard the familiar voice.

"Happy Birthday, Jandi! You're an older girl now."

"Yes," I said. "No kidding. I'm twenty-three!"

"Why don't I invite you for dinner tonight?" he said softly. "We can celebrate it for old time's sake!"

My heart sank again as I heard myself saying, "That would be nice."

"Good!" he said. "I'll meet you at seven by your club."

"That's fine," I said.

I sat there paralyzed after we hung up. What was going to happen now? Why did I agree to go out with him? What was there left to say or do? I knew that what had happened had created that irreparable void—and, so, why bother? The healing process was over now, and we were freer to go on living our lives—or at least I thought we were. Why meet now?

The telephone rang again, a bit early for a night place like the theatre. I usually came early so I could work in peace.

"Hello," I answered.

"Good morning, Janna. Happy Birthday!" I could never have guessed who it could be saying this in a million years. My sister Sema was calling to wish me a Happy Birthday!

Something had to be wrong. My birthday didn't exist as far as my family was concerned. What did she want? She sounded sweet and gentle, not at all like her usual self.

"Our father and I decided to celebrate your birthday at my place today, so you must come after work tonight as early as possible."

"Sema, I can't. I've already been invited out. Anyway, thank you—but the answer is no."

"Janna, why do you have to make it hard for us? Why don't you give us a chance? Maybe things could change, now that you've grown up. After all, we're family, and we're trying. You must come! I'm preparing a dinner for you and everything will be ready by four o'clock. Here's my address. I'm on Gertzen Street, right near Nikitsky Gates, Arbat, okay? You've never seen my place, so we'll be waiting for you." And she hung up.

I sat there even more shocked than I was after Valentin's call! I thought about it for the rest of the day. I supposed if they were really trying, maybe I should give it a chance.

At lunchtime, my staff gave me a little surprise party, which was really nice; I received a present and some flowers. By four o'clock I decided and was on my way to Sema's place. Of course I was concerned about my date with Valentin. I couldn't reach him personally, but I left a message to tell him that I would be at my sister's place. I also left a note with our security guard.

My father was already there with one of his brothers and wished me a happy birthday with a smile and gave me an unwrapped gift. It was a white duvet cover. But that wasn't the gift I cared about. The gift was my father wishing me a happy birthday. I had never in my life heard him say this to me before.

As the table was set for four, it was obvious nobody else was coming, but it all looked strange to me. The table wasn't prepared with our usual Russian generosity. It only had Olivier salad and a small dish with herring covered by onion rings, and there was a half-full bottle of vodka on the table as well.

Sema invited everyone to sit down, and she poured some vodka into the crystal shot glasses. My father took his in his hand and got up.

"My dear daughter, you are twenty-three years old now, which means you're a grown-up young woman. I can talk to you now. You see, I've spent my life devoted to my children. Unfortunately, you were orphans and I had to be both parents for you. That terrible woman, Polia, came to our family with only one idea and that was to get rid of all of you so she could be with me alone. Well, I wasn't going to allow that to happen." He paused, looking at each of us, obviously pleased with what he was saying.

"Anyway, I was never happy with her, not for one day. I buried myself in my work not ever wanting to come home. Only my responsibility for my children kept me doing this for years. Well, now you are all grown up and live your own lives, and I've decided it's time for me to live my own life too. I'm sixty years old now, and I think I deserve a bit of my own happiness. Therefore, I'm divorcing that woman, and I expect you to understand. After all, Janna, I'm your father, and she is nobody to you."

Still holding his glass, he looked directly at me. "I've decided to give you the sewing machine and the Persian rug. The rest will be split between Sema and Tania.

"That woman will get nothing. She deserves nothing! Let her die like a dog under the fence, for all I care!"

Now I understood why they had called me to come here. What a cruel son of a bitch! Did he think this vicious little speech he had obviously been preparing would make me change my mind about Mama and do what he wanted me to do? I'd sooner he saw me dead before I'd change my mind and leave my stepmother alone to "die like a dog under the fence."

Inside, my blood was boiling, and I almost burst out with anger but thought better of it.

What could I tell this man that he would hear or understand? Could I tell him that the woman he had married had nothing of the sort in her mind that he was accusing her of? Could I remind him that this woman had cured him of his ulcer? Or that she'd slaved for him and his children for eighteen years and in no way deserved to "die like a dog under the fence?"

What could I tell him to make him hear me? Nothing! There was nothing I could tell this man who called himself my father. Nothing!

I put my glass down on the table, got up, and left the room, which nobody even noticed. When I closed the door behind me, I felt dizzy. For a moment I almost felt like I did that memorable day of my eleventh birthday. Oh, no! That wasn't going to happen again! I wouldn't allow him to affect me anymore. I couldn't allow this man to kill me—no bloody way!

As I was approaching the subway, I knew where I had to go. I had to see Mama. I hadn't spoken with her for a couple of months. I couldn't waste one minute. I had to see her right then. She had probably gone insane worrying about what was going to happen to her, now that this bastard was going to leave her with nothing.

Thank God she was there! She greeted me with this strange smile on her unusually pale face. I asked her to sit down, and said I wanted to talk with her.

"It's very simple," she said. "One day he came home and told me he was getting a divorce. He hadn't come home for several days, and I already knew he'd bought a new cooperative apartment for himself a year ago and was waiting for it to be built. He moved in there as soon as it was finished and bought everything new for himself. He has lots of money and can do what he wants. He told me that I didn't have to go to court in person if I signed this letter. He said they'd give a divorce automatically."

"So, what did you do?" I asked.

"Of course, I signed it," she said. "At least I don't have to be shamed in front of public."

"Do you have a copy of this letter?" I asked her.

"Yes, I do."

"Please, Mama. Show it to me!"

It was two pages long written in his handwriting. My hair stood on end as I read the letter. It said that sadly he had lost his wife, the mother of his three children, while he was in the war. When he returned, he had to take care of his children alone. This woman that he married came to the family with only one purpose, to destroy his children! She wouldn't feed them. She abused them, making them slaves for her, doing all the heavy jobs around the house. In the meantime she was busy pampering herself. She even bathed herself in the milk his children needed! She was the cause of all his children hating each other and she forced the youngest one, Janna, to leave home at the age of thirteen. The eldest, Tania, was forced to get married at eighteen, and on it went. At the end of this letter he asked the judge to grant him a divorce immediately.

After his signature there was hers, with a very short comment: "I agree to the divorce."

"Why did you sign this letter, Mama, which is full of lies?"

"I could not see myself standing in front of the judge and the public," she said. "I'd rather sign it and have it over with. What else could I do?" She went on to tell me all kinds of things over which they had fought all these years. Of course she should have left him a long time ago, when she was much younger and the opportunity was offered to her. But it was useless explaining any of that, and so I just let her talk and talk.

When she was completely exhausted, we both went to bed. During the night I woke up, hearing strange laughter. I tiptoed to her room and saw her lying on her bed, her eyes wide open and just giggling from time to time. I realized that I was going to end up with a crazed woman on my hands. That was all I needed.

I knew what she was going through. She was an old-fashioned woman who thought that every neighbour would now think of her as wretched and worthless, making her ashamed to show her face on the street. Added to this was her fear of being fifty-four years old with no pension, no support, nothing.

The maddening part about Soviet divorce law at that time was that it was different for each republic. A housewife in Georgia would receive financial support for twenty-five years, in the Ukraine for ten years, but in Russia itself for only one year.

My father had decided to cut Mama off from even that privilege, which was why he wrote such a horrible letter to the court. He hoped that the judge would take his side. It was completely inhumane and cruel!

After hearing her crazed laughter, I made the decision to go to court with her and testify as her witness, although she told me she was not going to go.

Finally I said, "You don't have a choice, Mama! You must be there because I've already gone and put my name down as your witness, so they expect you to be there."

On the day of the court hearing we arrived early. There was nobody in the courtroom except the secretary who told me to wait outside the courtroom until I was called to testify. I stayed in the coffee shop until everyone was in the room, including my stepmother, and the doors were closed. Then I came and stood by the door, waiting to be called.

The red sign "Court in Action" was lit and the secretary asked for absolute order. There was complete silence in the room. It was so quiet I could hear my own breathing. In a few minutes the secretary spoke again. She was calling the first case: "Citizen Boris Isaevich Laidman, the applicant for a divorce from citizen Polina Isaevna Laidman."

Then she read his letter. When she finished reading, she asked him to confirm that everything that was written in it was the truth, the whole truth, and nothing but the truth.

My father said with great confidence, "Yes, your honour. And as you can see, citizen P.I. Laidman has put her signature on it, which means everything I have written is the truth."

When I heard him saying this I realized he hadn't seen Mama in the courtroom. I was pleased with her. I had asked her to make sure to hide herself, and she had managed it! The judge asked my father to sit down and then called for my stepmother to approach the witness box. I could only imagine my father's expression when he saw her.

The judge asked her the same question. "Tell me, is this letter the truth?"

My stepmother couldn't speak. She burst into tears.

The judge said, "Thank you. Please be seated."

And then my name was called as a witness for citizen Polina Isaevna Laidman. The door opened, and I was asked to walk into the courtroom. It was a big room, full of people, but no matter how many were there I intended to speak on behalf of my stepmother so that she could walk out of this room with her head up.

I wanted her to hear my words of appreciation for her hard work and loyalty and to get the recognition she deserved: to know she wasn't alone. I also knew how important it was for her that the public should hear her stepdaughter speaking well about her. It would be the best medicine possible for her.

When I got on the witness stand, the secretary asked me to swear that everything I was about to say would be the truth, which I did. And then they asked me to speak.

"First," I said, "I would like to establish the fact that I am here to testify on behalf of my stepmother, not my own father. It may not be to my advantage to do so from various points of view, but I consider it my obligation to speak on her behalf."

"Continue," said the judge.

"This person, who was described in my father's letter as selfish and heartless and other words of that sort, came to our family of three children who were raised apart from each other for six years during the war. She spent eighteen years doing her best, to take care of my father and all of us, which was very hard. Everybody knows it's not easy to raise one's own children, let alone stepchildren. I don't know why my father married her in the first place. Most definitely it was not for the reason of love because he didn't give her any support. On the contrary, he made it very difficult for her from the beginning.

"It seemed to me that he was looking for any and every reason to make it look as though everything she did was wrong. Yet he didn't divorce her when we children were at home and she was much younger. In other words, he used her until the children were gone, yet he made her feel guilty, which enabled him to justify his personal affairs with other women. My stepmother was faithful to her commitment till the bitter end, and I believe she deserves the recognition for doing what she did.

"Now I would like to ask a question of the court and everyone who is here in this room. How many women would agree to marry into a situation like this with three orphans to care for?" I looked around. There was no movement of any kind from anyone.

"No, I don't think there are too many. To do so, one has to undertake the most difficult task. One has to be hard working, good-hearted, and this woman had these qualities, which is why I am here to speak for her. If nothing else, the fact that all three of this man's children are healthy and have a good education should be recognized and appreciated.

"In his letter, my father said that three of us children weren't close to each other. Well, this is the only true statement he made. More than that, we didn't relate to one another at all. There was a lot of resentment, and why? In my opinion, it wasn't because my stepmother mistreated us. It was because my father opened his pocket to any of his children who sided with him and completely cut off the one who spoke the truth. He wasn't interested in hearing the truth.

"I don't want to take up the court's time by going any deeper than this, but there is one thing I want to make clear. This woman, after all her hard work and patience, should not end up on the street "dying like a dog under the fence," to use my father's own expression. I would like to see to it that she'll be taken care of as she so truly deserves."

As I spoke, I saw my father's face turn pale and his lips turn blue. I was familiar with that particular look, and I knew very well what it meant. Of course, he hadn't expected any of this to happen. He had gone to court feeling certain that everything would go his way, and it hadn't. I felt this was the one opportunity available to make my stepmother feel better about herself so that she would be able to function after the divorce.

After I finished speaking, there was a pause in the courtroom and then the judge got up and spoke.

"Unfortunately there is no law in the divorce act for punishment other than the divorce itself, which certainly will be granted. But I wish to express my own feelings in this case.

"If it were up to me, I would suggest that this man deserves punishment not only for misleading the court but for doing it with one reason in mind and one reason only—that is, to cut his ex-wife off from the financial support that he is obligated to pay to her. I therefore order him to pay her seventy-five rubles a month for one year, according to Russian Federation Law. I also order that all the furnishings and household items become hers, and which may not be removed from the house."

With that, the judge sat down and the secretary called the next case.

My stepmother and I got up to leave the courtroom. At the same time my father also left the room, and as we reached the stairwell we heard the door slam loudly behind him.

As we went down the stairs he came behind us, screaming, "You bitch! How could you do this to me, after I fed you for eight years?"

Mama and I ignored him and continued down, hand in hand. There was no sense reacting as he continued to scream. "I should be pulling each and every hair from my head for every piece of bread I gave you, you bitch!" he shouted. "You should have died before ever I met you! You killed your mother!"

CHAPTER 26

Frozen Ears

After the divorce I had to stay with Mama to make sure she was going to be okay, and as it turned out it was a complete necessity. In spite of the order, my father managed to convince the court that he couldn't afford to pay her the seventy-five rubles, because all he had was one hundred twenty rubles a month.

According to the law they could only take off 15 percent of it, which was barely enough for a week's food. We both knew he had money hidden away—lots of it—but nothing could be done, and so I had to support her financially.

Mama was a master economizer. She knew how to stretch a ruble in ten different ways. She would buy one kilo of meat with the bone in. Out of this meat she could make two four-course dinners for a week. She used to say that to make a good soup you needed a good bone.

The soups would be perhaps cabbage borscht with beets, carrots, and potatoes; a bean soup; a pea soup; or noodle soup. Out of the cooked meat she would make stuffing for a couple of other second courses, one of which was meat blintzes, which she was a master at making! Yes, Mama certainly knew how to stretch a ruble.

Her real problem was finding how to get a job. But who wanted to hire a woman of fifty-four when the retirement age for women was fifty-five and for men, sixty? In order to qualify for a pension one had to have a twenty-five-year working record—it was that or nothing. There were no partial pensions based on how many years one had worked. We could prove she had fifteen working years, but she needed to get a job for ten more years. The problem was how did a woman of fifty-four with no special training, who'd been a housewife for eighteen years, get a job?

Her last job had been during the war when she was a fabric painter. She and a friend painted Russian shawls made of the finest wool for export and which they hand-painted with traditional designs. Her friend had continued doing this work and by now had earned her pension, but Mama got married and had to quit.

We desperately needed to get work for her! There was another problem that had to be solved before she could go to any job interview. I found out she didn't have anything decent to wear and needed a complete wardrobe!

She didn't even have a regular pair of shoes, only quilted fabric boots. She had a quilted jacket that she wore for all her needs, a silk dress she'd bought when she got married, two summer outfits, and a couple of flannel dresses for fall and winter. Nothing she had was suitable for going out to get a job.

I had to spend at least three month's salary to buy her a few blouses and skirts, a couple of warm sweaters, two pairs of shoes, winter boots, and a winter coat, which I bought second-hand. Finally, she was ready to go for job interviews. I thought of every person I could ask to help. There was nothing much they could do, but at least we got a few interviews.

After about four months of futile appointments, I was referred to a director of personnel for Soviet Exhibits of National Industrial and Economical Achievements. It had functioned from the 1950s and was huge, with every industry represented in separate pavilions. It was an impressive showplace that millions of citizens and tourists visited all year round.

I was ecstatic to have managed to get an interview for Mama with this organisation, and thankfully she was hired to be a floor guard for one of the largest exhibits. The heavy industry pavilion was a gigantic space of ceramic floors and hundreds of pieces of heavy machinery.

They needed a person to keep an eye on people walking around and to make sure the place was treated with care. Besides this, she also had to keep the floors clean. I felt the job was more suitable for a man, but obviously the pay was too low. It was only sixty rubles a month, and no man would do such a job for that kind of money. It was two combined positions, guard and cleaner. Probably some of the administrators were receiving one of the two salaries, which was often the case in Soviet Union. One of the members of the family, officially on the payroll, would simply collect pay once a month. This would be for the benefit of their relative, most likely the boss, whose official salary was also too low.

They told her she could start work at the beginning of the next week. We were both so happy that I suggested we to stop at one of the exhibition cafeterias and have a feast. It was Mama's first time eating out in years. She talked vivaciously and even looked younger and more attractive than I'd ever seen her; she was even wearing lipstick, which she normally didn't put on. It was her big day! She had a chance to earn her own living, which made me glad but also sad. I couldn't help thinking that if she'd done this fifteen years before, by now she would have been okay.

After that day there was a great improvement in her—no more giggling at night. She would get up at around five and go outside and do the things she had neglected because she had been so depressed. By the time I got up, the kettle was on the table and both of us would have a cup of tea with her homemade strawberry jam.

Mama would leave the house two hours before her job started and arrive at least an hour before her time. Little did I know she was washing the floors first thing in the morning before the pavilion opened. The place was too huge for her to finish the job at night. She did half at the end of the day and the other half in the morning.

In the meantime, I wanted to organize some privacy for myself. I decided that if I had to stay near Mama until she could manage, I still wanted her to be less dependent on me. After all I wasn't going to be around all the time.

We had a very small house, which of course belonged to the state.

I asked Mama if I could close the connecting door between the two rooms we had and make my own separate entrance into the second room.

"It's good for me to be near you, Mama," I said, "but both of us have to have our own space. I may want to have company and I also study later. Or if I come home late, you wouldn't be disturbed."

Mama thought it was a great idea, and I decided to make the change quickly and cheaply with the help of some friends from the club, who were mostly actors or in theatre production. I got everybody organized and we did all in one day!"

I got all the material needed from the club's old set décor. We put drywall on both sides of the connecting wall and cut out a space for the door in the former bedroom, which was easy.

There was drywall on the side and two-by-fours on the outside, with some wood chips in between for insulation. We forgot one little thing, however, which was to put the chips back in the wall! Somehow, they had fallen out, and in our enthusiasm to get the job done, hadn't noticed this important detail! When the door was installed, everybody was in high spirits. At last, I had my own living quarters—something that was considered a luxury in Soviet Russia 1964. Even if it was only one room with no real kitchen and a toilet out in the garden I was thrilled to have it! In the next couple of days, I did a little interior decorating and got myself some inexpensive wallpaper. Also, I had the club workshop build me a wooden base for my bed, and when I covered it with an oriental rug, it doubled as a couch!

Now I had to come up with some kind of a makeshift kitchen in my little place. I hung some drapery from the ceiling, which gave the effect of a separate area, and I put in a small table with a gasoline burner. I couldn't do any gourmet cooking with it, but I could boil potatoes and make simple dinners.

I had my friends over, who all helped me to put my first dinner together. We had a great time being both intellectual and silly. The vodka helped, naturally. We told hilarious stories, mostly about the Communist Party leaders. Khrushchev was target number one, being the easiest personality of all to poke fun at! Everybody felt comfortable telling political jokes because we all knew each other so well, and the fun went on until five o'clock in the morning.

By mid-October, I was beginning to realize how cold it was in my room! There had never been much insulation to begin with, and nobody had taken care of the house for a very long time. With the loss of the wood chips in the wall during the renovation, plus having two windows on the other wall, the place became unbearably cold.

One morning I got up to get ready for work and found the water in my pail had a thick layer of ice over it! I couldn't break it, no matter how hard I tried, and then I realized one of my ears was numb and the other had very little feeling in it. They were in fact frozen! I went quickly to Mama's, but her place was frigid too. Apparently, she didn't want to leave the stove going while we were both out. My only solution in order to get warm was to go to the club.

Coming back after a full day of work and night classes, I'd find Mama sleeping, and I didn't have the heart to wake her up. In the morning she was gone by the time I got up. I kept missing her for the next couple of days until Sunday morning when she knocked on my door and told me that she'd been sick and in terrible pain all week with arthritis. When she told me about trying to cope with washing the impossibly huge floor area at the exhibition I couldn't bring myself to tell her about my problem with the freezing room.

I advised her to quit the job—that I'd find something better for her, but she couldn't afford to waste a single day.

"Janna, I need the work so I have a pension. What will I do otherwise?" She sighed. "Maybe they might hire me for a smaller and warmer pavilion. Oh! That would be so good!"

I knew people wouldn't be stupid enough to move from a good situation, especially during the winter. So, that same Sunday, I went to the club and talked to everybody, asking them to try and think of some job for Mama. I asked them to speak to their theatre administration to see if she could get a coat-check job. It would be a perfect situation for her but difficult to get because women who worked there stayed forever. Something had to happen for her soon. If not—I was afraid she'd get seriously ill.

One day that week, I had to go to the school of one of the club's top theatres. The head of the school was the father of one of my best friends, a young drama director Eugene Radomsky. He had worked in our club trying to organize a new contemporary theatre group and he had also given acting classes in the theatre school. When I saw him there I had an idea. When his students were on a break, I grabbed him by the hand and led him to his father's office.

Luckily his father was in, and with both of them there together, I told them they needed to create a new position for a receptionist.

"Every time I come to the school," I told them, "I have to wander around looking for people I need to talk to! Another thing: the dressing rooms are always wide open and unattended and I often hear students complaining about their wallets or other belongings having been stolen. I thing we need someone to look after this sort of thing," I said, "and you wouldn't have to pay this person a lot of money!"

Before they could respond, I added, "My stepmother could take on a job like this. And I promise you, you wouldn't regret it!"

They looked at each other and then back at me.

"What a good idea!" Eugene's father said. "I'm going to see to it right away! Mind you," he said, "we had a receptionist for a long time, but she died a couple of years ago and I suppose we just didn't bother to rehire anyone. But you're right. Let your stepmother come in tomorrow!"

I was happy beyond words, and the next morning Mama started her new job! She was in warm place, surrounded by students and actors who loved her right from the start. They shared all kinds of gossip with her and told her their troubles and cried on her shoulder. She was invited to see all the school performances too and, happily, the theatre school became her life.

The pay was very low—only forty-five rubles a month—fifteen rubles less than she received from the exhibition. Reasonable pay at that time was from seventy-five to ninety rubles a month. The ruble was then worth about ninety cents in American currency.

With Mama trying to cope with the low wage, yet so content with the job, I decided to write to my sisters, hoping I could persuade them to help her out a little.

I wrote first to Tania, whose husband was the chief engineer in a shipbuilding plant in Nikolaev, near Odessa. My letter was as diplomatic as I could manage about Mama's situation, and I asked her if she could spare just five rubles a month to help her out. I received a more or less non-committal letter back, saying she couldn't really afford the money.

Then I wrote her a second letter, trying to appeal to her merciful side. Her answer was blunt and straightforward—the real Tania was in this second letter.

"Even if I had the money," the letter said, "I wouldn't do it! Why should I? This woman is absolutely nobody and nothing to me!"

Tania was definitely out.

I tried Sema and this time used a totally different approach. I appealed to her pride rather than sympathy.

"Sema, you're the senior expert in your firm," I wrote, "and your husband is about to become a professor of economic science. How would you feel if you knew that the woman who looked after you for fourteen years—who cooked for you, cleaned for you, washed and ironed your clothes for all that time—had to beg for her needs?"

Sema wouldn't have liked that (being very aware of what people might think), and I knew it. She agreed to give her fifteen rubles a month. "Tell her to come to my house on the first of the month and I'll give her the money."

I practically ran all the way to the school to tell Mama the good news. Naturally, I wouldn't tell her how I had persuaded Sema to agree to give her the money!

"Guess what happened, Mama!" I said, "Sema called me and offered to give you fifteen rubles a month! She wants you to go to her house each month and she'll give it to you. And you'll get to see her little girl too. I know you'll enjoy that!"

Mama's response was, "No, I'm not going there! I can't go there! I just can't"

"Oh, come on, Mama! Now that Sema's a mother herself perhaps things have changed. I'm sure they have! They must have!"

She began to soften. "Well—maybe you're right. She might have changed. All right, I'll go then," she said, a bit reluctantly.

The first time she went, everything was fine. The next time was okay as well. But the third time, as she was leaving Sema's apartment, she overheard the husband say, "What's going on? Is she going to come here every month? And why do we have to give her supper too?"

Sema's response was, "I know! I don't see why we should do it! I'll put an end to this supper business and I'll mail her the damn money!"

I received a phone call from Mama at work. She was sobbing like a child and couldn't even speak. I asked her to stay by the phone booth, that I'd be right there. When I got to her, it took me a long time to calm her down. I kept saying, "Mama, Mama—there's nothing new about this. Nothing new, nothing new..."

That was the last time she received money from Sema.

I should have known better. In my heart I knew that some things never changed. And we were better off without them—so much more peaceful. I had been helping her all this time and I would just continue to do so. The good thing was she had a job and she liked it. She felt good about herself; she looked much happier too and had made friends and was earning her way toward a pension. Those were the most important things. Life would go on.

CHAPTER 27

The Magic Is Gone

Some time before the money episode with my sisters, I sat down with Mama in my little room one Sunday and said to her, "Mama, I want you to know the truth. I'm not interested in any man, except one. It's very unfortunate that this relationship between us really never worked and probably never will, but I can't seem to forget him. I keep thinking about him, and it feels like I have unfinished business with him.

"I'd like to ask you one favour, in case Valentin ever comes to the house looking for me. Tell him I want to see him or—better yet—tie him up if you have to and make him wait for me! I need to see him. I'm also telling you that if this happens, I'm not going to have him sneak in and out of my place, and I don't want to see you to be upset about it or judge me. I'm telling you now, I will be with him, if it's at all possible."

Mama said, "Of course I'll do that, whether I approve or not. It's your life, and I want you to be happy. Look what happened to me. I lived my whole life afraid of what other people would say. It's the way we were brought up. I can't change it, but you can."

Shortly after our conversation, I was at home, doing my Sunday cleaning, and I was about to finish the floors when I heard a knock on my door.

It was Mama. "He's here!" she said.

"Who?" I called out.

"Valentin," she answered. "That special friend of yours!"

"Oh! My God! Mama, I look terrible. I can't let him see me like this! Please, please, Mama, don't let him get away! I'll clean myself up and be ready as quickly as I can! When I am, I'll knock on your wall and then you can bring him to my door. But not until then—please!"

"Okay, okay," she said. "I'll do that. Don't worry!" I got so excited I kept dropping things, but I quickly dried my floors and then managed to have a sponge bath. I had some French perfume, which I only used on special occasions, and I dabbed some of this expensive, precious fragrance on. I had three pieces of underwear made of incredibly light silky material and I slipped into them but decided not to be too dressy, and I put on a black tracksuit.

Then came the hair and the face—but I left my hair wet and didn't put on any lipstick. It would have been out of place. Thank goodness the place was clean. My hands were shaking, and I had to try and calm down before I gave Mama the okay sign.

He was quickly standing there—and my heart stopped again! What was it about him? Why couldn't these unbelievable feelings when I saw him happen with other men? It was like a curse. Why did I feel so overwhelmed with emotion every time I saw him? I wished I could free myself from this burden. And that's what it was—a burden!

"Hi, Jandi!" he said softly.

"I am very sorry, Valia, about that day," I said. "I didn't think you'd want to talk with me ever again after that, so I didn't call. But I never stopped thinking about you."

Saying this, I went up to him and looked in his eyes.

He smiled his funny smile and said, "I know Jandi, and it's not only your fault." He looked around the room. "Do you have anything to eat? I feel like having a couple of shots of vodka."

"Sure, I have a couple of things, but I don't have any vodka."

"Don't worry," Valentin said with a grin. "I've got some." He opened his briefcase and took out a bottle of vodka. "When your stepmother told me I had to wait half an hour to see you, I ran to the store and got it. It was funny. She wouldn't let me go! She said you wanted her to tie me to a chair to keep me there so I left my coat with her to prove I'd be back! I'm actually cold now, so let's have a drink, I need it!"

I put everything out on the table in no time. There was kolbassa, bread, a couple of cold boiled potatoes, which I quickly fried, and a few pickles. It was all I had.

"This is just great!" he said. "What more do we need?"

While I was arranging the table Valentin watched my every move. It literally paralyzed my movements. He said I was like a professional I was so fast. That comment made me feel better, and I told him how much I liked cooking and that if I had more time and money, I would love to get into gourmet cooking.

He poured each of us a shot of vodka and raised his glass. "To you, Jandi!"

I looked at him and wanted to say, "To us!" But I didn't. I simply said, "Thank you."

As we ate and drank, he told me about his work in the Institute Korolev—one of the atomic firms in Moscow.

"My job is interesting and I'm learning a lot, you know," he said. "I'm going to start working in the field, which means exposure to a very harmful environment. But somebody has to do it. Especially as my job is designing rockets."

It was surprising to hear him share these things with me. I knew that what he was saying was top secret, and he had never spoken about any of these things before.

Then he took my hand in his, and I saw that familiar look in his eyes—the look I'd remembered since the first time he kissed me. And I knew what was coming next, of course. He would pull my head close to his and start to kiss me.

I wondered to myself why I had to wait for him to start everything. Why didn't I go first, ahead of him? What was stopping me? But the unspoken rule was that I had to wait for him—and I did. And when he kissed me, it was his way. I would have done things gently, from the depths of my heart, but allowing him to be the leader gave me no freedom and allowed him to be in command.

It was my fault. I shouldn't have let that situation go on and on. After all, I wasn't a teenage girl anymore! I had to change all this in time, but not now. For now, I'd allow him to lead me—and, of course, we went back to the way it had always been.

I was too much under his spell. It wasn't us kissing each other, it was him kissing me. And I let him; he had this incredible power over me. Yet even though I was aware of it, I somehow couldn't think, and it was too late to stop the momentum.

His hands were getting stronger and stronger, his kisses more and more urgent. I became his object, and I didn't have a chance. I was like a doll in his powerful hands and all thinking stopped. I just followed him. This man I had waited for all these years...I didn't want to screw it up now.

Something we had both wanted for so long was finally happening. It was supposed to be thrilling—but where was my excitement now? Why was his body just a body? Where was the magic?

I had dreamed of this for eight long years, and now I was lying in bed with this unforgettable love of mine, exhausted but detached. We weren't together the way we should have been. Something wasn't right. Something wasn't complete. It seemed to be a one-way street—for him. He was a leader, but where did that leave me? Very much on the outside. I didn't know whose fault it was, I just knew that the magic was gone.

That winter was the coldest and longest of my life. The temperature was often minus thirty, and I had to put up with it, even if it was almost killing me. Mama told me she was using double the amount of coal oil to keep the place warm, and I told her not to worry about me and not use so much fuel—that I would somehow manage to survive. The other important factor was crucial. If we were to run out of coal oil in the middle of winter, we would be even in bigger trouble!

The most difficult time was late in the evening, when I came home after my night classes and had to sit at my table in the freezing cold room and study. My ears hurt even when I covered my head. With the temperature in my room being minus three or four degrees, it was sheer agony. I told myself that this bloody winter would someday be over—and so would everything else in life! In the meantime, my winter exams were going to be starting soon, and I had to work and study with everything I had no matter what!

After that first night with Valentin, he came over every Saturday evening. He always brought something with him—usually canned delicacies—and always a small bottle of vodka. He said it was the best thing to warm us up!

Of course, I always provided bread, potatoes, and onions. I knew how to prepare potatoes in fifteen different ways. We had the same menu every time because that kind of dinner was all I could afford. That even though I received the top salary at the club after director, who was getting two hundred and twenty rubles a month. My salary was one hundred forty rubles, but it wasn't enough to cover my important needs. I had to take care of Mama and pay off the loan I'd taken out to buy her some clothes, so I had to cut down on my basic expenses. I was thankful my winter coat had been paid off by the end of the fifth year and it would last me for at least another five years.

Before Mama was divorced, I had everything organized and I didn't to struggle so much, but the divorce really put me in the hole again, and nothing could be done about it. It was just the reality of the situation.

Meanwhile, on Saturday evening Valentin and I always had a special time together. We talked about all kinds of things—our jobs and my university, which I wasn't happy about. If I decided to go to another university, I'd lose all my credits, so I was in a state of indecision, hoping the rules might change. So we talked about that.

But I couldn't bring myself to talk about what really bothered me, which was the sexual part of our relationship. I suppose both of us were still the product of our times. I knew I would outgrow these attitudes at some point in my life, but not with Valentin, who was far too strong-willed and set in his ways.

Every time we finished our modest dinner, we'd get undressed and go through the same routine—pretending to be quite casual about going to bed together. Immediately, he would take control, catering mainly to his own wants and needs.

The way he approached lovemaking was nowhere close to what I would have liked. I wanted us to move at a more leisurely pace so we could slowly feel our way with each other. Instead, I felt like he was attacking me. He was like a marauding lion and I was his prey, and I didn't know how to change it.

I figured it was the way it was, that it was the nature of the beast. I also knew I wouldn't be happy with the way it was—ever. It would have to end. It must end.

One night after he finished his solo performance, he fell asleep without saying a word. He just turned his back and in seconds was dead to the world. I lay there, wide awake, thinking about what was happening between us and how it was affecting me.

The magic we'd had was gone, and there wasn't a trace of it left. None. And I couldn't see myself pretending that everything was all right, either. I thought and thought until I knew what I had to do. He had to leave. And I wanted him to leave—right then!

"Valentin!" I heard myself saying, "I want you to leave!" I'd said it before I even realized it. I also didn't count on him hearing me. I was sure he was fast asleep.

There was a five-minute pause, after which he got up, without saying anything, dressed himself, and left. He was gone. It had happened shockingly fast. He was gone, and I was in my freezing room all by myself. It was the end. And why should I feel sad? I'd made this decision myself, and it was up to me to start feeling better.

CHAPTER 28

I Have To Make It

My freezing room turned into a prison during the winter exam session. I had two weeks off to do my exams. I studied day and night with only a couple of hours' sleep, during which I still couldn't warm up. I went to bed fully dressed, making sure my ears were well covered too.

Getting up was a struggle each and every time. I learned my lesson not to leave water in the pail but kept it in a kettle and a cooking pot and lived on tea. Every half-hour I washed my hands and face with warm water from the pot to feel at least a momentary sensation of warmth. Once I ran out of water I would go outside and bring in some more to fill up the pots. In between, I sat and memorized.

The Russian school system was based on memorizing. We weren't allowed to use any reference books during the exams and there was no multiple question system. Each student would get two or three questions that had to be reviewed in front of the examination commission, and after that other questions could be asked or not.

My feet bothered me a lot from being frozen when I was nine years old. From that time on they hurt a great deal, especially in the winter. Massaging them would help for a few minutes, but by the end of the fourth day being in my cold room destroyed my concentration. I did everything. I soaked my feet in warm water, which would get cold again in two minutes! Then my feet felt even worse. My hands weren't much better, and my writing looked so crooked I myself couldn't understand what I'd written!

Often, I'd find myself just sitting and staring at one spot in my book, with my head absolutely a blank. In other words, my studying productivity was next to zero. A couple of times I was close to simply giving it all up. Then I thought of how much effort I had already put into it, and I would force myself to go on, but not for too long.

The old questions "What can I do?" and "Where should I go?" were still unanswered. My choices were limited. To go to Mama's room was useless; there was no space to put my bed anywhere for one thing, and, secondly, I couldn't afford to rent my own place. After five days of going in circles, I decided to go to my Uncle Moisey's, my father's brother, who lived with his wife in the same building as my father. They didn't have children and lived in a comfortable two-room apartment with a good size kitchen.

I told him about my problem and asked if I could stay with them until the end of winter. He heard me out and told me to go home, pack my suitcase, and come back. I thought it was pretty nice of him.

When I returned, he met me at his apartment door with a key in his hand and said, "Let's go!"

I asked, "Where?"

"Come with me!" He took me up to the seventh floor and opened an apartment with the key, saying, "This is where you are staying. It's your father's place, so unpack and make yourself at home. I'll speak with him so he will listen."

"Uncle Moisey," I said, "don't you know about my relationship with my father? I can't stay with him. It's impossible! I'd better go back to my freezing room right now! Let's forget it!"

"I am telling you to stay here!" he said emphatically." I'm glad I have his spare key so I don't have to ask him. I'll just tell him! You understand? He doesn't have a say in this matter. You look terrible! Now unpack and take a shower, eat something, and get back to your studies! I'll see you later." And he left.

I knew my face looked blue and my hands were red, but my feet were killing me the most. I stood there for a few moments and decided I simply couldn't go back to my room. I would die there.

The first thing I did was to take a shower, and it was one of the most fantastic and unforgettable experiences! Centrally heated water! What a magnificent product of nature and civilization! I knew I would never take it for granted again! It made me feel alive and crispy clean! It made my brain function, made me want to eat and do all kinds of other wonderful things—like live life!

Then to have a simple boiled potato with a little butter was a glorious experience too, especially now that I was warm, and to lie down in a heated room and relax for a few minutes and then just to float away!

I woke up when I heard the key in the door. My father walked in and said nothing. Nor did he look at me.

I said, "Hi," but there was no answer. My father had this talent. He could be in a room with one of us and not speak for weeks at a time. I couldn't afford to react—I was staying in his place. I had to just concentrate on getting through my exams and through this winter. In another two or three months it would be over.

In the meantime I'd take care of his place and do the cooking. I knew what he liked and I would see to it all.

In a couple of days the fridge was filled with food, and then he finally spoke a few words to me.

"I've bought some meat," he said, "and there's also chicken and fish and other things. Just tell me what else you need and I'll buy it."

Besides all these items, he had brought in a supply of his favorite caviar, smoked salmon, good bread, a few tins of pickled vegetables, and other delicacies. I hadn't eaten such foods for a long time.

My studying went well. I passed all four exams with relatively good marks and went back to work. The first day I returned from the club, my father asked me point blank, "When are you getting married?"

What kind of question was this? Obviously, the message actually was this: "When will you be leaving my place?"

I decided not to challenge him. This time he was going to have to put up with me.

The next Sunday after I finished cooking, he told me to get dressed up.

"Somebody" was coming over to join us for dinner. It sounded rather strange.

He had never before shown any interest in what I was wearing, and I said, "What's wrong with what I'm wearing?"

"You can't wear that track suit when we have a visitor!" he said. "You have to look more feminine. Wear that red dress you have."

"But that's my evening dress," I protested. "It'll look out of place wearing it at home!" Then I thought better of it and said, "Okay. I'll wear it."

The visitor was a guy who lived in the same building. I had seen him a couple of times in the elevator. When he walked in my father had a broad smile on his face and the two of them sat and talked about politics for a couple of minutes while I was serving food.

Then it dawned on me. I began to see what my father was doing. I didn't like this guy, who wasn't my type at all. He had small hands, and I didn't like his voice either. I couldn't even look at him. Then my father started interviewing him.

"Do you live with your parents?" he asked.

"No, I live by myself."

"Where are your parents?"

"They have their own place."

"Are they retired?"

"No, they're still working."

"Who bought this apartment for you?"

"I did. My job pays well, but my parents helped me just a little bit with the down payment."

"How much are you making?"

This persistent questioning on the part of my father made me crazy!

"Two hundred and eighty rubles a month."

"That's a lot of money! And how old are you?"

"I'm thirty-three."

"Why aren't you married yet?"

"I'm thinking about it now."

"My daughter knows how to cook!"

"Yes, everything was really tasty!"

I sat there with my face absolutely burning! No doubt it blended in with my red dress!

After dinner, we had some tea with apple cake. My father's guest had three big pieces and then left.

My father said to me the next evening, "This guy, David, wants to take you out to the movies this coming Saturday. Don't make any plans."

"But I'm working this Saturday night!" I protested

"Look. He's a nice boy. He has his own place, and he makes good money!"

I said nothing.

The marriage campaign continued, and I started receiving phone calls from other men who wanted to meet me. It looked like my father and Uncle Moisey were working overtime to find me a husband!

I told my father that after my having been off work for two weeks I had a lot of catching up to do.

"That's all fine, but don't forget," he said with force, "you don't have that much time! You're twenty-three already!"

"I'll do what I can to find a place to live," I said. "Please, just bear with me for a little while longer."

"What do you mean a little while longer? Be more specific! I need to look after my private life too."

"You know my evening schedule," I said. "Try to be patient. I'm not home until after midnight, two nights a week, and if you need more time alone, just tell me and I'll stay out. On other days I leave at eight in the morning, and I'm never back before ten at night. I have class three times a week, so I'm only at home on Sundays."

I knew he was seeing someone, but Uncle Moisey had told me she had place of her own.

"That's not the point!" he insisted. "You still have to get married—and soon! You're too choosy and you act like a princess. You have many choices now, but it's not going to be like this forever. There are a lot of girls younger than you who are already married. Soon you're going to be too old."

This was typical of my time. Grown-ups wouldn't leave young girls alone. As soon as they were eighteen, everybody asked you the same stupid question: "When are you getting married?" At twenty, girls were made to feel there was something wrong with them if they didn't have a man who'd proposed to them and weren't busy planning their wedding.

I could see how Father was looking for an argument. A couple of times he told me not to come home until midnight—and these were days when I didn't have classes nor was it my night to be at work. I told him it was fine, but I could see he was waiting for me to say I couldn't, that I had to study or something. I knew he was ready to say, "If you don't cooperate with what I ask, you'll be sorry." I had to keep the peace if I was going to survive this terrible winter.

One day in January, my friend Luda from university asked me not to rush home after class; she wanted me to meet her boyfriend who was picking her up. He had a friend with him, and we were all introduced to each other. Luda's boyfriend's name was Leon and his friend was Maxim.

Maxim was of medium height, a bit taller than me, about 5'9". His nose was slightly red, which he apologized for, saying that his nose always got red in the frost. He was good looking and possessed a pleasant charm. His voice was both soft and deep at the same time, and I immediately had a feeling we would get along. He wasn't my type physically, yet he had something that attracted me.

After introductions, they invited us to a concert and dance in the Luzhniki Stadium, which always took place during the university student's winter break. Luda suggested we all to go together, and so we went off in Maxim's car.

To have one's own car in Russia in those days was very prestigious. Even so, he apologized for the smallness of the vehicle. Then he apologized that the car was so cold, that it would take a few minutes to warm up. They were normal remarks, but I thought the man didn't seem to be that sure of himself. In a short space of time he'd apologized about his nose, his car, and about it being cold. I immediately disregarded this thought, however. In fact, I took it as part of his charm.

During the ride, Maxim told me he was thirty-six years old and had graduated as an engineer-architect from one the oldest civil engineering universities in Moscow. After graduation he had been sent into the armed forces to serve as a naval officer in Vladivostok, which he said was the most exciting time of his life. I found out later that this period in his life held all his best memories. After he returned from Vladivostok he told me he'd worked in various research Institutions in Moscow and specialised in steel and concrete construction for industrial buildings and was working on his dissertation. Maxim was unusual. He lived apart from his parents and had his own apartment.

Everybody was already seated when we walked into the concert hall, and as soon as we sat down, the concert began. He and I were in good spirits and were very much enjoying each other's company. Before the intermission, he got up and told us he wanted to get to the restaurant before there was too big a lineup. I thought it was a pretty ingenious idea of him, and so we agreed to join him shortly after the concert.

By then the place was swarming with hundreds of people, but Maxim was sitting calmly at our table with red caviar, smoked salmon sandwiches, and a bottle of champagne. We all had a good time, with Maxim and Leon telling one hilarious story after another! It was great. Afterwards, we joined everybody on the dance floor. The place was huge and packed with people, and while we danced, Maxim invited me to go out for dinner and dancing the following Saturday at the Journalist's Club. I accepted happily. I knew the place because of my own club, which gave me access to all the professional clubs in Moscow, and I was glad he knew them too. At the end of the evening he dropped off Luda and Leon and drove me to my father's place.

We didn't stay in his car too long. It became too cold, so we said a quick goodnight to each other as he told me he'd call me the next day. As I went up to my father's apartment I said almost aloud, "Maxim is going to be my husband!"

In the morning, my father told me again that I'd had all these calls from different men.

"Don't worry," I said. "I'm getting married."

"When?" he asked. I suppose it was quite funny. He didn't ask me anything about my future husband. His first concern was *when*. Eventually I think even he understood that what he said had its funny side. So he decided to ask me one more question.

"Does he have his own place?"

When I told him he did, he looked satisfied and went back to his newspaper!

Maxim proposed to me at the end of the first week. During that time, we saw each other every night. We went to the theatre, movies, to dinner and dances, and on Sunday we went skiing. He said he hadn't been on skis in more than fifteen years. Afterwards, he invited me to his apartment in Warshavskoe Shosse, which was at the opposite end of New Moscow from my father's place, where he had a one-bedroom co-op apartment with its own kitchen.

He proposed to me quite casually while we were drinking wine and listening to music. He simply said that I was the first girl he had ever met who didn't make him feel uncomfortable! I didn't know what he meant. He didn't say, "I love you"—not even once. He only said that I had a great figure and a great smile. Perhaps it was the best he could do.

I liked him too—for his sincerity and for the fact that he wasn't pushy. I told him about my previous relationships and frustrating love for Valentin, which I didn't go into any details about. I simply said that the relationship had been a strange one and that it was over.

The next week, the students' break was over, so there were no more concerts or dances. Night school students weren't given a break, but most of us took advantage of the full-time students' holiday, and we felt as though it was a time off for us too. We all skipped classes and really didn't do much homework during that week.

It was back to serious studying again, but I was considering changing schools in the coming summer. I had decided to get a degree in the cultural industry; I'd already had some great working experience for almost five years, and I wanted to continue in the field.

As our courtship developed, Maxim did not disappoint. He proved to be thoughtful and creative, which continued to attract me to him. As it happened, in the first two months after we met, he went away for research purposes to the Republics of Latvia and Georgia. When he came back from Riga he brought me a few well-chosen gifts. One was a leather case full of cosmetic items, some perfume, and a few other things. The interesting thing was how it was assembled together. He bought everything separately and then found a smart leather case and put it together himself. I appreciated his thoughtfulness very much. He also gave me a leather belt and kid gloves. That too wasn't easy to find, especially the gloves, which were perfect for me. I had long fingers, and it wasn't easy to buy me gloves that actually fit.

From Georgia, he brought me cast-iron cookware and pans in six sizes because he knew I liked gourmet cooking. He didn't buy them in stores but from people's private houses—not for money but in exchange for one of the popular Russian perfumes. I thought it was a pretty original idea. This creative and resourceful quality of his was important to me. I had passes to all the theatres, but he never asked me to use them. He bought the tickets himself and invited me. That way we always had good seats. In other words, I really enjoyed his courtship.

The day he proposed to me I didn't answer immediately, but I seriously considered his proposal. That evening, he told me all kinds of things about himself and his family. The only memorable affair he'd had was with a ballet dancer during his five years in Vladivostok. She was married to a naval captain who was away most of the time, and as she lived quite a distance away from Maxim, he had to walk miles and miles back to his place after their dates. It took him so long to get back, it would be almost time to go to work. Since his return almost ten years ago, he really hadn't met anyone he would have considered marrying.

He showed me photographs of himself in uniform in which he looked very handsome with a great head of dark hair. He had lost a lot of his hair by the time I met him and tried to cover his partial baldness; I didn't care for his attempts to cover it up. I figured it was part of his insecurity and that perhaps I could make him understand that the cover-up drew way more attention than the baldness. Perhaps I'd be able to suggest cut it and just let the bald area show.

Telling me about his parents, he was very objective about both of them. They had been born and raised in a small town near Minsk. His father, Issak, was born in 1893, his mother, Sophia, in 1902. She was a local beauty and was tall—five feet ten with long black hair, which she wore in two braids. Maxim's father was at least four inches shorter than she was.

She was a seventh-grade schoolgirl when Maxim's father fell in love with her, and they got married shortly after her sixteenth birthday. She never went back to school, although Maxim's father was a great scholar. In fact, he was one the best-educated men anywhere, graduating in economics and specializing in Western agricultural economics. He had given two important dissertations and had published two books on the agricultural economy of the USA and Canada without ever having been abroad. He could speak and write in seven languages, including English, and was obviously an outstanding man. Maxim's father had also witnessed the Russian Revolution in October 1918. His father told Maxim that the soldiers didn't know which side they were on, the Reds or the Whites, when the Reds took over the Winter Palace.

His father was one of those men who lived in fear during Stalin's years of repression from 1934 to1938. Stalin got rid of millions of the most educated and high-ranking people. Many were scientists and doctors in the Soviet Union of that time; they were simply taken from their homes in the middle of the night and most of them never returned. Their families had no idea what happened to them. Some of them were kept in prison for as long as twenty-five years. Countless thousands were murdered and as many died in prison.

When the repression began, every family expected sudden arrests in the night. Men had small overnight bags prepared and kept them by their beds. When the KGB bandits came to a house they turned it upside down, searching for no one knew what, and then they would simply take the men away.

At that time, his father was a professor of economics. By sheer luck he wasn't arrested, but his closest friend and colleague who had a family of four children spent ten years in jail, during which time Maxim's father supported the man's family. When he returned, Maxim's father gave him his own second dissertation so that his friend could get his master's degree faster and get a better-paid job.

When he told me about his father I was dying to meet the man! Maxim told me about his mother too, who was very different from his father.

She wasn't an intellectual person at all; she had never risen above her seventh-grade education and wasn't interested in reading.

She was also domineering and never acknowledged her husband's uniqueness. They had very little in common, but being an old-fashioned gentleman, he didn't have the heart to divorce her. He was not a happy man and had lived very much his own life for many years. In fact, he was dreading retirement and staying at home so much that at the age of seventy-two he was still working full-time.

CHAPTER 29

Courtship and Marriage

Our courtship continued. We both knew we were heading towards marriage from the very beginning. My thoughts were that it was a comfort to have a mature man as my future husband. The thirteen-year age difference was a bit of a concern, but providing he and I had lots of things we enjoyed doing together, it would be no problem.

My main concern about Maxim's age was that he was ready to have a child right away. I wasn't at this stage yet. I wanted to complete my education, and that wasn't going to change, no matter what. I had made up my mind a long time before to get a university degree. Unfortunately, three years of law school would be, in a sense, wasted, but then again I didn't believe that any education was a waste.

Nevertheless, it would take me another five years to get my diploma. I intended to continue working and going to school, and having a baby in the early stage of marriage was not in my plan.

As far as going to bed with Maxim before we got married, my decision was no. He respected my decision, which made me feel a deeper attachment to him, and I trusted him more after that. Later in life, I realized that this was a major mistake on my part.

After telling him about my family, he wanted to meet my stepmother, and we went to see her in late February. She didn't have a phone, so we simply drove out to see her on a Sunday. She got very excited when I introduced Maxim to her, and I could see she liked him. We told her that we were planning to get married.

"Oh! If I had known you were coming I would had been better prepared!"

I told her not to worry, that we had brought wine and a cake.

"No, no, no!" she said. "No! We must have a dinner!"

After we'd had one of Mama's amazing three-course dinners, I took Maxim to see my room, which of course was freezing cold. It was so uncomfortable that even after a few moments, we had to quickly leave. He couldn't believe I had lived in such a frigid place during this bitterly cold winter!

On the way home, Maxim asked me for my passport so we could go to the Marriage Office and fill out an application. After this was done, we were given the date for our wedding: April 3, 1965. He suggested we go to the Arbat Café to celebrate. I felt so good and was looking forward to having an easier time from now on. It looked as though he and I were going to have a nice life together.

A couple of days before we applied for our marriage license, Maxim introduced me to his family. Although he'd told me a lot about his mother, nothing could have prepared me for this woman!

The first thing she said when we were introduced was, "So. It's you! Maxim told me you were an orphan. You certainly do have hungry eyes! See, Maxim? You don't know how lucky you were. You should kiss your mother's hands every day of your life!"

I had no idea what she meant. Maybe she thought orphans were different. I didn't know what to say. First of all I wasn't hungry—and even if I were, food would be the last thing on my mind. We were standing by the front door feeling awkward when Maxim's father appeared.

"Sophia, invite them in, at least," he said.

"You see?" she cried. "I can't say or do anything without being criticized! He always shuts me up. I don't know how I've lived with this man all these years!"

Maxim's younger brother, Eugene, who had stayed behind his father, said, "Oh, come on, Mother! Stop complaining and let's sit down and eat!"

"You see what I mean?" she went on. "They're all against me! They attack me for no reason. Oh well, we might as well have tea." She turned to her husband. "Isak, bring the kettle in from the kitchen. It must be boiling by now. I put it on a long time ago."

She led us to the table, which was set with hard-boiled eggs, bread and butter, a tin of sardines, and a package of biscuits. If this was the evening meal, it was unusually meagre and very un-Russian. Maxim had warned me that his mother hardly ever cooked—that she had always hated cooking. What was on the table was what she served the family every night.

His father was exactly as Maxim had described him—quiet and smiling, with eyes full of brightness and life. I liked him immediately. His brother was pleasant too, but I could tell he was a Mama's boy. She constantly deferred to him, which he was obviously accustomed to.

His mother continued to give me suspicious and penetrating glances. "I want you to know I am not gong to give a penny for your wedding," she announced, pouring herself a cup of boiling water.

"Mother, we didn't come here to ask for money!" Maxim exclaimed. "I just wanted you to meet Janna. Now let's talk about something else!" And he turned to have a chat with his father.

She ignored their conversation. "You can eat as many eggs as you want," she said, as if to encourage me. "By the way, did you know that I gave Maxim his car? I didn't want him to kill himself on that stupid motorcycle! He got it from the junkyard and was always repairing it! I decided to pay for his car and save his life."

Maxim interjected, "Mother, that's not how it was!"

"See?" she said. "He doesn't even remember that I gave him the money for it! And then he wanted to buy a place of his own so that when he got married we wouldn't all live together. Now he has everything he needs. When I got married, we didn't have anything. Isak was only interested in studying, so I had to save every penny and I still do!" she said triumphantly. "It's better to have money than anything else, in case something happens. Men don't know how to save. It's the woman's job.

If it were up to Isak, he would spend all the money he ever earned on books! We've lived simply all our lives, so I've saved lots of money! He should be so lucky to have had a wife like me!"

I looked around and saw that their furniture was old but not the antique kind. They were simply worn-out pieces of furniture. On one side, there was a couch that was falling apart, and I remembered Maxim telling me that his father always slept on it.

My heart went out to him. That this brilliant man—a professor of science who'd been published so many times, who was honourable member of the Academy of Science in the USSR—could sleep on this old couch! And everything in the room looked dusty and neglected.

The windows badly needed cleaning, and the shelves below the windows were loaded with empty cans and bottles.

Before we left, I took a peek in the other room. It was very small and had two beds in it. One was gigantic and the other was single bed where I presumed Eugene slept. I was relieved to get out of the place and to breathe fresh air. I felt completely drained, as though I'd just survived mental torture, and wasn't up to talking on the way back. I closed my eyes, using the technique I always called upon to disconnect my mind, and fell asleep.

When I awoke, I didn't recognize where I was. Then I saw that we were at Maxim's building and he was parking his car in front of it. I panicked. I thought he was taking advantage of my exhaustion and had brought me there without asking me.

The point was, I couldn't stay at his place because I didn't want to give my father any reason to look down on me. If I had stayed, I knew he would call me names and try to make me miserable again. If I wanted peace, I had to stay at his place until we got married.

I explained the whole thing to Maxim. I also told him that he should have asked me. He gave me all kinds of reasons why he hadn't, but none of them convinced me. The poor man had to turn his car around and drive me all the way from Warshavskoe Shosse to Medvedkovo—two absolutely opposite ends of Moscow. Then he had to drive all the way back to his place!

We planned our small wedding that week and booked a room in the Aragvi restaurant and selected our menu carefully, working out every detail. Maxim told me not to worry—he was going to pay for our wedding provided he didn't have to buy a new suit and shoes for himself. I had to somehow find a dress for myself and a pair of shoes, plus a few other things. It was important to me to look like a bride on the day of my wedding!

I hoped that because my father wanted me to get married so much he might give me a little money. I didn't expect it, but I hoped he'd at least return the money he owed me for my fur that he'd given to Lora five years before.

Of course I was afraid to ask him. I dreaded any conversation of that kind with him and decided to call my sister Tania in Nikolaev and see if she could do anything. She'd always had influence with him.

She agreed to do it and told me to call her in a couple of days. When I did, she said that Father didn't want to hear about it and that I should be grateful that he hadn't thrown me out of the house after what I did to him in court. So, that was that.

I couldn't count on getting any loan from Gosplan—I was already paying out one I had applied for after Mama's divorce. But after speaking with Alexander Comrade, our club director, he called the loan department and had them rearrange my loan. As a result, I was able to get a hundred and twenty rubles for the wedding! Maxim assured me that we'd pay it out in no time and not to worry.

I felt so much better! Now I could actually afford to have a dress made! I called my close friends and invited them to the Marriage Castle for the third of April and to our reception at Aragvi.

Lidia Vasilievna, our club courier, went with me to select fabric for the dress. We decided it should be short so that I could wear it later. She offered to make my dress and said there was no way she was going to charge me for it.

I said, "No, Lidia! Please! You can't do this. I have the money! It's not fair!"

"It's my gift to you," she said. "This way, you'll remember me because it's going to be in all your wedding pictures for the rest of your life."

I didn't know how to thank her. I was so touched. Strange that my father wouldn't even give me my own money and this woman was giving me such a gift. And she was right. I would never forget her generosity.

The white shoes to go with my dress would be a major expense because the local ones were badly made and uncomfortable. The only solution was to find someone who had bought a pair outside Russia, although, of course, the price would be high—at least a month's salary.

On the other hand, I could probably sell them after the wedding, which was an idea. I called Alla, whose marriage had taken place a year earlier and who might know of someone who had a pair I could buy.

"You can wear mine!" she said. "I only wore them once."

"No, no, Alla! I couldn't do that. Let me buy them!"

"No, Janna. Just wear them on your wedding day. No one will know."

I couldn't believe it! I was getting what I needed with almost no money spent!

This way I could afford to buy a pair of new white gloves and some beautiful underwear. It had worked out fantastically.

On the morning of my wedding, I got up early to take care of a few things. The night before Maxim had picked up my suitcase so I wouldn't have to go back to my father's place again.

There were a few things I left out of my suitcase: my best underwear I'd collected over the years, my perfume, a few pairs of my best stockings, all my makeup, and a few presents I'd received from different people. They were my personal treasures, and I wanted to keep them near me.

After my shower, I packed all these things in the leather case that Maxim had given me. My plan was to go to the hairdresser and then go to the club to dress. The staff was getting together at two o'clock for a little farewell party and Maxim was picking me up from there at three. We planned to go to his parents' place to pick up Eugene and his father, who were going with us. Maxim's mother refused to join us, saying she never went to restaurants. Maxim and I tried to persuade her to change her mind, but it was useless.

I had never had my hair done in a salon before. I'd made the appointment three weeks before at one of the top places with a hairdresser who was very popular. Unfortunately, it turned out to be the worst hairdo I'd ever had!

The man had no idea how to work with my kind of hair. First, he did a haircut that I knew would look terrible on me. When he went at it with his busy scissors, I felt like crying, but he just told me to relax and be positive. In the meantime, he kept yapping constantly with everybody in the salon about who did what the night before and about the previous day's famous clients who were actors, dancers, and so on. Then he splashed my hair with beer, put about forty rollers all over my head, and finally put me under the dryer.

When he began to comb it out, my hair bounced around in tight curls, and I looked like an old curly doll! It wasn't me at all. I couldn't wait to get out of there and wash it, which I was able to do in the club. I sneaked into one of the dressing rooms and did it so fast nobody saw me.

Lidia Vasilievna came in with the dress and was shocked to see me with wet hair. "Oh! You shouldn't have gone to the hairdresser in the first place,

Janna!" she said. "You have naturally wavy hair and it always looks so nice! Why spoil it? Why would you want to change it?"

My hair may have been a mess, but my dress made me feel much better! It was perfect on me—very simple, with no sleeves and a lovely soft collar around the neckline. Alla's shoes were perfect as well, and when Lidia Vasilievna did some interesting things with my hair, arranging artificial pearls and flowers in it, I began to glow. What would I have done without her?

When we walked into our office reception it was full of people including, of course, Maxim. Everybody was so happy for me! They were all talking at once, and then Comrade Konstantinovich opened a bottle of champagne, passed it around, and then opened another one so that everyone had their glasses filled.

They lifted their glasses to us, every face wreathed in a radiant smile. I felt as though all of them were my family—except that they were better than any family I had ever had. I couldn't help it. Tears poured down my cheeks!

We were also presented with a huge box and a beautiful bouquet of flowers. As soon as we all had some champagne, they begged me to open the gift. They couldn't wait for my reaction!

I couldn't believe my eyes! There were three boxes; one had a setting of silver cutlery for twelve, another the same number of dishes, and the third an absolutely gorgeous white linen tablecloth!

"Oh! Oh! Oh!" I screamed with excitement and hugged and kissed every one of them. We were all full of joy!

The whole bunch of them came downstairs with us, carrying everything to Maxim's car, helping to pack it safely in the back seat. My case with all my goodies was there too. Everybody wished us luck, and we drove away. I think it was the happiest moment of my life.

Maxim and I chatted excitedly all the way to his parents' place, parked the car in front of the building, and went upstairs.

We didn't have much time. We were to be at the Marriage Castle at five o'clock, but Maxim's mother insisted we have chicken soup, which she'd made for us especially. She had on her usual outfit: a dark floral brown dress with a brown apron over it. Apparently, she wore her apron from morning to night every day and always had a towel hanging over her elbow. Looking at her one might say she was the perfect housewife, but I didn't see her that way.

The soup was flat with no taste at all and it was cold, although, for that reason, we ate it quickly. She demanded that we have tea with biscuits as well, but this was getting to be too much. We really had to go. Maxim's father was all set and so was Eugene. Maxim asked his younger brother to put on a tie, but he didn't have one. His father offered him one of his, but he didn't like any of them.

"No, no, no!" he said. "They are thirty years old!"

Maxim's mother interrupted the argument. "Eugene! If you don't want to go, you don't have to. We can stay at home together and watch TV."

"Mama, what are you saying?" he responded. "If you don't want to go, does that mean I shouldn't go? This is my only brother and he's getting married today! There's no way I would stay at home on this wedding day! Papa! Give me that brown tie. I'll wear it. Let's go or we'll be late!"

As we came towards the car Maxim, who had gone ahead of us, screamed in shock. The car was empty. Everything had been stolen! The door had simply been pried open by an expert and everything that was inside had been taken.

We stood there in total shock. All my beautiful things were gone. I hadn't even been left with any underwear to change into tomorrow. My makeup—everything!

Suddenly Maxim said, "Where's your passport?" and started to search for it in his jacket.

I realized that if my passport had also been stolen, we couldn't get married. Perhaps there was a message in all of this.

"Oh! Thank goodness!" Maxim cried with relief. "It's here in my inside pocket! At least I was smart enough to keep it in a separate place. Let's go!"

And off we went.

Our guests were already there. Everything went smoothly. I made up my mind not to let the terrible theft affect me, and we all had a good time. I drank many, many glasses of champagne at my wedding!

CHAPTER 30

The Reality Check

I woke up with a strange feeling. Where was I? Oh! I'm married to Maxim, and it's my wedding night and I don't have to go back to my father's! This is my home! Maxim is my family now!

I felt such comfort at the thought of him being there, next to me. I wasn't alone anymore fighting on all fronts. I had my husband now. My lover, my friend, my protector. I would do my absolute best so he'd feel the same way.

I was filled with energy knowing I could do so many things now. I could make our home warm and comfortable. We'd have delicious dinners together. We'd invite friends and play good music. It was so exciting!

We weren't able to afford a honeymoon, and we both had to work. Maxim was working on his dissertation, and I had to prepare my entrance exams for a new university. At the end of the summer we were planning to travel by car to the Carpathians. I had never been to West Ukraine, the site of those beautiful mountains. It was going to be fun. There was so much to look forward to—so much to do!

Then I remembered...All my precious things had been stolen from Maxim's car! I didn't even have a change of underwear. And my makeup! I had no makeup! Now I knew why I had drunk so much the night before!

I had wanted to forget the whole ugly episode. I didn't want it to spoil my wedding or to have my friends see me upset. What else could I do—have a long face at my own wedding? No! It was my celebration!

Maxim and I had danced like crazy. Everybody danced, even his father danced with me a lot. This man was definitely going to be my friend. We'd invite him to our place and I'd cook all kinds of delicious food for his enjoyment. He deserved to be spoiled.

I thought of the beautiful dishes and silver cutlery and that gorgeous tablecloth, and I decided I wasn't going to tell anybody at the club about the robbery. It would upset them too much. We still had other gifts from friends who were at the wedding, which we hadn't time to open yet. Maxim had to go to work soon, but I didn't! I had a couple of days off, and I didn't have to go anywhere! I was staying here, in my home!

It was still dark, and I wondered what time it was. It was close to six already, and I had to wake up my husband and make him breakfast. My husband...It sounded so strange. I had a husband now. I'd get used to this word that sounded so new to me, but I liked it. He was my family.

"Good morning, Maxim-chik! It's time to wake up. Breakfast is ready!"

"Oh..." He mumbled something, but he was still asleep. He'd had lots to drink as well. We had driven home after two in the morning, although I didn't remember anything, except a vague memory of stormy drunken lovemaking and I was glad it happened that way. The one thing I had to watch now was not to get pregnant. We'd think of some way. We didn't need a pregnancy at this point in our lives.

"Ooh...What time is it?"

"It's ten after six. But you said you were leaving for work at seven thirty. I thought it would be good to get up now so we could both enjoy our first breakfast together. Don't you think?"

"It sure would be, but I'd prefer to have my wife instead. Come here, my baby," and he stretched his arms out. Before I knew it, I was in bed and he was all over me, kissing and hugging me with such hunger that it felt as if he could truly eat me for breakfast! It was another stormy, passionate session of lovemaking, and it felt good, but it was over all too quickly. We had no time. On the other hand, we'd have many times from now on when we wouldn't have to rush.

After Maxim left for work, I had a lot to do. I needed to go shopping for groceries so we'd have everything on hand for the next couple of days.

The store was a few blocks from our building, and it was a lovely April morning. I had married in the spring, my favorite time of the year. I loved it! And everything was going to be fine in my life.

The store was still closed, and I could see a lineup of people waiting. Most of them were older—probably pensioners. They were chatting away like a great gossip club. I overheard a few interesting stories—most of them about their sons-in-law who drank too much and didn't help their wives around the house. A few stories were about who was sleeping with whom and about their own rotten husbands and their unhappy marriages. Some of the stories were hard to make sense of because I hadn't heard the beginning of these long sagas.

I heard one woman say, "My Tatiana walked into his office to ask him to sign this document and she caught his secretary pulling down her skirt in such a hurry! No wonder that bitch always acts like she's the boss! She's got him by the balls!"

When the door opened, the crowd raced in, all wanting to be the first at the counter to get the best pieces of meat! Everybody was yelling and shouting and calling each other names. One woman grabbed another woman by the hair, trying to push her out of the way. She turned around and in the rush dropped her big duffle bag on the woman's head! Then peace was immediately restored and everybody became happy! They knew they were going to get their meat that day. After all, they wouldn't have gotten up at six in the morning to stand in line for almost three hours for nothing!

I was back home by eleven. Almost five hours had gone by, and I had so much to do before my husband came home. I went to work quickly, but when I opened the fridge, a horrible smell hit my nostrils. I had to take everything out and clean the whole thing. In the meantime, I started cooking the stew and soup. The stove needed a good cleaning too, but what did I expect from a man who spent his entire day at work? He was rarely at home, especially in the three months when he'd been courting me.

I planned to organize things and have a clean home. I couldn't stand a dirty place, and I was glad Mama had taught me how to clean. But I wasn't going to be like her. She was absolutely obsessed with cleanliness. I just wanted our place to be reasonably clean, and I knew Maxim would help me too.

I needed a big pot for the soup, and although there was one in the cupboard, it had some kind of mess in the bottom of it where something had been burned a long time before.

I scraped until it shone and then washed and swept and washed and swept the whole place for the next six hours! By five o'clock, the place looked and smelled like a home and everything was ready for dinner. The only thing I had to do was to take shower. The bathroom had been more or less scrubbed, although it would take a couple of more good cleaning sessions before it was really shining.

I could hardly stand on my feet when I turned on the tap! My knees were shaking from all the work I'd done, but it was okay. The hot water did wonders for me. I still had to set the table, put the music on, and have the candles lit. When Maxim walked in, our place would feel cared for and romantic, and we'd relax and have a great time!

CHAPTER 31

What Do I Do?

It was May, and my period hadn't started. I began to realize that it could be pregnancy—what would I do if it were? It was out of the question—impossible? What was impossible? To get pregnant or have a baby? Both! I didn't want to think about it.

By the end of May I knew I was probably six weeks pregnant and I had to have an abortion. I would have loved to have a baby, but it was too soon. How on earth could I handle a full-time job, go to university, and on top of it all have a baby? No way! I couldn't handle it! I'd have to find somebody to perform an abortion for me, and fast. I couldn't lose a minute! But how could I do this without Maxim knowing about it? He was my husband—I had to tell him.

We had just finished dinner, which I had hardly touched. "Maxim!" I said in a gloomy tone, "I'm pregnant."

"What?" He dropped his fork. "Did I hear right? You're pregnant?"

His eyes were shining with happiness, but what had I expected him to say? "Oh, no! That's terrible"? I knew he would welcome a baby 100 percent. The sooner the better.

We had talked about my plan to complete my education and about waiting to have a baby. Of course in the meantime, there could be no guarantee.

He would try to keep me from getting pregnant and so would I. The fact was, in spite of everything it could happen anyway. All it took was one time.

"Maxim!" I said. "We cannot have a baby now. It's too soon! We just got married. We haven't even been on our honeymoon and you know I have to work and go to school! We also don't have anybody to help us. It's impossible! I have to have an abortion."

"Abortion? No! What if they screw you up and you can never have a baby? You know it happens! It's out of the question! Please, don't think about abortion. It's too risky! If anything happened, you would never forgive yourself. Please, I beg you, don't have an abortion! We'll manage. I'll give you full support, I promise. You'll have a university diploma. It may just take a little longer. And you already have a great job. They're not asking for your diploma, are they?"

"No. But they may. Any time. Who knows? If the director should change or a new one comes in who may have somebody of his own for my position? He may use my not having a university degree as an excuse to fire me. I think about this all the time. And if that happened I wouldn't be able to find another job I like without it. I was lucky to get this kind of job without one, but I cannot live my life depending on luck! I need to have my diploma. That piece of paper means everything in the USSR!"

"Yes, I know all of this, Jannachka, but having an abortion could end up tragically. You know Tonia and Lenia Petrov? They've been married for ten years and can't have a child because of her first abortion. They butchered her. Same thing with Galina and Alek Rudov! And remember Alla? Every time she gets pregnant, she has a miscarriage and it goes on and on. Please, baby, we cannot afford an abortion. Besides, all these people aren't thirty-six years old. I don't have time to take this risk. Please, I beg you. Let's have this baby. We'll be okay."

"Maxim", I answered, "I can't say yes now. I have to think about it." I was remembering my first abortion and how I suffered after it. I began to realise how lucky I was to get pregnant in the first place. Maybe I shouldn't push my luck any further.

In the next several days I received phone calls from several women who confessed that they would do anything to have a chance to get pregnant. It seemed that Maxim had literally organized a "Do not have an abortion!" campaign.

The message was coming at me from every direction until finally one day I said, "That's it! I'm throwing the idea of abortion out of my mind. I'm keeping the baby!"

"Oh thank God!" Maxim cried. "I knew you'd come to your senses. This is so wonderful! You watch. Everything is going to work out. Now we can plan to go on our honeymoon. We'll have a great time! We'll outfit ourselves comfortably and have everything in the car so we can stop anywhere we want. We'll even take folding cots and mattresses so you can rest any time you feel like it. It's so great! Our baby is going to travel with us!"

We had a wonderful month's trip. We travelled with our tent and two folding beds, and we had a portable burner. Every evening we cooked simple meals so we could stay overnight in the most secluded places.

Maxim was a passionate driver and loved going long distances. He was in his element! He watched my stomach growing with great curiosity. He couldn't believe he was finally going to have a child of his own!

On our trip we met tourists from different parts of Europe, from Germany and also from Switzerland and Finland. All of them drove these comfortable motor homes, which I had never seen before. I was fascinated by their appearance and convenience. Each one had places to sleep and kitchens! Even their pots and pans were different: they were practical and looked so colourful! There was no unique cookware to be found in the USSR.

One morning as we were getting ready to leave our site, we saw a motor home driving away with five nuns in the vehicle and a nun in the driver's seat. I had never seen a nun behind the wheel. In fact, I had never seen a nun in the flesh, and these were tourists. They all smiled and waved at me, noticing my fascination. Truthfully I stood there with my mouth open. No wonder they took notice of me!

We met Carpathian skiers, student travelers, and local villagers. We went to the markets and bought their delicious sour cream and farmer's cottage cheese—fresh, rich, and tasty—I had never tasted anything like it!

West Ukraine was full of richness and beauty. We went to Lvov, the capital and visited the ancient cemeteries, where every stone seemed to symbolize love, money, and history. It stretched for a couple of kilometres, and we spent the entire day just browsing amongst the monuments. I kept thinking about my mother the entire time. I didn't even know where she was buried.

In the grand cathedral in Lvov, we heard the most incredible singing. In the coffee and pastry cafés we met poets and writers. The whole experience was interesting and different. In fact, the trip inspired me to write my own poems, which seemed to flow from me naturally.

This was a most happy holiday and honeymoon.

On the way back to Moscow, the night came down on us about 150 kilometres from home. We had driven all day and decided to stay overnight somewhere until it got light again. We finally came across a hunter's lodge, and the man in charge invited us in and told us to take any bed that wasn't occupied. The room we were shown was large with several beds, some of which were empty. We found two side by side and we fell into them, utterly exhausted.

I woke up with a start. The light was on, yet it was still dark outside. Why on earth would someone turn the light in the middle of the night? Then I saw everyone in the place sitting up, swearing and scratching their badly mosquito-bitten bodies! It seemed that no one had slept for hours. They were all being attacked by thousands of bloodthirsty mosquitoes! I wasn't touched by one. Apparently, they didn't care for the taste of my blood.

Shortly after we returned from our trip, Maxim came home one night and said, "We have to move from here in two weeks."

"Why?" I asked. This was the last thing we needed!

"Well," he said, "some time before I met you, the university where I gave my dissertation started to build a new cooperative building very close to the centre of Moscow, and I liked the area. You know how it goes in Moscow. If something like this comes up, administrators and professors get first choice for their families and friends. It was very fortunate that my professor didn't want one and he co-signed for me. So I had to get a sum of money together quickly in order to secure an apartment. The rest of the money was to be paid as soon as construction began, which is now. I received a letter today. The money has to be paid in two weeks or I'm out, which means we have to sell this apartment we're in to the cooperative, get the money for it, and then pay for the new place. It can be done in a week. There are always hundreds of people on the waiting list."

"But, Maxim, where we are going live until it's finished?" I asked, thinking about my little room back at Mama's. I threw the thought out immediately. How could we possibly live in that little place with no facilities?

He seemed to read my thoughts. "I know we can't live in your old place, but it's not going to take long. The apartment will be ready in a couple of months. The ground floor is already finished, and the building only has nine stories. And this is a civil engineering university. It's their own project; they know what they're doing! Don't worry. This isn't going to take long at all. I mean, if we want to live in this area we have to take a step back temporarily. And don't forget, we'll save a lot of time travelling to and from work—both of us. And especially when you go back to school. As it is, you and I spend an hour and a half every morning getting to work and another hour and a half at night. That's three hours every day out the window. It'll only take fifteen minutes from the new place. It will free up a lot of time for both of us."

It was true.

"What about your parents?" I said. "Couldn't you borrow the money from them until the building is ready so we can stay here?"

"Are you kidding? My mother? She wouldn't part with her money for five minutes!"

"What about your father? Doesn't he have any say in it? After all, he's the one who earned the money! Your mother never worked a day in her life. Can't he say something about it?"

"When it comes to money my father doesn't have anything to say, as far as my mother is concerned. She puts away every penny. All he gets is a little pocket money. He even has a limited budget for his important books."

"But, how come? He's the one who brings in the money every month!"

"Right. But the day he brings home his earnings, she takes it from him. She's in charge of it and always was, from the day they got married more than forty years ago. She keeps on bragging that she saved tons of money because she knows how to manage the household. They even have a summer cottage! No, I know my mother. It's out of the question."

I had nothing more to say. My own father had all kinds of money. Could I ask him? Not in my lifetime!

At seeing my sadness, Maxim said, "Look. Let me go to my mother and try. Maybe when she knows they're going to have their first grandchild she'll feel differently about the money. I mean we could pay her interest. Maybe that's the key! She should like that. Why didn't I think of it before? That's it. The interest!"

We both felt better at the possibility of finding a way not to have to move out.

After work the next day, Maxim went immediately to see his parents while I sat tight, waiting anxiously for his return. It would be the perfect solution if we could only get the financial help we needed! At just after eight o'clock, I was surprised to hear his key in the lock. When he stepped in, the troubled look on his face was not very reassuring.

"Forget it!" he said before I had a chance to ask how things had gone. "We're moving out."

"What happened? Tell me!" I said. "And did you have anything to eat there?"

"Of course not! But right now, I could do with a shot of vodka!"

I quickly poured him a drink and put some food on the table. After three shots, he managed to speak. "She's simply out of her mind! Completely out of her mind!"

"What do you mean?"

"Just what I said!"

I could see he wasn't able to relax or talk, even after three shots. "Maxim," I said gently, "I know you're upset, but if you can talk about what happened, you'll feel better."

"All right." He rubbed his face and forehead for a few seconds. "It was like this," he said after a pause. "When I asked her if she could lend us the money for three months—and I offered her twenty percent interest—do you know what she said?"

I was all ears.

"'I'll give the money,' she said, 'and you can pay me the interest—on one condition: that when your apartment is ready we move into it and you live in ours. It's time we lived in a decent place!'" He looked at me, pain and disgust written all over his face. "Can you believe it?"

"That's horrible!" I said. "And what did you say to her?"

"What do you think? I said, 'Mother, how can we possibly live with those neighbors of yours? The man's a chronic drunkard! I worked so hard all these years to save money for my own place so that when I got married we wouldn't all have to live together. I've managed to make this happen and now you're asking me to do this? If you didn't have the money of your own I could understand it and perhaps we'd have done what you ask.

But this isn't the case! Why don't you buy a co-operative apartment for yourselves? You can afford it! You can afford anything you want!'"

"Did she agree?" I asked. "After all, it's true, isn't it?"

Maxim gave a short bitter laugh. "Agree? Do you know what her answer was? She said, 'It's none of your business what I have or can't afford! I'm telling you that if I lend you the money, that's my condition. We've lived around this drunk for thirty years! What's wrong with you putting up with him for a few years yourself? We're not going to live forever! When we've gone, the new place will be yours and Eugene can move back here.'"

"Oh my God! This is unbelievable," I cried. "And impossible!"

"Of course it is—and I told her flatly no! It's out of the question! I'm not doing any of this! Her reply was, 'In that case, you're not my son anymore! And I won't set foot in your new place. Don't ever ask me because I won't go!' So that was it. I just left."

I was shocked.

The only question I asked him was, "And your father and brother? Were they there? Did they hear the conversation?"

"Yes. Both of them tried to say something to make her change her mind. She just told them to shut up—and they did."

"Don't worry," I said. "We'll move into my room at Mama's. We'll have to put in insulation, though, and buy a lot of coal so it'll be warmer. And we could get a couple of burners so we can do some decent cooking. If we do it this way, we can manage. Don't worry, we'll get through this together."

Maxim hugged me with relief.

In the next couple of weeks we organized everything. The apartment on Warshavskoe Shosse was sold back to the cooperative—for the same price as it was bought for years before, of course. The money for the new apartment on Serpuhovskaya Street was paid, the insulation for the room was put in, and two truckloads of coal were delivered. After we bought the burners, Maxim and I moved in. Of course, Mama was very happy. I heard her singing at five o'clock every morning.

It was September—a golden month. We hoped that by December our new place would be ready. Maxim was at the construction site almost every day after work, and when he came home he reported on the progress. He told me it was moving really fast. The building was constructed out of pre-fabricated steel and concrete panels. In a month and a half the workers were working on the roof. Everything was going according to schedule, with our baby due in the middle of January.

Gradually, I bought things for the baby, the most necessary being diapers. There was no such thing as disposable ones—we had never heard of such a thing. At least fifty cotton diapers were needed, both linen and flannel because they had to be washed, dried, and ironed to keep the bacteria out. Diapers were most important items for babies until at least five months old. The baby had to be tightly wrapped in them from head to toe all the time, according to the doctors.

There were all kinds of theories about the wrapping. The baby's arms would wake them up unless they were held in. Or the babies might scratch their faces. The legs? Same story. The babies would wake themselves up if they were free to move. The funny part of this theory was that the baby's legs were supposed to grow perfectly straight if they were tightly wrapped.

Another thing I was preoccupied with was learning how to knit. I knew how to crochet from childhood, but I wanted to learn knitting because I wanted to knit all kinds of interesting sweaters, leggings, and little vests and hats for my child since it was almost impossible to buy anything out of the ordinary for children. However, yarns weren't available hard to find. It was up to the knitter to create a colourful combination, and I had a good imagination when it came to colour, learning how to knit was a challenge for me because of being left-handed. Every time someone tried to teach me I couldn't follow the person because she knitted with her right hand. I actually wrote with my right hand because in Soviet schools, they trained you to write only with the right. And so I tried to knit with my right hand, but it felt too clumsy and I had to give up.

The second week of January, Mama's niece Lusia called me. She had been married for several years now and had a two-year old son. That day I shared my knitting problem with her and told her how I wanted to knit things for my baby if I could only overcome my problem.

She said, "How silly! Why should you learn how to knit with your right hand? Do it with whichever hand you're used to."

"But nobody seems to know how to show me."

"Look, Janna," she said, "I'll gladly help you, but you'll have to come to my place. We can spend as many hours as you need until you're comfortable. After that you'll be able to knit on your own, I promise you!"

I was very happy about this and the next day, on January 12, I left early for Lusia's place. She lived quite a distance from me, and after a lengthy walk to the bus and then a long bus ride, I arrived at her place at eleven in the morning.

Thanks to her patience and perseverance, I finally got a handle on the process. I started one little sweater for my baby in royal blue thick wool. Both of us wanted to make sure I knew what I was doing, and we got so carried away that before we knew it, it was dark out. I thanked her many times for her help and on my way to the bus I went over and over the process in my mind.

The lineup for the bus line was long, and when the bus arrived, everybody squeezed themselves into it, preferring not to wait for another one in the cold. The buses weren't regular. It could take almost an hour sometimes until the next one. I expected the baby any time and felt extremely awkward hanging onto the railing.

Directly in front of me were two middle-aged men, sitting down and happily chatting with each other. It was hard for me to keep my balance as the baby was kicking furiously. The woman standing next to me noticed my discomfort and asked the two men if they would give me their seat.

"Why should we give her a seat? Why is she so special?" asked one of them, looking pained.

"Can't you see she's going to have a baby any moment?" said the woman. "Look at her! Are the two of you blind?"

"So she is going to have a baby! So what?" Both of them spoke up now. "She isn't sick, is she? The two of us are invalids and we have the papers to prove it...here!" And they took their papers out. "Does she have papers to prove she is sick? No, she doesn't!" and both of them continued to talk, looking smugly satisfied with themselves. The woman looked at them with disgust and turned away.

The rest of the ride was a nightmare. By the time the bus arrived at my stop I was too tired to walk. I had to stop and rest a few minutes before I slowly walked home. My first sharp pain happened before I got there, and I knew what it was. My time had arrived.

I had read some literature about birth and knew it would take a long time for the baby to arrive. The contractions were to come every half an hour or so in the beginning, and then the time between them would be gradually less and less. Since there were no painkillers to be had in the

Soviet Union for women in labour, I didn't want to suffer all the pain lying in a hospital bed, listening to other women screaming. I knew some women took twenty-four hours before the baby came—especially if they were first babies.

I decided to simply stay home and occupy myself by keeping busy between the contractions. I would go to the hospital when the intervals were five minutes or so. Four hours later my plan was still good. By now, I had ironed all the necessary diapers and other things. I folded them carefully, while repeating my knitting formula, hoping not to forget it, since I knew it would take me sometime to go back to the knitting after my baby was born. When I felt my next contraction coming I looked at the clock making sure to register the intervals. Then I would go lie down and start breathing in and out. The pains were hellish, and I wished there was something to ease them, but I knew very well there was nothing. One had to get through it. That was all there was to it.

After six hours of contractions, Maxim looked exhausted, and insisted on taking me to the hospital. He was beginning to panic, so I agreed to go.

During the ride, my contractions were almost nonstop, and I knew it wouldn't be long before the baby came. I filled out a long questionnaire at the hospital, took a shower, and was brought into the pre-labour room. No one was allowed past the reception area, including husbands.

There were four women in the room, all of them screaming. The minute I was in bed my pains became continuous—less than a minute between intervals. I called to the doctor who was busy, and the nurse came in. She told me not to panic, that I had just gotten there and it would be a long time before the baby arrived. The four other women had come in the night before she told me and were still in pre-labour.

I tried to tell her that I had spent all that time at home and that I was well into my labour, but she was gone. I thought they'd know by reading the questionnaire, but they obviously didn't bother. One of the women was screaming hysterically and her voice was driving me crazy. I was at the end of my rope with my own pain. Something had to happen fast.

In the meantime, there were two things going on with the hospital staff. First, the shift changed. Secondly, January the thirteenth was the Old Russian New Year, and both shifts were busy celebrating it. They had a party going on right in the labour room! They were all confident that none of us was ready for the final stages.

I was in total agony with absolutely no relief. I demanded that the doctor pay attention to me! I had a feeling the baby was ready to come out, but something was holding it back. Finally, the woman doctor appeared by my bed.

She put her hand in me to find out what was happening and said, "Oh my God! You're quite ready, young woman. In fact, I have to do something right now."

And I heard a sound like a blown balloon losing air, and suddenly I felt wet all over. Whatever she did, I immediately felt much better.

"You should have called me much earlier!" the doctor said. "Your placenta is very thick. It wouldn't have broken on its own, and it could have affected the baby."

She called for the nurse to bring a wheelchair, but nobody responded, so she urged me to get up and go to the labour room quickly, that she would assist me. While I was walking along I felt the baby's head coming through. It was the strangest feeling! A minute later I was on the table, and in two minutes the baby came out.

It was a purple colour, and I knew that if I hadn't demanded that the doctor come immediately, I would have lost him. My baby boy. My first thought was, "Thank goodness, it's over!" The baby's cry meant it was okay, and the nurse told me his colour would change in a couple of days.

"Don't worry!" she assured me. "You have a normal, healthy baby boy!"

Our son was born January 13, 1966, and we named him Aleksei.

I looked at the baby again and for the first time I realized I had a son! He had lots of hair on his head, which was dark and wet. I was exhausted! My eyes were closing. I couldn't keep them open, but the nurse wouldn't leave me alone.

"It's not over," she said. "We have to wheel you into the operating room and sew you up!" The stitching was a nightmare. There was no anaesthesia and they paid no attention to my gasps as the needle was thrust in and out of my flesh.

In the Soviet Union, the name of the game seemed to be pain and suffering.

Skipping such details as the shortage of linen, terrible food, twenty-five beds in a room, and no peace for even a split second, one other detail was even more bothersome than all the rest. In the maternity ward there were no visitors allowed, not even the fathers. They had to go through their own struggles, isolated as they were on the outside. Not knowing what to do with themselves, they either got together with friends and drank themselves silly celebrating the baby's birth or they stayed close by hoping to catch a glimpse from afar of their wives with the new baby.

And far it was. The maternity ward was on the fourth floor of the hospital. There were no telephones. Communication was done through a little window on the first floor, through which they could pass flowers, food, or letters. Once that was done, they would sit and wait to hear from their wives. After the baby's birth the hospital stay was ten days, provided the baby and mother were okay.

The baby and mother being discharged from the hospital was like being released from jail!

The nurse on duty would come out, proudly holding the infant, as though she was the one who had given birth to the baby! Of course, the fathers had some money to give to the nurse as a gesture of appreciation for their care. This moment was supposed to be a poetic and emotional one. Finally, they would let the mother come out.

Normally, the parents of both the husband and wife would be there in the hospital waiting for the baby to be received.

Maxim was there alone.

CHAPTER 32

The Baby

If anybody ever wanted to know what it was like to have a baby in the middle of January 1996 in northern USSR in a place without water or a washroom, I could give a graphic picture of the whole experience. But why bother? It was all our own fault for wanting to relocate for the sake of future benefits.

When we moved out of the Warshavskoe Shosse I was almost six months pregnant. Who guaranteed us that our new apartment would be ready in three months? They told us it would be finished in a couple of months, but a couple of months could turn into any number—however, no complaints. We had made our choice.

One thing that really helped was Mama's stove. We had to have a huge pot of boiling water on it at all times. Maxim carried in at least five pails of freezing cold water from the street every morning before he went to work so I wouldn't have to carry it too far. Some of it we stored in Mama's tiny kitchen so it wouldn't freeze, which was helpful.

Mama didn't miss work even for one day because of earning her pension. But she also had arthritis, and I only let her help me with the ironing, especially in the beginning. How to dry the diapers was a real problem; we were always completely surrounded by them hanging everywhere! The baby couldn't take being in a wet diaper, and the minute he felt the wetness he would cry until he was changed.

Baby Aleksei also had an excellent appetite. Following doctor's orders, the baby had to be fed no more than every three hours. But what if the baby got hungry in an hour and a half? Too bad, he had to wait. And the baby in the meantime? Nonstop crying!

By the end of March, our new apartment was far from ready. At this point Maxim and I didn't care how ready it was. We simply moved in. We didn't care if the elevator wasn't working even though we lived on the seventh floor. The heating also didn't work, so there was no hot water the first month, but we decided to ignore those things. We had space, and the rest would come later.

We were the only family living in the building before everything was finally organized a month later.

We had great plans for decorating the place based on space layout, comfort, and simplicity. In the USSR no apartment had closets or storage space, which we were determined to install. The kitchen was spacious—twenty-one square metres with a door and a window. This was paradise, and it all belonged to us and nobody else! The living and dining room combined was large—thirty-three square metres, which led to the bedroom. It was fifteen square metres. And the washroom had a shower! That in itself was a miracle! It was Khrushchev who'd come up with the idea of cooperatives. People used to call these buildings *"Khrushchevskie korobochki"* (boxes), but it was thanks to him, Nikita Khrushchev, that we had this wonderful apartment all to ourselves!

Our plan was to close the connecting door between the living room and bedroom by building a wall-to-wall unit, which would become a closet for clothes, books, suitcases, and everything else. It would be just shoulder width so we wouldn't really lose any space.

We bought the material for the unit through Maxim's connections in the building industry. We managed to get inexpensive pressed-wood panels, and we had enough to build everything we needed. We wanted to begin immediately, so Maxim borrowed an electric saw and began our project. He was the master carpenter, I was his assistant, and we worked all kinds of hours and never felt tired.

We opened the wall between the bedroom and kitchen, put the door in, which originally connected two rooms, and it was done in a day. After that, we built the storage unit. It took two weeks, and when it was finished the entire apartment was covered with sawdust! I cleaned everything, and in no time the apartment looked great. By doing what we did, we not only cut down on the need for furniture, which was costly and hard to find, but this way we also had storage space. The plan was brilliant.

We had only one little problem regarding the construction. We could live without any of it for the moment, but my approach was "Let's do it now!" It took a few heated discussions, but in the end Maxim was happy and proud of what we'd created, especially when it was all finished.

We had bought at bargain price a dining table with six chairs. All the pieces had deficiencies and they also weren't a set, which we found more interesting. I found them through my connections. We also had two armchairs that didn't match. Nobody wanted two different ones, but all l I had to do was match them with window coverings to make it all work together.

The kitchen was another story. It had no built-in cupboard—just a stove. Since multi-unit apartment projects had been planned under Khrushchev's leadership, the demand for kitchen units far exceeded the supply. Kitchen cabinets became a huge money-making business for people to make money—all illegal, of course. Stores that imported kitchen cabinets had thousands of people waiting to buy them, so deliveries were limited. Speculators got their hands on them first, and they didn't have to buy them either. All they had to do was to sell a numbered ticket, which was usually the price of the unit. When the shipment came in, the cabinets could end up costing double the original price, but at least you had a kitchen that could be organized. The same games went on with getting a refrigerator.

Luckily, I was able to buy two numbered tickets and our kitchen was put together beautifully.

Then I began to decorate. I painted the corridor ceilings and walls, used fine bamboo curtains as a partial wall covering, put a couple of wicker rugs on the floors, and hung another exotic bulky bamboo curtain to cover our coat shelves. We had a huge mirror, which I hung near the entrance, and the result was a tropical paradise! This was my first interior design, and I was very proud of what I'd created.

I only wished I was as happy about my private life with my husband.

What was wrong with it? Many things, but the root of it was in the bedroom. Our sex life was the same old story I had become familiar with: a one-way street. At times I felt as though I might as well not be there, it had so little to do with me. My husband focused on himself. He had his routine, which never varied and that I figured probably never would.

I thought at first it was because he was starved sexually, which would explain why he couldn't last long. I was very patient, hoping that eventually he'd be able to bring me into the picture, but I began to realize it was a habit he was unable to change.

In time it got worse; I felt like it was often over before it even began. Was it his fault? Maybe not. Maybe it was like this with every man at that time. But how was I to know? Who could you talk to about it? One thing I was certain of: it wasn't the way it should be.

There was another disappointment. Maxim, who was very inventive and thoughtful during our courtship, was not this way after we got married. Perhaps he thought there was no need for romance, that once you got married, the romance was over. I didn't see why this should be the case. I felt there should still be a room for some fun!

It was March the eighth, International Women's Day. In the USSR this occasion was widely celebrated. On that day, every woman was treated with a gift or taken out for dinner and, of course, given flowers. Everywhere you could see men lining up to buy flowers. There weren't too many choices at that time of the year, but there were lots and lots of mimosas, which were sold at every corner, especially in Moscow Centre.

That day, Maxim came home from work and I was looking forward to receiving something special from him. But when he came in he just asked me, "What are we having for dinner?"

I was so upset, I nearly burst into tears. How could he forget or ignore this important day? What was this all about? What had I done to deserve such ignorance? What did he think was going to happen between us? Could I be as loving and caring after this? What should I do?

There was no question that we were both good parents—but what about us? And me in particular? I was only twenty-five. Did I have to live the rest of my life being just a parent? What about me as a woman? What about that?

CHAPTER 33

Masha

Someone who played an important role in my life was Masha Levova. I met her about a year after I got married.

At the club, a new position was created to cater to children's entertainment, and Masha was hired for that position. She was forty-five and was married with two grown-up children, both of whom were university students at the time. After our working relationship was established, we became close friends in spite of our age difference. Her life had not been a simple one, and I soon found out what was really wrong.

Her husband was an alcoholic, and a bad one. I asked why she lived with him, and she told me her story.

She had married Gennady Levov, who was a very talented accordionist and a composer too, right after the war. Their son Alexander was born shortly after they got married, and at that point Gennady was hired as a musician for the dance ensemble "Berezka" under the choreographer Nadejhdina.

Berezka was very unique and became famous all over the world. The group had at least a hundred dancers, all female, and each one of them had incredible costumes—floor-length traditional Russian dresses, all handcrafted. As the dancers moved, they slowly formed very complex arrangements to music that was composed by Gennady Levov.

The group became so famous that to get tickets for their home performance was a matter of prestige. They travelled to all different parts of USSR with their concerts and later started going abroad.

Going abroad meant more money for everybody, not only because of the higher pay but because all members of the group were able to buy things that weren't available in Russia. They could purchase them and sell them for a high price to those who wanted them back home, and there were plenty of those.

Masha and Gennady were very happy together and had their second child, a girl.

Before the war, Masha had taken philosophy in university, but the war began right after her second year, when the entire university was evacuated. She couldn't continue her studies at that time because of having to look after her aged parents who lived a distance away from Moscow.

One of the most startling things about Masha was that her features and her colouring were almost like a mulatto. She looked totally different from the rest of her siblings. Masha's eldest brother had become a writer and on doing a family tree, had found a possible answer to the puzzle.

He discovered that their great, great, great-grandmother was one of the Hannibal slaves. Hannibal, a Negro, was one of the most notorious of slave drivers. In Russian history he was also known as one of the ancestors of the famous classic Russian poet Alexander Pushkin, who, like Masha, was also born a mulatto to parents who were pure Russian.

Hannibal used all of his female slaves sexually, and countless children were conceived as a result. Apparently one of Masha's ancestors from way back had been a mulatto, and although generation after generation appeared to be pure Russians, the gene cropped up again, in the person of Masha.

After she had given birth to her second child she went to medical school but wasn't able to graduate because of what happened with her husband. On one of his trips abroad in the United States, Gennady was accused of shoplifting. The incident caused a big scandal and hit the papers under the headline "Soviet Entertainers, Thieves!" Nadezhdina had to pay a large sum of money to prevent bad publicity, and when Gennady returned to Moscow he was no longer included in the concerts outside of the USSR. Someone else was asked to go in his place, and Gennady was only allowed to perform inside the USSR.

Gennady didn't take it lightly. He became extremely depressed and eventually hit the bottle, losing interest in performing in Nadezhdina's group and then resigning.

The family income was reduced drastically. Masha had to drop out university and search out all kinds of jobs in the entertainment industry. Gennady was out of work for a long time, although at one point he got himself a job as a music teacher, which Masha hoped would turn things around for them. However, when he received his first paycheck he went out and got totally drunk on the way home and was hit by a truck. Now Masha had a husband who was an invalid as well as an alcoholic.

Gennady went downhill quickly. He began selling their personal belongings for vodka, and Masha was so afraid she was going to end up with nothing that she took every item of value they had, sold them all for the best possible price, and put the money in one of the first cooperatives, which was to be built for Moscow entertainers.

It was the best she could do, and this way at least the family had a decent place to live. By the time she paid for the apartment, she had no money left to buy decent furniture, but that was the least of her worries. Her goal was to give her two children a good education.

To be able to support her family she took all kinds of jobs. Most of them were in the children's entertainment industry, which didn't pay much, so she had to take whatever jobs she could get in the field. Masha became a real expert in the industry.

In spite of her home situation, Masha kept her optimism and never lost her sense of humour. She found salvation in her various love affairs and in writing poetry. She wouldn't divorce Gennady even though he'd started to become abusive. She knew if she divorced him he'd become a street person and she and the children couldn't have lived live with that.

By the time Masha was hired to work for the club, her son had graduated from the university as an architect and her daughter was in her fourth year at the University of Foreign Languages, specializing in Hindu and Urdu. Obviously, both of her children were well on their way.

When I heard Masha's story, one thing bothered me: her pay was much lower than mine. Before the club created a children's entertainment position, I was the one who took care of both the adult and children's entertainment.

It was too much to be expected from me, and I had brought that fact to the director's attention constantly. I thought that if we separated children's entertainment from the adult, we could create interesting events for the kids, which was how the position was finally created.

It took three years to make the decision because the issue was money. In the end, the money was found, but it wasn't very much, even though Masha accepted the terms. I knew if she had a university degree, she wouldn't have had to accept such low pay. If she had her degree she could have had double, or even triple, the pay!

I was preparing for the entrance exams to my new university at the time, and I thought of Masha and how great it would be if she could do them too. We didn't have much time, of course, as the exams were starting in two months, but I decided to talk to her about it.

At first, she laughed at the idea. "At my age?" She said, "I'm too old to become a student again!"

But I saw the dream, the longing in her eyes, and decided to persevere. "If anybody deserves to be recognized as a specialist in kid's entertainment, it's you!" I said. "But you don't have a piece of paper, and, therefore, you don't get paid the way you should! Masha—all this could be changed! Tell me. What are you going to do? Sit at home and wait until Gennady gets drunk again and starts insulting you? So your love affairs keep you going, but what about ten years from now? Maybe there won't be these love affairs anymore, and will you be happy with your life then? I don't think so!"

It must have made her stop and think because the next day when we met at work, she picked up the conversation.

"Janna, I can't do these entrance exams for university because I don't have my original high school diploma, I only have a copy."

That was at least a beginning. I wanted her to get hooked on the idea and to forget her age. Once that was accomplished, I wasn't going to take no for an answer no matter what. It became my whole focus and inspiration from then on.

"Okay," I said, "you have a copy of your high school diploma. Why don't you bring it tomorrow?"

The following day she handed me her diploma.

She had graduated from high school in 1937 with excellent results. Masha was in fact a "gold medal" graduate!

I was overwhelmed and felt even more inspired to help her find a way. Furthermore, she handed me three other documents from her purse, which were her three university exam books. When I saw them I nearly fell off my chair.

The first was from her university where she had studied philosophy. The marks were all straight A's. Then there were her two years in medical school, which were also straight A's, and there was a third book, from one year of journalism school, also with straight A's.

I screamed at her, "You are one stupid idiot! You are so gifted and you're sitting here, working your ass off with these children's programs getting half my pay! That's it! You have no say!" I cried. "I'm taking care of this no matter what it takes! I don't care, you're going to the university this year with me!"

I knew what I had to do. First, get the copies of all her documents notarised and send them with a letter to the minister of Culture and Education, Ekaterina Furtzeva. She happened to be the first and only woman minister in the crooked government of the Soviet Union.

In fact, I took the letter in person to Furtzeva's executive secretary.

It was a good thing I knew how the system worked! Most of the time, personal letters never got into the minister's hands but got lost somewhere down the line. Besides that, one could wait for months for an answer. When I delivered the letter I pleaded with the secretary to answer quickly, and, indeed, I received it in record time—one week.

I was sure the answer would be positive, but I was wrong! Unfortunately, the new law, which came in to being in 1960, had to be the same for everyone, no exceptions, the letter stated. Otherwise there would be too many exceptions, like this one. To apply for university exams one had to present the original high school diploma.

This was laughable. I knew what this really meant. It took money, which had to be paid to the "right person," and we weren't going to do it that way. Masha would get those university exams, no matter what!

I had my next move planned.

I said to Masha, "Look. Your first university was evacuated out of Moscow during the war and it's now been operating for a long time. Now, nothing would have happened to their archives. What if your original diploma was there?"

Masha said, "It couldn't be! I already checked. It's not there."

"Oh, really? You checked it and it's not there? We'll see."

She looked at me as though I were absolutely crazy. "What are you talking about?"

I said, "Let's go there now!"

She didn't know that I had with me one of the best boxes of chocolate money could buy. I had my plan in my briefcase! These chocolates weren't only hard to find, but they cost a whole lot of money and my plan included them.

We walked into the University of Lomonosov on Lenin Mountain and asked the oldest archivist there if she would be kind enough to look up the file under Maria Aleksandrovna Ivanova, who was a student from 1937. The woman asked us to fill out a requisition for the search, checked Masha's passport, and told us to come back in two weeks.

Of course, I expected this, and now I made my move. I slowly removed the chocolate box from my briefcase and thanked her for being so cooperative and understanding. The woman's face changed immediately and she told us to come back after lunch!

I knew she'd get to work immediately, but Masha told me that I had wasted my money because they'd already searched for it and couldn't find it.

"Are you sure they looked for your file?"

"What do you mean? Are you suggesting they didn't?"

"Masha," I said, "I am surprised you're so naïve! You think if you're doing your best no matter how little they pay you that other people are the same? Don't you know that when people are underpaid and overworked, they aren't exactly happy campers, and, therefore, have no reason to give their best?"

Masha thought for a moment. "Maybe you're right. Maybe they didn't look for it because it could be simply misplaced."

"Well!" I said. "I think you're finally getting it!"

The elderly archivist was waiting for us when we returned. "You are such lucky girls!" she declared. "Here is your file!" And with a smile on her wrinkled face, she handed Masha the precious folder.

Masha's hands were shaking with excitement as I helped her go through the papers. Sure enough, her original diploma was there! We both screamed and hugged each other, and the woman looked happy too. Thanks to the box of expensive chocolates, Masha had a chance of being accepted for the university exams that year!

We both studied like crazy. She and I stayed up together night after night and never missed a day's work. The exams were a piece of cake for both of us because we each had had a lot of experience with them in previous schools. We were incredibly joyful when the university accepted us. Seeing Masha get the chance she needed and so richly deserved made me deeply happy!

Shortly after that I received an offer from Moscow Central Television and became a researcher for their theatre review programs. Masha was hired in my place in the club, and her financial situation improved from her first years at university. Things were looking up.

Masha became my confidante. Until then I had no friend with whom I could share my marriage problems. Masha, being an experienced woman, suggested that Maxim talk with one of the best-known sex pathologists who happened to be a close friend of hers. I knew Maxim wouldn't go for a consultation but that the way to do it was to bring Masha's friend to our place. I suggested making it a social gathering on the weekend. It was all organized properly, and we invited an agreeable group of friends that Saturday.

Everyone had a good time, except that Maxim didn't share his problem with the doctor. At one point that evening, the two of them were alone in the kitchen. They got into politics and other matters, and the doctor told Maxim that in his practice he dealt with all kinds of marital problems as a result of sexual ignorance or negligence.

Maxim expressed genuine sympathy, saying that it was very unfortunate when such things happened with married couples. He then excused himself from the conversation, suggesting they join the rest of the company in the dining room. That was the end of the story. It had been a useless exercise, and the doctor could go no further. Unless Maxim acknowledged his problem, there was no way he could interfere.

Of course I was fully occupied with my job, studies, our little son, and all kinds of domestic responsibilities. But in spite of my busy life, my marital problems bothered me a lot—and it seemed it wasn't going to get any better.

CHAPTER 34

Raya

I met Raya in the beauty salon next door to our apartment building. These salons had no appointment system; it was always first come, first served. If you liked a particular hairdresser and wanted your hair done by that person, you simply waited your turn. Sometimes, if you weren't there early enough, you could spend a day waiting in line.

I passed by the salon many times and often saw people lined up before the hairdressers came to work.

I didn't have my hair done often, but all kinds of fancy styles had come into fashion, so I grew my hair long and decided to try one of them.

It was my first time there, and I watched the stylists, trying to figure out which one I would like to go to. Eventually my attention was drawn to a young woman who had something special in her face and in the way she moved. The more I watched her, the more I felt drawn to her personality, and so I decided to wait for this girl.

When my turn came, our eyes met in the mirror and I knew we'd become friends—although I didn't know we'd become soul mates for life.

She and I didn't say much while she was doing my hair, but I knew I was in good hands. I felt very relaxed and silently observed her expression and hand movements.

Her looks fascinated me. She was young, but there was something in her face that made me think she'd been through some personal tragedy. Her eyes looked too mature for her age. She also didn't involve herself in the usual superficial chat amongst hairdressers. She was in her own thoughts while she worked, and at the same time her hands moved with the confidence of a real artist. When she was done, my hair looked beautiful and I was extremely pleased.

I told her that I lived next door, and I asked her if she would like to come to my place after work. She accepted my invitation happily and we arranged for her to come to my apartment after three o'clock that same day.

It worked out perfectly. It was my day off, and I went back home looking forward very much to Raya's visit. Something told me that getting together with her was going to be important, and I wasn't wrong.

When I opened the door, she stood there smiling radiantly as she held out a cake she'd brought for us and a bottle of wine. Raya had a wonderful mass of straight reddish-brown hair that framed her very simple face and prominent chin, an indication of strong character. But her eyes were full of pain as well as wisdom and purity all at the same time. She was as tall as I was and had a solid figure. Everything about her seemed solid.

I led her to the kitchen where the table was set with plates and several tasty appetizers. We had time to ourselves, and my baby, now ten months old, stayed sound asleep in his crib while we filled our glasses and began to enjoy the food and each other.

Somehow Raya and I felt that we'd met each other a long time before or rather that all our lives we had been waiting to meet. We both started to pour our hearts out to one another, and when Raya's turn came, I found my instincts about her had been right: she had truly experienced deep tragedy in her life.

"My father left my mother and me when I was only three," she said slowly. "And you know—I've never seen him since. I looked and looked for him but he never came back. I couldn't ask my mother about him because she cried all the time. I wanted to help her, but I couldn't. She changed so much. She was beautiful, but I began to see bottles around her bed and her hair became—I don't know. She didn't wash it. It smelled bad and so did her breath. She wasn't beautiful anymore. Then she would leave me alone. I was very frightened, but there was no one to help me or explain where she had gone. I felt so afraid. But I knew I had to be brave, and I tried. I think she met other men, but I didn't know them."

"Oh Raya," I said. "I can picture what it was like for you! I was afraid and alone when I was three too. I had no one either. I know what you've suffered, believe me! But please continue."

"Things got worse. My mother would fall down so much and hurt herself, and she would scream. Oh my God. It was terrible! And what happened was, they took her away. She looked dead, but I know she wasn't. It was her eyes. They were—you know—dead. And she didn't say goodbye to me."

She paused to collect herself. "I heard later that she was shipped out of Moscow. I don't know where they took her, and she died."

"What did you do? How old were you?" I asked.

"I was about five. It was my grandmother who took care of me after that."

"Was that okay?"

"Not really. She was anything but a saint. She loved wine and couldn't live a day without drinking a bottle. When I watched her I made up my mind I was somehow going to have a better life. I used to pass these hair salons and sometimes watch women having their hair done. That was going to be my work. I wanted to be a hairdresser. Clean hair. I loved clean hair, and I watched how they did it. So at sixteen, I trained, and I love it. I'm so happy doing this!"

When she was eighteen, Raya met her husband, Slava, at a dance where he was a singer with the band. He had returned from doing his army service and had graduated from technical college as a radio mechanic. They had married only few months before we met and the two of them were living with her grandmother. It wasn't their choice. It was simply the way things went in the Soviet Union!

Their place was in one of the oldest communal apartments in Moscow, with eleven families sharing one kitchen. The building had deteriorated so much that there was no point in repairing any of it, and the city had decided to demolish it. All the tenants had waited for years in hope of receiving decent accommodations.

Slava didn't have "Moscow *Propiska*"; in other words, he wasn't a citizen. He and Raya had to marry quickly so that he could be included in this communal place as a tenant.

The quota for living space for individuals was up to six square meters. But if he was allowed to live there, their space could be increased to eighteen meters. Thanks to Raya's aunt who was a veteran of the war, they were able to get an individual one-room apartment with a kitchen and washroom of their own. They considered themselves very fortunate because had they not been married, Raya and her grandmother would only have been entitled to twelve square meters.

From that day on, Raya and I became inseparable. She was loyal and devoted, my number one friend; she was really family to me. She was the only one who knew how to work with me in the kitchen when we had parties. Cooking together as we did gave us time to relax and talk about important things.

Although she hadn't gone back to school, she began to read the literature I had around for my studies. She had good sense of comprehension and had a different and refreshing point of view about the books she read. Also, because going to the theatre was part of my job, I sometime took her with me.

Raya loved my little boy and was a big help to me. She and Slava stayed over often, and she stayed over even if he wasn't with her. It seemed as though she wanted to be near me most of the time, and I asked her if our friendship might affect her marriage.

"That's the way it is," she shrugged. "Slava will just have to understand, that's all."

Many of my friends couldn't comprehend our closeness. When I invited them to our place, I would often hear snobbish remarks.

"And I suppose your hairdresser will be there too?"

"Of course!" I would say lightly. In my heart I was hurt by this kind of attitude. Raya didn't have a degree, but that didn't make her any less intelligent. Actually, she was more intelligent than those who thought they were superior. They had parents who had put them through university and had used their connections to find positions for them. Where would they have been without all this help?

In spite of the veiled criticism, Raya and I simply adopted one another. I gave her the sense of belonging and family she wouldn't have known had she not met me, and in turn she gave me all the love she could. She was a deep thinker, had incredibly high moral standards, and was more sophisticated than many who had high opinions of themselves.

A year after we met, I learned about a position with Moscow Central Television in the beauty and makeup studios. It seemed like the perfect position for Raya, but it took me some time to persuade her to try for the job. She was very reluctant and felt sure she would never be hired, but after continued coaxing on my part, she agreed to make the necessary appointments and went along to several interviews after that.

In Soviet Russia, it always took a long time to get the results for these positions. There were many bureaucratic committees all meeting to look through their notes and discuss the various applicants and come to a collective decision about who should be hired. This decision-making process took at least two months. When we at last heard the results, to our great joy the position went to Raya! She was stunned and could hardly bring herself to believe her good fortune!

The summer after Masha and I graduated from our first year in university happened to be a turning point in my marriage. At the same time, I was offered a month's job in a summer camp on the Black Sea for the Gosplan children. Masha and I talked about it and she suggested I take it because of the opportunity to be on my own without any distractions. This way, I could perhaps come to some decision about Maxim and me.

Raya offered to help with the care of Aleksei, who was in kindergarten during the day and was happy and doing well. Raya was six months into her first pregnancy and said, "I really want to do this, Janna! It will give Slava and me a chance to practice for our own baby!" So everything was settled.

The time at summer camp flew by quickly, and I had a great time with the kids. The administration offered me another month and allowed me to have my son with me if I wanted to, but I said no. Much as I would have liked to, I didn't think it was a wise thing to do under the circumstances.

The day I came home, Raya prepared a special feast for us two couples, which we really enjoyed. It was great evening, and we all had a hilarious time. On the surface, of course, everything seemed fine, and I kept them laughing with all kinds of anecdotes about my life as a counselor for the thirteen-year-olds.

In order to discipline the youngsters, I'd spent a lot of the time being a kid myself, coming up with different ideas for contests that we held.

My best idea was for an international song, which was about all the children in the world uniting. The girls painted their dresses to match their chosen country's flag, and the boys painted their shirts as well. We collected small drums to be worn over the necks of the thirty kids so they could walk and beat their drums at the same time. Of course we won the first prize and became the camp sensation.

That night after dinner when everyone had left, I began to feel very awkward and uncomfortable around Maxim. The old problem was still with me, and I wasn't looking forward to going to bed with my husband—but there was no way out of it. Once there, I tried to suggest doing things differently, hoping to get him out of the usual boring routine, but he refused to go for it.

"Wives don't do things like that!" he snapped in a furious tone. "Only prostitutes do!"

Having no other option, I went along with him, but for the last time.

After it was all over, I felt depressed and used, and I knew I couldn't continue this way any longer. I wanted to speak with him about it right then, but he was sound asleep. I got up and showered and stayed there for a long time. It was as though I were trying to completely scrub the memory from my whole being, mind and body. It must not and could not continue. Max was a good man and a responsible father, but as far as our marriage was concerned it was over.

I knew better than anyone how important it was for a child to have a mother and father to grow up and to have good memories of childhood. Happy memories developed confidence and security. Ugly ones damaged lives.

Therefore, the welfare of our child was my prime concern, and since his future was in my hands I wondered about myself as a human being—as a woman. How could I make my child's life happy if I wasn't happy? There had to be a way, and I had to find it.

The next morning before Maxim was awake, I left earlier than usual to take Aleksei to the kindergarten because I had to catch up on work at my regular job. All the counselors from the summer camp had planned a night out after work—something I wouldn't have missed for the world.

I called Maxim and told him I'd be home late and that Raya was picking Aleksei up and staying over. She had an early doctor's appointment near us and it was difficult in her condition to travel all the way from where she lived.

When I came home shortly after midnight, Raya was asleep in our bedroom and Maxim was on a foldout bed in the dining room. I undressed quietly and went right to our bedroom, making sure not to disturb either Aleksei or Raya.

I was almost asleep when I heard the stereo blasting loudly. The next minute Raya was awake. Our first thought was Aleksei. The last thing we needed was for the baby to wake up at two o'clock in the morning. I crept into the dining room and found Maxim standing on the balcony holding an almost empty bottle of vodka in his hand.

"Max!" I exclaimed, as quietly as I could. "What are you doing? Why are you behaving like this?"

He whirled around, his face full of rage. "You're asking me what? I'll tell you why! Because my wife is cheating on me! You went away for the whole month because you have a lover!"

Before I could say anything, he grabbed me and slapped me so hard I heard bells. I pulled away from him and ran out of the room, shutting the door tightly behind me. Instantly, there was the sound of him throwing objects that shattered against the door. I saw no point in dealing with him at that moment, so I went back to bed.

I thanked God Aleksei was asleep, but Raya was sitting on the edge of the bed looking ashen.

"What's going on?" she asked. "I don't understand! What's the matter with Maxim?"

"Don't worry, Raya," I whispered. "He's upset, but I'm going to talk to him tomorrow. We'll work it out. I just can't deal with it now. Please relax and go back to sleep. Please!"

Somehow she fell asleep, or at least pretended she did, but I lay in bed with my eyes wide open for the rest of my night.

Maxim left the house before we were up, which made us feel much better. We couldn't have faced him that morning and he knew it.

I made sure Raya was okay, trying to lighten things, making her laugh, while we picked up broken pieces of former treasures from the floor. I knew Maxim had intended for these objects to hit me on the head.

Of one thing I was absolutely sure: it was never going to happen again.

It was Maxim's turn to pick Aleksei up after work, and I came home after eight o'clock when he'd been put to bed. I tiptoed in and talked with

Aleksei until his eyes were safely closed and then went into the dining room where Maxim was sitting.

"Max," I said, "we have to talk."

"Yes, of course," he answered, with a guilty look in his eyes.

In a quiet voice I said, "Max. Here's how it is. We have to get a divorce."

He looked stunned. "What? A divorce?"

"Yes," I said. "A divorce."

"But why? Because of what happened last night? Look, I'm sorry about that. It'll never happen again. Please forgive me!"

"No!" I answered. "It's not because of what happened last night. It's because we cannot be husband and wife any longer. From now on we can only be parents to our son, which is why I suggest a legal divorce."

I knew he didn't know how to respond, and I also knew what his next question would be.

"But what about Aleksei? Do you want him to grow up without a father? You should know better than anyone how that would be for our little son."

"Yes, I do. And that's why it's important for us to divorce at this point so we can concentrate on being good parents to our son. Can you see this?"

"But how can our son grow up to be happy if one of his parents isn't there for him every day?"

"That doesn't have to happen! Our divorce doesn't mean that one of us would be out of Aleksei's life. It just means that we won't have any marital obligations. We'll have only parental obligations. If we separate these two issues, we could be much happier and our son can grow up with both parents with him for the rest of our lives."

"How can we do this?"

"Simple," I said. "After the divorce, we can continue living together—just as parents. This way, I don't have to lie to you or pretend anything and neither do you. We can be good friends as well as good parents. If you're prepared to do this, I am too. This way, we'll be winners in the end."

I saw the release of tension in his face.

"And what about all our friends? How would they react at seeing us living together and leading our personal lives separately? This isn't how things are normally done."

"Normal?" I asked him. "What's normal? To divorce each other and take away parental privileges, which in turn damages children or to continue with a marriage that's over, pretending it isn't? In the meantime, we'd be secretly hating each other! And what good would that do to a child? So think about what's called normal!"

"I can see what you're saying," he said slowly. "And I agree."

We applied for a divorce the next morning and within a week we were no longer man and wife. The judge said our divorce was the fastest and easiest he had ever seen in his entire practice, and Maxim and I felt 100 percent better about each other when we walked out of court.

From that moment on, our lives together improved every day. We talked about all kinds of things we didn't dare touch while we were married. We took care of each other sincerely and committed ourselves to do so for the rest of our lives. We didn't have to ever lie again—and what a relief it was!

CHAPTER 35

The Fire

When I walked into my office that particular day, the secretary, whose expression seemed extremely tense, told me the director wanted to see me.

"Looks like trouble," I said to myself. It was very unusual to be called into the boss's office that early in the morning.

"Good morning, Janna," he said, standing as I walked in. "Please sit down."

I tried to read his expression. I could see he was having difficult coming out with what was in his mind. Was he about to fire me? What was it?

He cleared his throat. "Janna, this is difficult," he said, hesitantly. "But I want you to know that your son is alive and your stepmother is alive too."

What was he talking about? Why shouldn't they be alive? Aleksei was staying with Mama during her vacation while Max and I worked on insulating her house. One more week and it would be done. We had been there two days and were going back on the following Friday right after work.

"Your stepmother's house burned to the ground last night," he said gently. "But she and your son are both okay. Please don't panic. Just call Max. Tell him to pick you up and take you there. Or do you want me to call him?"

It hit me. "Oh my God! Mama's house burned down? No! That's impossible!"

The secretary came to the door, saying something, but I couldn't make out what it was. I felt dizzy.

"Max is on his way," she said, "and should be here any minute." She came over to me. "Janna, here's a glass of water. Drink it. You'll feel better. The main thing is, they're alive! Please," she said again, "drink this glass of water, won't you?"

I don't remember the drive to the house. The house...the former house. There was no house there—only a pile of ashes. Our little boy was walking amongst the rubble that was heaped up under the two maple trees. This pile of ashes was all that was left of the place.

I tenderly took my child in my arms and felt his little heart beat. He was alive!

When I let go of him. I looked at Mama. She was sitting on the garden bench with blackened hands. She had been searching through the ashes for whatever she could retrieve. I ran to her and hugged her, hardly able to believe they were both okay.

"Mama!" I said. "How did it happen? Please! Let's get out of here. We can all climb in the car and go somewhere. There's nothing left here! Come on, come on! Let's go!"

I was talking rapidly, as though the faster I spoke, the faster we'd be removed from this shattering scene.

"Shhh! Slow down!" Mama said. "We have to act as though nothing out of the ordinary has happened. We mustn't forget that Aleksei is very young and anything shocking can affect him for the rest of his life. So far, he hasn't shown any unusual behaviour, so he must be okay. Let's talk calmly, so he can see that everything and everybody is perfectly fine."

"Yes, you're right, Mama," I said sitting down beside her and forcing myself to take a breath and slow down. "Please tell us what happened, will you?"

"Well, we went to bed as usual, around eight o'clock. I woke up when the roof was about to fall on our heads. My first thought was not to wake up Aleksei, so I carefully picked him up and just walked out of the house. I was very lucky because the door had already fallen in. I found my way out without rushing and carried him in my arms until I got to Luba's house. Then I knocked on her window trying not to do it too loudly. When she finally heard my knocking, she opened the door and I whispered, 'Shh, don't speak loudly! Let's put the baby to bed and then I'll tell you what happened.' When Aleksei was sound asleep, I told her that my house had just burned down, and then I collapsed. I was so tired! That's all. That's the whole story. I woke up this morning and called you, but you had already left for work. So I called the office."

"My God!" I said. "Mama!"

"Unbelievable!" Maxim said, shaking his head over and over. She looked at me with a wistful expression. "I don't have a home anymore," she said.

"Mama, don't worry," I said. "You'll have a home soon—and for now, you're staying with us!"

Yes," she said. "Maybe I'll get a small place with water and central heating. I'm getting too old to carry water from outside." She reached behind her. "And look what I have left! My crystal vase...It's the only memory. This was the first thing I bought when you father and I got married, and you know who saved it? Nikolay Georgevich! After I got out of the house, he went back in and this was the only thing he was able to save. See? I have a good friend! I knew he was a nice man. Let's pack it in this blanket I brought from Luba's."

Max and I sat staring at Mama. Neither of us could find words. She had saved our child.

As strange as it sounds, because Mama's house burned down, I was able to get a place for her within two weeks! And there was running water and central heating in her apartment. She also had a toilet and shower in her new place. We bought her a television and fridge, and her two sisters got her a bed, a couch, and a table with three chairs, and other things were collected for her.

Auntie Luba, who was a good soul, gave her all she could, and her many friends at the theatre school brought her clothing and helped her to settle in. Everybody lent a hand, except my sisters, who didn't lift a finger.

There were many occasions when I felt like calling my father. I wanted to say to him, "See? You thought when you left Mama without anything, she'd die like a dog under a fence! How wrong you were! She has everything she could possibly need—and she has friends. Many friends! She's richer than you could ever hope to be!"

But he didn't even deserve the time it took to think about him!

CHAPTER 36

The Discovery

My university studies continued. Masha and I spent countless hours together preparing for our assignments and exams. She, being a perfectionist, kept me in line.

A lot of subjects didn't make sense to me, and I had a hard time memorizing such material. In my opinion, subjects on politics and economics took too many hours and didn't leave enough time for the courses I was really interested in. But we didn't have a choice. All the subjects were mandatory.

Studying with Masha made everything more bearable for both of us. She was tough on me. Most of our studies went late into the night, and I was a morning person whereas Masha was not. Many times I wanted to skip the endless memorizing that seemed to put me to sleep. She would force me to continue working by making pots of coffee, and when coffee didn't work, she would get me to take a cold shower. Our last resort was to go for a walk, but I still managed to fall asleep with my eyes wide open!

My job was exciting. I had been meeting interesting people and I also had several admirers who all ended up being my friends. I had no intention of remarrying. I just didn't believe in the concept of marriage anymore.

One of my affairs started shortly after my divorce. I had been selected to work on a committee whose goal was to develop cultural activities in large industrial plants. Every member of the committee was assigned to work with one of the plants, mine being the Electro-Mechanical Plant of Vladimir Ilich Lenin.

The chief reason I liked this particular company was because I lived right across from it. Our apartment windows overlooked a memorial park with Lenin's statue, which apparently was the spot where an attempt had been made on his life, and right behind it was the plant headquarters.

My work with this company had to be done with the cooperation of their club of culture, and I had to work closely with the director of the club, who was a divorced woman of about forty-five. She had bleached blonde hair, which made her face very hard, and she had an extremely deep voice, probably because she smoked war-time papirisas called "*Kazbek*," which only soldiers smoked. Her name was Larisa, and although I got along with her fairly well, I couldn't see her as a possible friend at all.

The company head of the Communist Party was another important person I met. The company had ten thousand workers, and the leader of the party was no more important than the director of this plant—Anatoly Ignatieff.

I was impressed with him right from the beginning. It was unusual to see a young man in his position. He was in his midthirties, tall and handsome, with a rich, resonant voice. We chatted about all kinds things, and I was surprised at how informal and casual he was yet at the same time somewhat reserved. I left his office and looked forward to working on my task, knowing I would be getting all the support I needed from his end.

I was a little surprised when I received a call from him the next day suggesting we meet outside the plant for dinner. Something told me he had a personal interest in me, and the fact was, I felt quite honoured to receive this invitation—which is how our affair started.

It turned out to be a very passionate one. He was the first man in my life who knew something about women. He and I had no hang-ups at all about intimate relationships and were well suited to each other, including a similar sense of humour. We started seeing each other at least once a week. Soviet corruption was a favourite topic of ours, and he admitted he really didn't like being part of it.

"If I had a choice, I wouldn't be doing this job. But you see," he said with a smile, "I'm good at it and I couldn't possibly go back to being an electro-mechanical engineer! The position I'm in pays well. It allows me to travel abroad and gives me and my family quite a few benefits."

In my opinion, we all had to do things under the Soviet regime that we disagreed with, but to be a leader of the party organisation, one had to believe in it—or at least so I had thought. On the other hand, I was beginning to discover that this wasn't necessarily the case. In many instances, people used it as a ticket to a better life.

Anatoly was one of them.

He was married. He told me that if he hadn't been in such a top position he would divorce his wife in five minutes, but it suited my purposes that he had a wife and couldn't divorce.

Our dates weren't long, but they were very fulfilling. My own divorce helped me a lot and made me feel free. On the other hand, because I had made a commitment to raise our son together, I treated Max with respect and care and he did the same for me. It really was the best possible arrangement.

Basically, we had a good family life together. We never had any financial arrangements between us but simply trusted each other. In the beginning when Maxim brought his salary home and as usual handed it to me, I told him to keep at least half of it for himself. He refused and suggested I continue to be the money manager because I ran the household so well.

Once in a while Maxim had projects outside of Moscow. During those times he would rent a little place close to where he was working and come home on Friday for the weekend. I think he made himself available for these projects so that he and I could have more freedom in our personal lives. But it didn't mean I brought any dates home when Aleksei was there. The only company I had at our place would be Raya, who stayed overnight, or Masha when we had to study late.

For the most part Anatoly and I met at my place during lunchtime. They were very exciting moments. Anatoly was an intoxicating man to be with. He never walked into my place empty-handed. Many times he brought me flowers, champagne, chocolates, and a few times after his return from abroad he would bring lovely presents for me. I prepared my gourmet lunches for our dates. In spite of the time limits that we were both aware of, we never felt rushed. We both were very attracted to each other sexually and intellectually.

Our lovemaking was like a beautiful symphony played by the masters, and he helped me to discover a world of intimate pleasures. My first orgasm was a totally shocking experience. My body suddenly turned into a glorious flower of incredible shades and colours and gave off the most delicate perfume. I thought, Oh my God! Was this what life was about? It must be! And was it wrong to think this way? I didn't think so! I'd heard many love stories, but no one had ever told me anything about this. I had to live to be twenty-eight before I experienced this summit of being!

Well, at least I now knew there was nothing wrong with me—that I was healthy, normal woman. How could one learn about sex if there was no literature available and people didn't talk about it? No wonder there were so many unhappy women in Russia! For the most part, they just catered to their men's needs and put their own in the deep freeze. Was it too much to hope for, that one day all this might change?

Our love affair was interrupted by a totally stupid turn of events. At one point I had a hard time dealing with the club art designer. The problem was that the man, whose name was Eugene, had three or more jobs on the go and was not very punctual in delivering the items necessary for our project. There were also times when he simply kept on delaying the completion of many of the things we had to have. Every time I talked to Larisa about this problem, she seemed to ignore it, and I began to feel that Eugene was the one in control, not her. I couldn't figure out why the situation was like this

One day I found out that Larisa and Eugene were lovers, which explained a lot, but the problem still existed. I had to do my job. And I decided to handle Eugene in my own way. I would simply go to his studio and stay there until the job was complete. It was a time-consuming way of doing things, but at least the job would be done in time. Little did I know that the club staff had started to gossip about the length of time I spent in his studio. Eventually the gossip reached Larisa. Of course, I wasn't aware of it for some time, but I'd noticed a change in her attitude towards me and I had no idea why.

One day I decided to speak with her about it and invited her to my home for lunch. I had prepared some food for us before I left for work that day and also I knew she liked vodka. I had set the table for two by the window in my favorite room, the kitchen, and when we came in, she immediately had a couple of straight vodkas before we set down. I finally asked her to tell me what the problem was.

"Why have you changed towards me?" I asked. "Did I do something wrong?"

"What do you mean, did you do something wrong?" she demanded. "You knew perfectly well you set out to seduce Eugene, so how else would you expect me to react?"

"What? I seduced Eugene?" I couldn't believe my ears. He was the last thing on my mind! What an accusation! And this was how my spending time in his studio had been interpreted? Somebody was obviously making it his or her business to create this problem between us. I tied to tell her why I had decided to do what I did, but no matter what I said, her mind was closed against me. She was convinced that I had gone after her lover.

I knew we couldn't work under these circumstances. I had to do something about it, and after thinking about it for a minute I decided to share my secret with her. Of course it turned out to be a major mistake. I told her I was involved with Anatoly.

At first she refused to believe me. Then I thought of a solution. I dialed Anatoly's number and when he answered, we had an intimate conversation during which we both came to our windows—something we did whenever we were on the phone.

Normally, it was highly entertaining to have these conversations while we gazed at each other from across the park. I kept my eye on Larisa's face and saw her expression change from suspicion to one of relief and satisfaction. After I hung up, she poured me a drink and said she was sorry. I was very relieved and thought our problem was solved, but I wasn't aware of the risk I had taken by doing what I had. A week later, I received a call from Anatoly.

"How could you do this to me?"

"Do what?" I was shocked by the coldness in his tone.

"Why did you have to tell Larisa about us?"

I tried to lie. "Tolia! I did no such a thing!"

"How else would this woman know that we look at each other through the window when we talk on the phone?"

So she had told him. Why would she do such a thing? It had to be blackmail—and indeed it was, according to Anatoly. She had come to his office and demanded that he give her a new apartment or else his wife would know about the affair and the director and everybody else. He would certainly lose his job.

Anatoly was so angry he wouldn't allow me explain what had happened and we ended up not seeing each other for six months. During that whole time I was in agony and had torturous dreams about him constantly. I would see his face in my mind as well and, for some reason, would have this urge to get up from wherever I was and rush to the window. It was unbelievable. I would catch sight of him each and every time this happened! I began to smoke cigarettes too, one after another, but there was no relief from the pain I felt over this whole episode.

I ran out of cigarettes one night and dashed outside to the nearby café to buy some. As I entered, I caught sight of him sitting there having a coffee, and I immediately turned and fled. I felt as though my chest would burst as I rushed back to the apartment, my heart pounding and the tightness in my throat killing me.

I wanted to die.

It was late that same night when my phone rang. I didn't feel like talking to anybody, especially at such a late hour, but Raya urged me to answer it in case it was Slava.

It was Anatoly, and my heart sank. Now what?

"Good evening. Janna."

"Good evening, Tolia," I managed to answer.

"It's not too difficult to remember my name, is it?" he said gently. "I just thought it was time to stop this craziness—this running into each other and pretending we're strangers. Isn't it time we at least say hello? How do you feel about it?"

"Oh, I'd be happy to do that," I said.

"So why don't you come out right now and we'll talk ?"

"Where are you? I asked. "And how did you know I was at home? I don't have any lights on, only a candle."

"I could see the faint glow from it," he said. "And I'm right here in my office."

I looked out the window and was surprised to see no light at all in his office. In fact the whole building was in complete darkness.

Raya, who knew better than anyone what I'd been suffering these many months, was signaling to me. "Go! Go," she whispered.

"Okay, I'd like to see you. But where do we meet?" I asked.

"Right across the street, in the park!"

A quick exchange with Raya, who encouraged me to be brave and tell him everything, and I was gone.

He and I talked for at least an hour, and I felt as though a huge load had been lifted off my shoulders. Finally I could breathe.

I told him how sorry I was and gave him the whole story in detail. He also told me what he had done about Larisa. He simply didn't fall for her threats. He said that he'd almost wanted her to go ahead and tell everyone, that maybe it would be an opportunity for him to straighten his life. So her plan didn't work. He absolutely refused to make an exception. Just like everybody else, she'd have to wait for her apartment.

"She could see I wasn't afraid of her threats," he said. It seemed that shortly after we broke up, Anatoly had started having terrible nightmares about running into me and was constantly waking up in a cold sweat. Then it actually began to happen, which disturbed him to no end. Finally, he decided to call.

We were stunned to find out about each other and felt incredible relief that the pressure had lifted at last. Back at home, I felt at ease for the first time in ages, and Raya and I talked long into the night.

Anatoly and I continued our affair whenever we could, until the one from my past—Valentin—resurfaced.

CHAPTER 37

Life as It Goes

Life in Moscow. It was considered a privileged city, the jewel of the Soviet Union. It was supposed to look glamorous, rich, and successful. The food supply was directed to Moscow as a first priority in order to give stores a look of plenty and to demonstrate prosperity. It was the same with other merchandise: clothes, furniture, all kinds of domestic items, arts and crafts.

The second priority were other large cities, which received less than half of what Moscow did; the last on the list were the smaller cities and towns. They got what was left over, which wasn't much. As a result, hundreds of thousands from all over the country flocked to Moscow to buy goods.

People took their vacations and sick leave to shop and therefore had the time to stay in lineups and purchase what they couldn't get in their hometowns.

What it did to Moscow's citizens was to make their lives more difficult. They didn't have the time to stay in lineups, of course, because they were working. Actually, in order to manage our lives we needed to have many talents and connections. That was the normal lifestyle. You worked your network of contacts, used your charm, paid double for things, and bought gifts to keep your contacts interested and to stay on the priority list. Friends kept us in mind as well when they bought things for themselves through their contacts, and, in turn, we did the same for them.

The most important people in everyday life were the butchers, store cashiers, and cleaning people. To know the manager of any store was like having a superstar as a friend. When you accomplished this, you had it made, especially as far as your grocery supply was concerned.

Other very important people to know were the speculators. These people were primarily the ones who came and went out of USSR. They were diplomats, big-name musicians, singers, and dancers. They were members of the Bolshoi Theatre, Kirov Ballet, the Moiseyev Dance Ensemble, Berezka, and others. Before they left the country, they collected all kind of orders from friends and friends of friends for clothes, shoes, cosmetics, anything and everything they could buy abroad. In other words, every item was presold before those who were going had actually left!

Moscow's citizens had to have a passport stamped with their address on it. Without that stamp, one couldn't live in Moscow, and in order to get that stamp, one had to be born in Moscow or be married to a citizen of Moscow. Of course, to become a citizen of Moscow was the dream of many thousands from all over the USSR, and this demand for proof of citizenship created a lot of corruption.

People paid huge sums to make it happen, and bogus marriages had become a popular practice. The city had always experienced a great shortage of residencies. Hotels were always full, and to get a hotel room a person had to slip at least a hundred rubles in their passport—and a hundred rubles was the average monthly pay for a professional. Normally, it would do the job. Somehow the room, which hadn't been available, suddenly was!

My own life was built on the basis of such contacts and connections. I had my fish-store connection, my butcher, my fruit-and-vegetable person, and so on. I always had to maintain these contacts, often bringing gifts, although many were satisfied to just see my sunny smile. I knew I had lots of charm, and so I used it! Naturally, I would still slip in extra cash here and there.

It was tiresome, yet it was the way of life in Moscow at that time.

In spite of all the difficulties, I loved getting together with my friends and did so regularly. We often had great times with someone in the crowd who had a good voice and played the guitar and with whom we would all sing for hours and hours!

There was always somebody new and interesting in our company: a comedian, a talented joke teller, musicians, singers, and poets.

I used to love cooking for our gatherings, and it was nothing for me to prepare food for twenty-five people in less than three hours. I was known for filling my table with luxurious, delicious food and for very little money. I found out that most of my friends didn't know how to do it. In fact, hardly anybody knew how little money I actually spent on these elaborate festivities. One thing I did invest in without regret was my hard labour.

I loved to get people together to enjoy good, tasty food, and I was a good hostess. Once everything was ready, I would make myself look glamorous and be part of the fun, as though I were one of the guests. I felt it was the secret to a successful party. There were many hosts who let their guests know how hard they'd worked and how exhausted they were, but that wasn't my style.

I had several hobbies besides cooking and entertaining. I loved all kinds of applied arts. I loved making cards and writing my own poems in them. I also learned how to create my own knitting and crochet patterns. Another of my interests was changing a person's outward image, as the girls in camp did for me, years ago. I started with their hair, which I did quite successfully for many people. Eventually I was paid quite generously for doing it.

I loved dancing! I could dance all night long and never feel tired. I was known to be a great believer in life—in a happy life. I knew my chief motivation was to prove to myself that life was worth living. My reason for this came from my early life and having to fight for survival. I was driven all my life to achieve my major goal in life, to create something useful.

And now Valentin was back in my life!

One day he wrote me a letter, and my heart began to pound when I saw the familiar handwriting. It took me a long time to open it as my thoughts went back to the last meeting I'd had with him.

It had been December 1965. I was eight months pregnant and was coming down the subway escalator when I suddenly saw him on the one going up. We both caught each other's eye simultaneously, and he motioned me to wait for him at my end.

"Jandi!" he said. "You're pregnant with my child!"

"No! Absolutely not, Valia!" I replied. "In fact, our last time together was more than eleven months ago, you know."

"I don't believe it!"

I could see he didn't want to acknowledge this fact. He wanted the child to be his baby.

"Are you happily married?" he demanded to know. Before I could reply, he said, "If you aren't, I want to be with you and the baby. I don't care if it's someone else's I want us to be together!"

I tried to make light of it. "Valia," I said, "that's a good one! You and I both know the answer to that and you get ten out of ten if I say no!"

He sighed. Then we both talked a little longer and regretfully said goodbye, wishing each other luck.

And now, almost four years later I was holding a letter from him in my hands. My heart went on beating furiously and I questioned myself as to whether it was a good idea to opening this letter of his.

For some strange reason, my heart belonged to this man, but I also knew that going back to him was not a good idea. It hadn't worked before; why would it work now? At the same time my heart was screaming, "Go for it! Do it!"

I opened it.

"I know that you're divorced," it read, "but, Jandi, you're the only woman I've ever loved! We owe each other another chance!"

Right. Another chance...

I would have loved that, but somehow I didn't believe in it. At the same time, he was on my mind so much! Maybe we should meet and talk. What harm could there be in that?

And so we did, in a nearby café.

He had changed quite a lot, and in my mind I thought, "What's so extraordinary about him that I should feel the way I have for so many years?" Was it his looks? No! His mind? Not really. He may have been a good professional in his field, but what did I know about it? Not much. We really didn't have a lot in common. His songs? Yes! His poetry! And the way his voice sounded and his eyes looked when he sang!

Was it enough to be in love all these years and then find out time and time again that somehow it didn't work for us?

But he had been my first love, the first human being who had ever hugged and kissed me and who had given me what I needed and had been searching for—a sense of love. Of course, I'd been a fourteen-year-old girl then, and now I was a woman. On the other hand, maybe some people never grew up.

I just couldn't say goodbye to Valentin. Not yet.

I analyzed all the things that were wrong about us and came to the conclusion that most of them wouldn't change. I even wrote a poem about it—in Russian, of course. It basically said that most of us became the victims of our own crimes, that we tended to come back and visit our wounded souls over and over, as if asking for more punishment.

Ah, how sad...

So we met, and for the first couple of hours we were quite detached, talking about our lives. It wasn't until later that evening as we walked through a small park that we both realized we were prisoners of our past. At that moment, we flung our arms around each other, and we were gone. In a split second we were back on our first date. The skies above us were flying high, and we were flying with them. The air smelled like a delicious wine, and we drank it thirstily until we were both completely intoxicated.

We both knew we'd be together again. It was undeniable.

In the following months we saw each other whenever there was the slightest opportunity. Valentin talked a lot about his life during our separation, and to my surprise I could see that we'd both gone through the same things emotionally. What else did two people need to be happy together? I even started believing in a possible future with him until one incident took place that jolted me back into reality.

We both agreed to spend a weekend with Aleksei, and we made our plans. First we went to a children's theatre. It felt so good to have Valentin on one side and Aleksei on the other. Afterwards, we went to a theatre restaurant and had delicious tarts and lemonade and Aleksei had an ice cream as well. We walked down the streets of Old Arbat and then into the park across from our building, where Aleksei showed us how he could ride his bicycle. Finally we went home to have dinner, which I'd prepared the day before.

My son had his food first and then went into the living room to play while Valentin and I had our candlelit dinner in the kitchen. It all felt warm and cozy. When we had finished and were chatting, Aleksei came back to the kitchen to ask Valentin to draw him an airplane. He knew Valia was an aviation engineer.

"I don't know how to draw a plane. Sorry," was the abrupt reply.

I'll never forget my son's look of disappointment. "My papa knows how to do it!" he said, turning his back on us and marching back into the living room.

That was the end of a possible life with Valentin. I would not allow anyone, not even him—my first love—to be part of my life until my son was grown up.

Later when he had gone home, I sat down with my son and told him a white lie: that Valentin couldn't draw the plane for him because he'd been very tired. In my heart I knew the answer to the whole situation and never again brought Valentin to my place while my son was there.

I had separated the two of them once and for all.

CHAPTER 38

The Orphanage Counselor

Masha and I had many memorable experiences throughout our university years.

Masha really became the centre of our group. Everybody loved her. The fact that she was the only student in our group who was twenty years our senior helped her in many difficult situations. She had an outstanding personality and more energy and sense of humour than all the young girls put together. In fact, everybody acknowledged that both Masha and I had an entertaining approach to all kinds of serious and boring situations. We used to come to class and tell everybody all kinds of funny stories and poke good-hearted fun at our professors.

Masha and I invited our professor of philosophy for a drink after the exam. Three hours later, we both realized that he was a drunk! We looked at each other knowing we couldn't let the man go home alone. It was all we needed! We'd worked all night preparing for the exam, then spent all day waiting for our turn at school, and now we had to help this man get home! What would the poor wife think of us allowing her husband to get this drunk? All that aside, we weren't going to let him go home in the shape he was in.

It was a tough trip. We had to go across a frozen lake, and halfway across he fell through the ice. It was terrifying, but it didn't sober him up in the slightest. When we finally got him out of the hole, he seemed even drunker and kept falling while we kept picking him up and pushing him in the direction of home. By the time we arrived, both his ears were frozen and his wife met us at the door without being in the least surprised. We got the picture. For her, it was nothing new!

Masha had a habit of telling a professor of any subject before starting her exam, "You realize I'm much too old to write this exam. I simply am too old! I can't memorize anymore! I should quit school and just let the younger ones be the students. It's too late for me!"

Without fail the professor would tell her it wasn't true! In fact she had more ability than many of the young ones and always got the highest marks. This conversation would go on for at least twenty minutes or so, during which all the students would have a chance to pass written notes back and forth and help each other.

Eventually the professor would ask Masha the right questions, and she would express her personal opinion on the subject, which was quite apart from the textbooks. All the professors allowed her that. After the exams we laughed hysterically about Masha's performance, and, of course, she was the first one to laugh at herself.

During the last years of university we had a group of fifteen who got together for studies at her place. Those were great times. Each one of us had to prepare one or two questions in depth, and then we reported what we'd researched to each other. This system worked fantastically for everybody. We did it seriously, yet we had fun. At the end of the day we cooked some simple food and had a party around her table. We even had entertainment afterwards.

Masha had a friend who lived across the hall from her apartment, an older man whose knee had been badly injured during the war. This handicap didn't stop him from flirting with women. In fact, he was married to a woman who was at least thirty-five years his junior. She was madly in love with him and he with her.

Igor was a great singer, and he loved to come for a visit when all of us got together. When he sang and played his guitar, all of us fell in love with him. His style of performing was completely unique. He sang classical romantic songs, all the best lyrics of Pushkin and Lermontov together with quite a few of his own. He had an incredible charm, and even though he was in his late sixties, he had a full head of slightly gray hair with such a handsome face—it was no wonder his young wife was jealous!

Apparently, they had met many years earlier when Igor's first wife was still alive. Galina, who was then eighteen, worked as a nurse in the hospital where Igor suffered one of his numerous knee surgeries, and it was there that she fell in love with him. They had an affair for at least fifteen years and married after Igor's wife died.

After he sang for us, everybody looked forward to hearing him again and begged Masha to invite him when we got together the next time.

"Ask Janna to call him," Masha would say. "He can't say no to her."

He called each one of us by special names. Mine was Nefertiti. Pointing to me he would say, "Oh, where is my youth? She wouldn't be safe then!"

Gennady, Masha's husband was drinking heavily and getting worse and worse. There was no way out for him. He was an avid fisherman, however, and the only break she got was when he went fishing. Sometimes he would be away for days.

She and the children were always worried that something might happen to him on one of his trips, and one day he did have a terrible accident, which resulted in serious head and back injuries. Deep in our hearts we all hoped that his aimless, unhappy life would end. He died shortly afterwards, without regaining consciousness from his accident.

Amazingly, Masha stayed in the hospital day and night helping the nurses, and at his funeral she cried bitterly. I hoped that after his death Masha's life would be easier. He had been a huge burden on her shoulders for many years.

Several months after Gennady's death, Masha and I were on the subway going to our evening classes. She was in one of her romantic moods, telling me about her great love affairs when she was younger. This one was about a young, handsome officer who had been in love with her during the war. She was telling me in detail how they met and what had happened. At the time she was working in an orphanage as a counselor.

"There were some sweet little ones there I just loved!" she said. "But I also was in charge of such a group of boys! Difficult teenagers. I mean, I knew how to handle them, but there was one—oh my God! He was impossible—always in a rage, always making trouble. I used every technique I could think of to manage him. I tried softness, toughness, I got him on his own and tried to reason with him—nothing! I remember I lost patience with him and he tried to strike me! He was actually dangerous.

"One time, when I had the whole group together, he began to punch the boys around him, and I had to stop him. I gave him hell, and I'll never forget the look of pure hatred in his eyes. I didn't realize then that he was going to find a way to actually kill me! It was fate, I suppose, but a little kid overheard him telling one of the boys that he had a butcher knife and was going to use it on me that night. It's difficult to believe, but she hid herself under the stairway in a box and began to scream at the top of her lungs! Because of the kid screaming on and on, he was caught. I was very lucky!"

"Masha!" I turned to her, dumbfounded. "Where was this orphanage?"

"In Serpukhov, which is where my parents lived. Remember, I told you I had to go back there when the war started?"

"Was the name of one of the counselors Anna Ivanovna? I don't know her last name, but she was tall and soft-spoken."

"Yes," Masha replied. "She was my best friend for years, and then she got married and left. We saw each other only once after the war. I still miss her. How is it you know about her?"

"Masha—do you want me to describe the orphanage? As you walked in there was a large room, like a hallway with a table in the left-hand corner. The kitchen was on the right and we always had the most delicious borscht and cream of wheat. Am I right?"

She and I looked at each other as though we had just met. We were both speechless. Masha had been that counselor —the one who was supposed to have been killed that unforgettable night!

"Oh my God...Oh my God..."

That was all we could say. Our tears flowed as we hugged each other right there in the middle of the subway train.

CHAPTER 39

The Important Decision

Masha and I successfully graduated from university in 1971.

Both of us felt an incredible sense of accomplishment. Her life improved immediately after she received her diploma and she was hired as a director of the top school of art, The School of Surikov.

Her salary was at least four times more than she'd made at the club, which alone was worth her going to university at her age. Of course, making more money gave her the chance to earn a much higher pension for her future. The improvement in her life gave me great satisfaction. After all, she wouldn't have done such a thing had we not met one another.

For myself, getting the diploma was purely a matter of proving my own worth. I had decided to do it and had accomplished my goal. My job would be secure from now on, and nobody would think of questioning my position.

Shortly after graduation, I was offered a part-time job at the Institute of Patent Expertise. The job didn't require any office hours, so I did the work at home and earned about the same money as I had in my full-time job.

Sema had worked in this same firm since her graduation I strove to be more diplomatic with her, even though she never changed in the slightest and was the same selfish, self-centered person as always.

After she married and had given birth to a daughter, she gained so much weight that she was barely recognizable, and she was envious of my own slim figure. There were times when we'd accidently meet in the cafeteria and mutual acquaintances would compliment me in her presence.

"Oh, Sema!" they said. "We didn't know you had such an attractive sister!"

Sema would turn pale, and her expression seemed to say, "Never mind her! What about me?" I almost felt guilty hearing these admiring comments, and I did everything possible to avoid meeting her anywhere.

Her husband, Sergei, completed his master's degree in economics, had a good job, and was a member of the Communist Party. He worked on projects that involved some traveling to Mongolia, which meant that Sema was able to shop in the foreign currency stores.

Working in Mongolia wasn't the same as working in Western countries or Europe because it didn't give the Soviet workers the use of dollars. However, it did give the workers some foreign currency, which in turn allowed them the privilege of buying a few things in these stores. What it really meant was that those who worked in the soviet democratic sector couldn't buy in these particular stores. Only those who worked in capitalistic countries were given the dollar equivalent—therefore they could buy anything, and everything that was available there. Others could buy only selected items.

Ever since Sergei had started this job, Sema had been able to buy some of her clothes in one of these stores. Yet now nothing looked stylish on her, and I sometimes thought of the good taste that she once had before she got married.

Tania's husband had died of cancer at age forty. It happened very quickly, and, in fact, I didn't even know he'd been sick. Tania started to write me letters asking to help her move back to Moscow with her two children, a son and a daughter. She didn't want to live in Nikolaev as a widow, but although she'd been born in Moscow she had lost her right to be a citizen because of being away for ten years. I felt sorry for her and especially for her children and decided to help her.

An opportunity presented itself when a former actor I knew—a widower in his late sixties—needed money, and Tania was prepared to pay for a marriage. It all worked. Tania married him and got the necessary stamp on her passport. She came to Moscow with her children and moved in with father. Only then did she discover how difficult he was.

When I saw Tania for the first time in many years, there was nothing left of that exotic-looking girl I'd once known. She looked short and was very overweight.

In the early seventies, Max had begun to talk about the chance certain people could get to emigrate. In our conversations we had to treat this as a hush-hush subject. Nothing like that was ever heard of anywhere during those years, and it seemed unbelievable that the Soviets would allow anything like that to take place.

Apparently, the Soviet government had made a commitment to let a limited number of people emigrate in exchange for wheat. The deal came through the tireless efforts of a group of Americans who were fighting for human rights. It happened during Leonid Brezhnev's leadership, and people who had taken the chance and applied had him to thank for being granted this long-awaited freedom.

And taking a chance was what it was. Those who applied were automatically considered traitors. They either had to quit their jobs or they would be fired, and their children would be expelled from their schools or universities. Yet, the fact that one applied for a visa didn't mean they were guaranteed to receive it. That was the risk, and those whose application for a visa was rejected became *"Refusniks"*

When Max began to talk about a few cases that he knew of I didn't pay much attention to it. The fact of emigration had never crossed my mind.

But Max had let the whole idea remain deep in his heart, and he started to plant the seed in my own. He talked endlessly about the Soviet regime—the corruption, about all the kinds of things the Soviet people had to live with.

All of these were facts of life that were hard to live with. Yet I couldn't see myself even thinking about emigration as an opportunity.

I had just graduated from university and had a job. Also, my profession would only be in the USSR, nowhere else. And I had practically built my family around my treasured friends. How could I think of separating myself from them? Lastly, I was a divorced woman with a child. Emigration was a more likely possibility for solid families.

Nevertheless, the idea had been planted. Emigration was an opportunity of a lifetime, especially for our son's future. We all realized that the opportunity could disappear at any time.

That was how it was in USSR.

In 1971 we started to prepare our son for school. We wanted to enroll him in a special English-language school, so we hired a tutor for him. One of my friends who lived in our building was teaching English at the university of foreign languages and agreed to give him the necessary tutoring. Aleksei knew her and liked her, so learning went well.

By the time the school test came, Aleksei could sing a few songs in English, knew the alphabet, and could count to one hundred. He could also read a few short sentences. It was a great disappointment, therefore, that he wasn't even asked to show what he could do, so we were in and out of the school in five minutes. The administrator informed us that the list of accepted pupils would be on the board in a couple of days.

Indeed it was, but Aleksei's name wasn't there.

I was so outraged that I had to do something. I asked the why his name wasn't on the list and why he hadn't even been tested. The clerk looked through his application and said, "Oh, his parents are not members of the Communist Party."

Talk about discrimination! I was surprised at how openly it was being carried out. Obviously somebody had gone overboard in this direction.

When I realized the situation, I wasn't going to leave it alone. No way! I had to do something about it, but what? Go to the school administrator only to hear some kind of lie? No. I wouldn't give them the satisfaction. I went to the Ministry of Education and told them exactly what I'd found out. They assured me they would look into it—and they did. In a week we received a postcard informing us of Aleksei's acceptance in the school. Out of curiosity I visited the school again. The mistake had been corrected: there was one name added to each class of a child of a non-member.

However, the principal, as well as Aleksei's teacher, couldn't forgive me for going to the ministry and let us know it. All of a sudden, our child wasn't bright enough, his writing wasn't tidy, his hair wasn't cut properly, and the result was that our child wasn't happy at all.

Finally, I went to the principal and was told that they had accepted him as a favour and that he had better be good!

Then it got to me.

I soon began to listen to what Max had been telling me about emigration. He had been absolutely obsessed with the idea for a few years by then and he said that if we ignored this opportunity, we could end up regretting it for the rest of our lives.

I still couldn't see myself leaving. I suggested he emigrate by himself, but he wouldn't hear of it. He would never leave without his son.

"What kind of life is he going to have if his father's declared a traitor! Look, either we all go or we all stay. Even if it isn't for our own future, we owe it to our son to take the chance! And there's the time factor! This opportunity could be gone any moment—then what?"

But my God! What did it really mean, this emigration? It really meant going away forever!

Another thing to consider was that applying for a visa to emigrate (which was the only way it could be done) meant complete exposure.

We already knew about several families who had become "Refusniks." They had lost everything, including the right to live in Moscow. Their lives had turned into a horror story: no jobs, no rights.

Of course they hadn't given up but were fighting on all kinds of fronts and wrote endless letters and petitions and waited for their case to be reviewed again. Nobody knew how long they would be able to survive, and, in fact, some of these people became seriously ill from their new living conditions and stressful circumstances.

Applying for an emigration visa was therefore a huge risk. Yet there were those who were successful in receiving theirs and were already on their way.

Now I went to bed and woke up with this persistent thought: "I have to make a decision...I have to make a decision." Again and again I tried to plead with Max. "Please! Go alone! Please!" but it was out of the question.

"What's going to happen to our son?" he said to me. "He'd have to go into the army because he'd never be accepted into university. That's not the kind of life he deserves! Please—think about it!"

"What do you think?" I cried in frustration. "That's all I do now is think!"

"Well, think positive! We're giving our son the chance for a different life where he can make his own decisions and where nobody will be doing him 'favors' accepting him into whatever school he decides to go to. Wouldn't it be wonderful?"

"True, Max, it would, but what about me? Where would I work? There's no way I could use my profession anywhere in the world—so what would I do? Wash floors? It's a different story with your profession. You're a civil engineer, so your degree would be recognized and eventually you'd get a job. You'd just need to learn more about the specifics, right? But I don't have any hope! I'd have to start from scratch, and that's the difference. I've spent so many years getting to my goal, and now it's all going to go down to drain!"

I was tired of debating. I wanted to scream. But the bottom line was I knew I'd have to go. I had to make a firm decision and the sooner the better.

One morning I found myself in the AVIR, the emigration office, and I sat and wrote out all the requirements.

To apply, one had to have the following:

- *A qualifying passport*
- *A visa issued*
- *Personal references from one's last job, stating the reason for leaving, i.e., emigration*
- *When a visa was received, the following procedure had to be followed (with all original documents):*
- *Birth certificate*
- *Passport*
- *Book of employment*
- *All certificates and diplomas to be returned to the organisation that issued them*
- *Soviet citizenship relinquished*
- *Education costs repaid, including high school*

LIST OF ARTICLES PERMITTED TO BE TAKEN OUT OF THE COUNTRY:

- *Personal clothes*
- *Linen*
- *National souvenirs*
- *One icon (not older than nineteenth century) with permission of Ministry of Culture*
- *One photo camera per family*
- *One hundred dollars per person (US) NOTE: Diamonds or any jewelry with diamonds not permitted*

I had it all written down word for word in my notebook. Now we had to act.

CHAPTER 40

Applying for Emigration

When I decided to apply for emigration, I had to resign from my full-time job for one vital reason: anybody applying was supposed to have a character reference from his or her job. You had to state in writing your reason for asking for it, such as looking for another job or returning to school. In my case it was "emigration."

At that time, it would actually have had about the same effect as a bomb dropping—and not just on yourself.

Your character reference would be discussed by the head of your union, the head of your organisation, and the Communist Party representative, even if you weren't a party member. The head of your organisation would be at risk of losing his job and would be blamed because such a "bad element"—a traitor—had worked under him.

Not only that, but everyone in your organisation would be suspected of taking part in a conspiracy and they would all be questioned. Some would probably be fired, especially anybody wishing to emigrate. They couldn't be trusted anymore on the grounds that they could be planning to do the same. I had lots of friends there, and I thought it would be extremely selfish of me to continue working in the job under the circumstances. So, in actual fact, I didn't have much choice but to resign.

On the other hand, I still had my other job with the United Institute of Patent Expertise. Since it was just part-time, it didn't require any official references.

Normally, I went to the institute once a week, took a pile of applications home, and returned them edited and rewritten the following week. By the time we decided to emigrate, I had worked there for a couple of years. It was a convenient job and paid very well.

My plan was to continue there while I applied for emigration. Once I received my visa, I was planning to tell the administration that I was taking a leave of absence for a while, so nobody would know I was leaving the country. I knew that my plan was realistic and under no circumstances would my sister's job be endangered. The organisation was very big and had hundreds of part-time workers, and nobody cared much about them or knew them personally as long as the work got done on time.

I needed the job to survive before leaving—if, in fact, I received my visa. I also didn't have the slightest idea how long it would take before I knew anything definite. It could take a year, perhaps longer. It took me six months to gather and deliver all the papers they required. One could ask why it took so long, but that's another story. The reality was, nobody knew the answers. One simply had to comply, no questions asked.

One day about a year before the OVIR accepted my visa application, I had brought my completed work to the office and picked up another pile of work and was walking along the narrow corridor on my way out. Suddenly, I saw my sister Sema coming towards me. She didn't look at me, but as we came closer, she angled herself away from me until she was almost against the opposite wall, obviously trying to keep as much distance between us as possible.

As she passed she kept walking but hissed at me, "Get the hell out of here immediately and never set foot in here again, never!" She kept on walking as I stood there stunned.

That was my last "meeting" with her, because she would have made it too difficult to continue, I had to quite this job, as well. It was one more blow to my heart.

As for my father...

I had not been in touch with him for a long time nor did I wish to be, and as far as I knew I didn't exist for him. But because, unfortunately, I had to ask for his written consent to emigrate, there was no way I could avoid seeing him again.

The thought of it made my stomach turn with fear and disgust. I knew he'd make me suffer and even force me to pay some exorbitant price. In his book he had a lot of bad memories he would make me pay for. He would make me pay for all the fights when I took Polia's side and never his, all the fights in which he didn't want to hear the truth because he preferred to keep Polia feeling guilty and accused. That way she would go on slaving for him and he would have an excuse for having other women on the side. He'd make me pay for going to court as a witness for Polia and for telling the truth to the judge. And he'd simply make me pay for being born a girl and surviving my mother's death. Oh yes. This was a perfect opportunity for him to make me pay...

It was exquisitely pathetic, but this is what he did. In his later years he had started collecting foreign cognacs and brandies, which in Russia at that time were very hard to get and weren't sold in stores. Only vodka, champagne, and a couple of kinds of wine were available once in a while, and domestic cognac as well, with only one, two, or three stars. To be a collector of foreign cognacs and brandies one had to have a lot of money and contacts because practically the only way to get them was from the stores that dealt in dollars, and to operate in dollars was illegal.

The only people allowed to have dollar coupons were diplomats and their families who lived abroad and those lucky enough to have jobs with the Ministry of Foreign Affairs, as well as famous musicians and dancers who performed abroad. It was a criminal offence for anyone else to have dollars or dollar certificates.

When my father told me he wanted cognac I had to find a way. It was a long and complicated process. As soon as I got him a couple of bottles and hoped to get his consent he told me to get him some more and even named specific brands. My assignment became even more complex and took even more time and money.

I had to be introduced to those who had the right to go into the American money stores and buy for me. Of course the only reason they would agree to do it was for a profit, and one bottle of good cognac was equivalent to the cost of a good winter coat, a pair of imported winter boots, or a pair of fashionable Italian shoes. In other words, the cost of a bottle could be as much as three or four months' salary for someone who highly paid.

Almost every friend of mine and friends of my friends worked at getting connections for me, but no one understood why I had become such an obsessive cognac collector! Every time I went to my father, he wanted more. By the time he was finally satisfied, he couldn't come up with any new brands and had probably run out of names. In the end I had brought him eighteen bottles and he never tasted one drop. He was purely a collector.

After about four months, he finally signed the permission form, and I was home-free as far as my father was concerned. It was the last document I needed. How much we had gone through in the last year and a half to be able to leave!

I remember the morning when we first applied. We were taking the most important and most dangerous step of our lives. Whatever happened, life would never again be the same.

That day, Max and I were up at four in the morning. We showered and dressed, and by five thirty we were outside the OVIR hoping to be among the first in line. That day we were exposing ourselves, telling "them" that we didn't want anything more to do with the USSR. That day we were joining "those who were traitors." We hoped we would be among the lucky ones who obtained visas, and we refused to even think about what would happen to us if we were turned down.

That day we were putting our future lives in the hands of those stupid clerks, who all had their own reasons for saying yes or no—reasons that had nothing to do with logic. It was like a lottery.

It was very clear that they had orders to let a certain number of people go, but they were also instructed to discourage too many from applying. They did this by sticking a knife in somebody's ribs—by saying no for some arbitrary reason so that others would be too frightened to apply. Even if our applications were accepted we would be living in fear day and night, waiting for the verdict.

How long would it take? Nobody knew and nobody asked. One had to wait and live in fear.

If our applications were accepted that day we'd be joining the crowd that gathered every Saturday morning outside the one and only synagogue in Moscow—not inside, of course. Nobody ever went inside. No one was allowed to practice religion in the USSR, and if anyone was caught doing so, it was regarded as a criminal offence. Yet, they had this one synagogue in Moscow for tourists and correspondents so they could tell the world there was freedom of religion in the USSR. The Jews actually have a synagogue! Everything is okay for them.

In the late sixties and early seventies the synagogue became the unofficial meeting place for people who wanted to apply to emigrate. It was also for the "Refusniks" who hoped to speak with foreign correspondents and to receive some moral and financial support.

The crowd usually gathered in small groups talking very quietly, almost whispering, and of course, always looking over their shoulders, just in case. The gathering was often broken up by the militia on their white horses. "Go home, you people! What are you doing here? There are no services today! Come back on the Jewish holidays."

That was their spiel for breaking up the gathering and their way of pretending to any foreign spectators that there actually were services in the synagogue and that Jewish holidays were normally celebrated there. When the militiamen came charging forward on their white horses, the crowd dispersed quickly.

Today was the day of decision, but not for me. By the time our names came up to see the clerk we were cold and hungry. All we wanted was to get through it and go home. As we walked into the clerk's office, the female clerk looked up and down from head to toe, and I sensed her negative vibes. I knew something would go wrong.

First, she read every document of Maxs, and then she read Aleksei's. She put them aside. Then she started on mine. I could see in her face that she was looking for a loophole, and she found one. She was holding my mother's passport for the longest time, saying nothing. Watching her, I could almost read her mind. She was thinking hard what to do with me. She certainly wanted me to jump through some more hoops before she could accept my application.

Finally she spoke. "And where is your mother's consent?"

"I cannot get my mother's consent. My mother died in 1941, only a few months after I was born, and this is her cancelled passport."

"This proves nothing!" she said. "As far as this passport is concerned, it could have been lost and she could have another by now."

"But how could it be found if my father was away during the war when I was born?"

"This proves nothing! It could have been lost anytime before the war."

"But what do I do now?" I asked hopelessly.

"Go and get the certificate of her death. That is the only document we will accept other than her written consent."

"But my father was in the war when it happened, and nobody knows how it happened or where. I was only told that she evacuated Moscow for some far-off place right after I was born."

"That's exactly the point," she said. "As far as she is concerned, she could have been alive this whole time and you have a responsibility to take care of her. Unless you bring her consent or her death certificate, we cannot accept your application."

And she called out for the next name to come forward. That was it. We gathered all our documents and left. The next family was already in the office.

I was left out in the cold, not knowing where to begin the search for my mother's death certificate. My poor mother, whom I'd never met. Oh, how I wished I could fill this unfillable void that I'd lived with all my life. How I would have loved to take care of her if she were alive!

Could this spiteful woman in the OVIR be right? Was it possible my mother was alive and needed me now? Might I find her? Was there hope that we might meet after all? These thoughts and questions ran through my mind as we left, and I made up my mind I would do anything to find her...

CHAPTER 41

Finding My Mother's Friend

But meeting my mother was not to be.

My father never spoke of my mother's death. In fact, any discussion of it was off limits. I'm not sure to this day if he ever knew the truth. My eldest sister told me a story that painted a horrible picture in my mind, that the Germans had buried my mother alive. That was all I knew about her death. No one really wanted to talk about it, so I had to start my own search in 1973 for the actual facts of her death. It took me almost half a year, until by sheer luck I found my mother's friend from more than thirty years before.

How I found her is a story in itself. At first I tried going through official channels to see if there was any record of my mother's death. There was nothing. I tried retracing my father's search for his wife and children after he got back from the war, finally finding me in my orphanage and a little while later my two sisters. But I still could find out nothing about my mother. It was as if she had simply disappeared from the face of the earth without a trace.

My father's family was no help. They weren't interested and refused to talk about her. They all knew I was applying to leave the USSR, and in their eyes this made me an outcast and a traitor. By this time, my Uncle David who had helped my mother and her friend get out of Moscow in 1941 was dead. My grandmother, who could probably have told me something, had also died. Everyone else in the family simply shrugged and shook their heads when I asked about my mother.

In desperation, I went to see my Aunt Rita, my father's eldest sister, and asked her if she remembered anything at all about my mother when she'd left Moscow. At first she said no, but I kept pushing her to tell me something—anything.

She finally said, "Oh! Come to think of it she had this crazy friend, Ania...Ania Rotfield...who had two kids, Baiba and Mikhail."

At last I had managed to get a name, and I had a place to start! I went to one of the information kiosks in Moscow where they had lists of the entire city's registered citizens, somewhat like a census list. I asked about Ania Rotfield, but the clerks said they could do nothing for me. They needed her patronymic or second name and also the year and place of her birth. Of course I knew none of those things. I begged them to make an exception One girl said coldly that she was forbidden to give out information on anyone without proper information, but another girl took pity on me and offered to help.

She turned to the name Rotfield and showed me that there were about fifty listed. I asked her to read out the first names of all that were on her list, which she did, but there was no record of an Ania or Mikhail Rotfield living in the city of Moscow. When I asked her to check the lists for towns on the outskirts of the city, she said I would have to go to one of the stations outside the city limits and ask there. She called ahead and appealed to them to help me because I was looking for my long-lost mother. She also gave me directions where to go, and I took the train to Mytischi, one of the first stops outside the city. I began to get excited when the woman there said she had three Mikhail Rotfields on her list.

"Could you possibly give me their addresses?" I asked.

"I can't give you all three of them," she said. "I need more information." My heart sank. Then I remembered something else Aunt Rita had told me. "He would have been born around 1930," I said eagerly.

And there was one! "Mikhail Efimovich Rotfield was born in Moscow in 1930," she said. "He lives in a small town further north near a city called Bolshevo."

"Thank you! Oh thank you!" I said. "I'll find him now! I'm sure I will!"

There were no telephone directories in the USSR, so I couldn't simply look up his phone number and call him. Besides, very few people had phones of their own. So I took the train to Bolshevo hoping I was on my way to the right Mikhail, and if he was the one that I would find him at home.

The man who opened the door was tall and unattractive with a sour expression. He seemed quite uncomfortable when I told him my name and who I was looking for. He volunteered absolutely nothing.

"Is your mother's name Ania?"

"Yes."

"And you have a sister Baiba?"

"Yes."

"And you lived in Moscow before the war?"

"Yes."

"And at the start of the war your mother took you away from Moscow?"

"Yes."

"To somewhere in the East?"

"Yes, for a while but not for too long."

"Do you remember anything about my mother?"

"No. I can't tell you anything about that."

"What about your mother? Is she still alive?"

"Yes. I think so."

"Do you know where I could find her?"

"She's probably with my sister in Tashkent."

"Can you give me her address?"

"All right." He wrote something on a piece of paper and handed it to me. "Here's my sister's phone number. I suggest you call her."

He seemed relieved to get rid of me, but I was ecstatic! I knew I was a step closer to finding out the truth. I called Tashkent immediately when I got back to Moscow and found Baiba to be the total opposite of her brother. She was enthusiastic and obviously excited to hear from me after thirty-two years. She remembered me as a baby and asked all kinds of questions about my two sisters and me. Baiba remembered my mother too and how sick she had been, but she said she really couldn't tell me anything about her death. Her mother was still alive and had lived with her for a few years in Tashkent. Then her mother had married a man from Ukraine and moved to Kiev. She was widowed again, living alone and with no telephone, but Baiba was happy to give me her address in Kiev. She wished me good luck.

I hung up the phone feeling exhilarated! I wanted to fly to Kiev right away to meet Ania Rotfield, but there were no plane tickets available. I would have to wait at least ten days for a seat, so I decided to go by train that very night. The trip took two and a half days. God knows why, but all through it I hardly slept. I was shivering and trembling with excitement. Finally. After all these years.

A taxi took me to a huge block of senior citizen flats in the Podol district of Kiev, where a large, warm-looking woman in her sixties answered the door.

I said, "You are Ania. I am Janna."

We fell into each other's arms. She invited me in, put on the kettle, and made tea. I stayed with her that night and most of the next day. We talked and talked and cried and cried. She told me more about my mother than I had ever known.

They had been the closest of friends for many years, and she spoke about my mother's character, how soft and loving she was. She described her as having been tall with a very good figure and lovely soft dark hair.

She said, "You have her eyes and you have some of her sweet charm about you," she said. "Your sister Sema was a very difficult child, miserable and selfish."

"And Tania?" I asked. "She was always laughing. But oh, your father! He was jealous and possessive of your mother! It hurt me to see how he mistreated her. I'm sorry to say this to you, but he was a brute."

I nodded. "I know," I said softly. And now I felt even closer to the one who had given birth to me: She and I had both suffered at his hands.

Ania talked about their decision to leave Moscow and of the long tortuous journey to Tataria.

"That was when your mother started to become ill. That filthy train—no proper food—no doctor, of course."

"What do you think she died of?" I asked.

"I think it was some kind of cancer. And, I believe, a broken heart too." She dismissed her own heroic efforts to save her but simply said, "I loved her. She was my closest friend."

I heard about Ania's own sad life too. She hadn't spoken with her son, Mikhail, for more than ten years, and he never wrote to her, which was probably why he'd been so uncomfortable with me. She then brought out pictures of herself from before the war when she'd been young and pretty, and she even had a picture of my mother.

For the first time in my life I saw my mother's face! I could hardly breathe. I stared and stared at the photograph. This was the face of my very own mother!

"I want you to keep it," Ania said. "It has been waiting for you!"

"Oh, thank you!" I sobbed. "It will be my most treasured possession!"

The next day, Ania wrote out an affidavit for me stating everything she knew about the circumstances of my mother's death. We took it to a lawyer to have it sworn as the testimony of the only known living witness and parted in tears.

On the train back to Moscow, I thought about my father. He had always said how much he loved my mother, but he had never bothered to find out the exact circumstances of her death. Now more than thirty years later, I had found out the truth. How much more easily he could have found out all these things right after the war. So much for his love! I never showed my mother's picture to him.

CHAPTER 42

The Last Thirty Days

The last thirty days in Russia were the strangest of my entire life. We received a postcard ordering us to show up at the AVIR offices on the twenty-first of January 1974 at 9:00 a.m. sharp. I held the postcard in my shaking hands while my thoughts raced a mile a minute. What was the answer to be: YES or NO? If yes, it meant the end of doubt, and I doubted everything.

Was I doing the right thing by leaving my hard-earned education and my career behind? Was I wrong to leave everything and everybody—Mama, Raya, and Masha, in particular—and take my son away from the country of his birth, just to start a new life? I would be in an unknown new world without language, profession, or money! These questions had occupied my mind day in and day out for over a year. Yet, if it was yes, there would be no way to change my mind and that would mean the end of doubt.

But what if it was to be no? That also meant the end...the end of hope. How could I ever forget those forty-eight hours before Max and I walked into the AVIR office? There the clerk silently handed us two purple pieces of paper: our visas, stating clearly that we must leave the USSR on the twenty-first of February 1974, in exactly thirty days. We had thirty days to finish our lives in Russia. To finish everything! Everything!

We had to pay enormous amounts to leave Russia. Everything had its price tag. Our education: high school, university, all the courses we had taken and all the courses we didn't even remember taking. All of it was assembled and a price tag put on it. A huge number—more than twelve thousand rubles was paid out for Max and me. In 1974 the Russian ruble was worth about ninety cents US.

Then there was the price of the visa itself, something like four hundred rubles per person, including children under age. And to put these numbers in perspective: a monthly salary of a top executive was 200 rubles. And then the plane tickets were about 1,300 rubles each.

But the most painful issue, the most psychologically painful, was the price of giving up our citizenship. It was 400 rubles for each citizen of the USSR. This was the amount people were forced to pay to give up their citizenship—one of the many ironies in the corrupt Soviet system. In other words, when leaving the country, people were forced to give up their citizenship and yet pay top price for the privilege!

How did they come up with this number? How do you put a price on your identity? You leave the country in which you were born and raised, and someone puts a price on the sum total of your entire life in this lousy numerical way! As well as this financial psychological burden, they allowed you only one hundred dollars per person to take with you and not a cent more. You couldn't take anything of real value: no gold, diamonds, or other valuable jewels. They allowed you one icon per family, but the really valuable Russian icons dated from the fifteenth and sixteenth centuries!

So you have a hundred dollars in your pocket to start your new life in a new country where you don't have a job, where you don't know a soul, where you have no place to live, and where you don't speak the language. Could it be any tougher?

But then came my last day in Russia…

Everything would be for the last time. That night would be the last time in our now empty apartment. It belonged to the cooperative now. We couldn't sell it to anybody who wanted to buy it and who had the money. It had to be handed back to the cooperative for the original price, which we'd paid years and years before. My apartment, that had been my pride and joy for so long, now looked cold and bare. The only reminder of the past was the big wall-to-wall storage unit that was empty now. Everything was gone…Where? I didn't know.

All I know is that during the last thirty days this place was like a flea market. People I'd never seen before came and took my things—my books, even my own book of poems; my records; my jewelry. They took my collection of carved masks, my dishes, my silverware, most of my clothes, leaving a few lousy rubles behind...and emptiness.

In those days in Russia you could sell anything. Just tell one friend and in half an hour you had ten strangers going through your most precious private things. While it goes on, all you can do is just smile and say, "Thank you."

Our place had a strange sound that last day, our empty place. It sounded hollow, like my heart did. Nothing inside—empty. No meaning. I moved like a robot. I spoke like one. I was tired beyond the normal meaning of the word.

Every minute of those past thirty days was focused on one objective: to dispose. Dispose of my university diploma. I went back to the university and gave it back to some clerk, who looked at me with obvious disgust and at the same time barely concealed jealousy. I went back to the last place I worked and gave them back my workbook to the head of personnel who didn't even look at me (it was as though I might infect him with some kind of incurable disease). I went over to the passport office and allowed them to take my passport away, making me feel like a criminal. Then to the Ministry of Health to give them my birth certificate where they so kindly let me know how sorry they were that I was born...

You go and give...give away and dispose, dispose...

And then the people came. The telephone rang. Everybody said things they meant and some things they didn't mean. At times I felt like a wheel, like a wheel that was just going round and round and would never stop until the plane would take off, and then it would stop forever...

CHAPTER 43

Goodbye, Father

I had two more contacts with my father.

The first was a couple of days after I got his signed permission to leave. I had to call Tania, who lived with him at the time, and he answered the phone. When he heard my voice, he sounded surprised and confused and asked if I was calling from my new home.

I said, "How could I be, already?"

"But I gave you my permission five days ago already."

I couldn't help but laugh when I realized how out of touch he was. He actually thought that the minute he signed his permission I would jump on the plane to leave.

My last contact with him was even more pathetic. Tania kept asking me to come to the house to say goodbye to him. I kept saying, "No. What for?" As far as I was concerned, I did not exist for him. Apparently, all my life I had been like a "bone in his throat" (his own expression), and he had never wanted me around. But Tania kept coming at me with all kinds of different reasons why I should say goodbye to him. One of the most convincing was that he was old and I should forgive and forget.

"After all, he is your father, and you'll never see him again."

In the end, I agreed. "Okay, I'll come, but only for a few minutes," and I walked into his house for the last time. Tania had prepared the table, putting out white linen cloth and lots of food and, of course, vodka. My father's eldest sister, Rita, was there, and a couple of other people were sitting around the table. It looked like they were preparing for a party. Well, I was not. I was going to stay no longer than an hour.

As soon as I was seated at the table, my father got up holding a shot of vodka in his hand. It reminded me of the day when he told me about his divorce from Polia and his decision to leave her penniless. The memory sent chills through my body, and I thought, "Oh, no! I cannot take this again!"

But at that moment he burst into tears!

I was shocked. "What's wrong?" I asked. "Why are you crying? It can't be about me! You never wanted me around in the first place. I was always a thorn in your side! You must be relieved now that I'm finally going away for good."

He swallowed his tears. "Yah! But just the same, you are my daughter."

Oh God! How many bitter memories arose in my mind when I heard those words.

The times when he brought chocolate bears and rabbits for Tania and Sema and never for me!

The piano lessons he promised me on the condition that I shut my mouth—and that he took away the minute I opened it!

My skates that he threw into the outhouse in the garden and how he pushed my head down the hole to make me watch them disappear in the filth below.

And my frost-bitten feet!

My eleventh birthday party when he kicked all my little friends out of the house and humiliated me to the point that I collapsed with an epileptic seizure.

So many terrible memories...

No, I couldn't take it, and I wouldn't! To forget all this past brutality towards me? I could not and I would not! And I got up and left—forever.

CHAPTER 44

Goodbye, Valentin

A knock at the door brought me back to reality. I had been so lost in my thoughts I had forgotten about Valentin completely! Oh God, I must look like hell, I thought to myself. I cannot see him like this. I'd better do something with my face, quickly!

"Yes, Valia. Just a minute!" Oh, what the heck? I couldn't do much; it was too late. Just comb my hair and touch up my lips. It was futile. The lipstick would be smeared the minute I opened the door. Oh, God. Why are women so silly?

While I was doing this useless exercise, a thought ran through my mind. Why wasn't I excited? For almost twenty years I'd fallen apart every time I was about to see this man. My hands and knees were always trembling. Why not now?

I suppose something in me had died. Something told my body that it was over. It seemed to say, "You will never see him again. The great love of your life is over. You are one step away from a new life, and when that new life begins, it will have nothing to do with your past."

Yet, I took my time before opening the door. I somehow wanted to prolong this moment...

Ever since I'd told him that I was going to apply for a visa, he hadn't believed me. He even wrote on his bedroom wall, "You are NOT going, Jandi!!!"

Funny how he still believed that my love for him would keep me from going. During all those years, I must have made him feel that my love had no limits.

During the last year and a half he had done everything to make me believe he was capable, responsible, understanding, and so on. He'd even rented an apartment nearby so I could see him more often. Men! Once they realize their loss, they show incredible improvement! At first, he didn't believe that I'd have the guts to apply. Then he didn't believe that I'd get my visa. He kept on dreaming that if I became a refusnik, he would support Aleksei and me.

As for him applying, even if we were married it was hopeless. He worked in the biggest institution for the designing and building of rockets and missiles, and he had a high position there. He had been involved with a lot of nuclear field tests that were dangerous to his health, so he knew perfectly well that "they" would never allow him to leave.

In the end, when I received my visa, he simply started to drink. He would come home from work and drink alone, waiting for me to come and see him for at least for a couple of hours. And I did go see him from time to time; we would spend long hours making love and talking. We no longer had the time for secrets or games. We both wanted to talk, to ask each other the questions that had bothered us for so many years.

He told me how his heart had been broken when I went into hiding after I was raped by my boss. He had no idea why I avoided him then, and he told me about the endless hours he spent waiting for me by the subway station—waiting for one simple reason, to see my face again. He revealed how hurt he had been almost a year later when I finally admitted my reason for avoiding him—hurt because I had shown him no trust or respect. Instead of facing the truth, I'd preferred to hide and make him go through months and months of misery. He confessed that no matter how hard he had tried to fall in love with someone else, he couldn't do it, and then every time we had tried to make it work between us, something went wrong.

When we said goodbye for that very last time, Valentin was almost forty and still single. He hadn't been able to force himself to marry someone he didn't love as he had loved me, and because of this his life was empty.

He had a very dangerous high-pressure job and had nothing else to look forward to. Besides which, it was a job he told me he hated.

He knew that every Russian professional's brains were being used up and sucked dry, and that many of his colleagues were dying of cancer in their prime—and nobody cared. He realized that his life was on the line too, but there was nothing he could do about it. He had nowhere to turn. It was too late. And now, he had lost me...

I revealed a lot of my stuff too. How destroyed I felt after the rape and how I didn't have anybody to turn to for advice. My stepmother wouldn't have understood the situation because she was a perfect product of her generation that considered even the word "sex" dirty. If anything happened to a girl, it was her fault. Her life was finished and she would never be respected by a good man. Good girls preserved their virginity until they were married.

Those were the stupid rules of society—this crooked society that pushed most girls into marrying the wrong men and to marry for one reason.

I asked Valentin if he'd had sex with anybody during our first five years, and he said, "Yes, of course. There were plenty of available married women. I had to use them while you were a virgin."

"And why did you never really make an attempt to make love with me? We had so many opportunities."

"You see how screwed up we were?" he said. "Just because of this sick attitude, look where we are now! Both of us are unhappy. But it's too late... too late."

CHAPTER 45

Goodbye, Russia

The morning before I got on the plane to Vienna, leaving Russia behind forever, I pondered the magnitude of what I was doing. Leaving. Forever. How could I live the rest of my life knowing that I would never again see my dear Raya or Masha or all my other close friends? Never to see Moscow, Gorki Street, Pushkin Square, my dearest Mama Polia, everything and everybody I'd known—ever again!

How could I live with that pain for the rest of my life? This system was so cruel! Taking away my citizenship just because I wanted to leave the country. I didn't want to go away forever! It couldn't be forever; it was too painful…but I didn't have a choice. That's just the way that it was. Those who left the USSR were considered worthless. If they left they could never come back.

I had a few hours to spend in the apartment by myself. Max and Aleksei were staying the last night with Max's parents, saying their last goodbyes. Max would never see them again. They were in their late seventies. I was spending my last night in Russia with Raya.

My Raya…she was the last one in the world I ever wanted to hurt. And I knew I had hurt her badly. I was so afraid of telling her the truth about leaving that I'd said nothing until I got my visa.

After all, there was an equal chance that we wouldn't get the visas and that we would then be put on the list of "refusniks" who couldn't get a job anywhere. If you didn't work they could send you out of Moscow or even put you in jail because "you were a threat to society." They called you *"tuneyadetz"* or "a parasite."

All these things made us hate the system and want to leave, but not the people we loved. How could we possibly want to leave them—*forever*?

Oh! If I could have taken them all with me, or at least my Raya.

I will never forget the day I received my visa and I had those thirty days to go.

My heart was torn apart. On the one hand I was lucky that my agony of waiting was finally over and that I was not a "refuznik." On the other hand, this was the end—a fait accompli. Those thirty days screamed at me as if they were saying, "You wanted to go, so go quickly! Get the hell out and forget that you ever lived here! But before you leave, give us every bit of money you have or don't have. If you want to go, then you'll pay for it!"

I called Raya that day and told her I had something important to talk with her about. She was at my place in half an hour. I sat her down, put cold vodka and our favorite foods on the table, and started to tell her. With Raya I never discussed political issues much. We had many other things to talk about. So now, I couldn't come right out and say I was leaving for good.

I told her how difficult we were finding it to live in the USSR due to the discrimination because we were not members of the Communist Party. Raya looked at me with questioning eyes, as if to say, "Where is this leading?"

But she was the most tactful person I ever met in my life. She could be dying of curiosity but never interrupt me. Then I told her what had happened with Aleksei's school and that Max, with all his credentials, couldn't advance in his career. She was listening. And then I told her that Brezhnev had made an arrangement with the Americans. Under it, he would allow a certain number of people to emigrate in exchange for wheat; otherwise, the Americans would stop selling it to Russia, and Russia needed the wheat badly.

Suddenly Raya stopped me. "Janna—are you leaving?" Her eyes were full of terror. I didn't have to answer. She answered for me. "You are leaving. And what is going to become of me?"

We sat there at my kitchen table for a long time with the vodka and food untouched. We couldn't speak. We felt beyond any words. How else could it be? We were deeply and truly fond of each other, we two orphans, we two lost souls, whose hearts were bigger than the planet, full of love for each other. Since we met we'd followed in one another's footsteps and had planned to do so for the rest of our lives. No, this could not be happening...

"But, Raya, we are two soul sisters! Nothing can separate us from each other, even my leaving."

It was true, so true. Nothing could take Raya out of my heart.

"But, Janna. You are going away forever."

"But, Raya, what can I do? Max is going, and I cannot have my son fatherless nor can I take his son away from him. I must go"

From that day on, for thirty days, Raya was my shadow. The first day she went to work everybody in the studio asked her what had happened. Her eyes were swollen. She looked sick. She burst into tears again. "My Janka is going away...forever."

They told her to go home and be where she had to be until the end... And she was beside me every single one of those agonising thirty days. And her husband, Slava? He let her be with me. But even if he hadn't she would have done it just the same. Slava! He was in tough position through all those years of our sistership. He had to accept the fact that Raya and I were inseparable, or rather he had to learn to live with it. And he did. And I will be thankful to Slava for as long as I live.

He did something more. One night I stayed over at their place. We talked long into the night, and after Raya fell asleep, Slava said, "Janna, I want you to know how deeply Raya is attached to you, and I want you to understand how important it is for you not to let her down."

"What do you mean? How can I let her down?"

"Oh, you may get very busy," he said, "or become successful and rich and then your closeness could slip away, who knows? Your leaving is so traumatic, so traumatic for Raya now, but it would be even more so if you failed her in any way. So, I want you to know that you two have my complete cooperation in corresponding with each other directly to and from our home address. And also be very open when you write. I don't want this system to stand in the way of your correspondence because you see, from now on, your letters will be the only thing that can keep your relationship alive."

"Dear Slava! What a heroic gesture! But do you know how risky it is? You work in one of the most secretive organisations in the USSR. You realize that any correspondence with the West could get you in a lot of trouble?"

"Yes, I know that."

"But they can even arrest you and send you to jail! You know there are cases like that, so it could happen to you too."

"Yes, I know, Janna, I know. But I am willing to take my chances for two reasons. First, you two cannot afford to lose each other because of the stupidity of this regime, and, second, I am sick and tired of being a puppet of this system. I am really ready to fight."

And he did fight, but that happened much later.

One day, a few years after I left Russia, I received a letter from Slava that made me cry:

> Dear Janna! I have to confess that for many years of your friendship with Raya it made me very unhappy. But I felt if I didn't accept your closeness I would have a big problem with our marriage, and it was at Raya's insistence that I did accept it. I did it for her sake and for the sake of peace in our family. As the years went by, I learned to live with it.
>
> But what I saw happening at the time of your leaving and during these three years since you left made me realize a lot of things. One of them is that you two represent an incredible example of the deepest and strongest friendship, such as very few people have in their lives. I wish I had a friendship like yours. Will you now please accept my apologies for giving you some hard times in the past? Forgive me! All I can do now is to admire the two of you from the bottom of my heart. Slava.

About fifteen years after that memorable letter, I learned that Slava had been called to the KGB offices and questioned severely many times over. He was also threatened with arrest if the correspondence to and from the West did not stop.

His answer was, "Go ahead, arrest me! Do anything you want! I am not going to ask my wife to stop the beautiful relationship she has with her friend!"

Eventually they left him alone. The incredible thing is that Raya knew nothing of this at the time. Slava never said a word to her.

But that night, my last night, I was spending with my dearest Raya to say my last goodbye and to ask her to forgive me for the pain I was causing her.

I still had a couple of hours before she came over and I still had to sort out a couple of thoughts and finish unfinished business...with Valentin. He was coming to see me for the very last time.

Here I was leaving my country forever and my heart was breaking, yet I had to stay calm. I could not fall to pieces at the last moment.

What was going to happen to Polia? The woman who had walked into my father's house when I was an ugly six-year-old, when what I needed the most was to be loved.

The woman who would leave my father's house that same day with her beautiful niece Lusia whom she loved and not me.

The woman who stayed with my miserable father for eighteen horrible years because I called her "Mama." "You are staying with me, Mama, aren't you? Please say you are!" And she did.

The woman who was abused by my father and my two sisters, and whom I stood by until I got sick of the situation and left my father's house at fourteen to survive. Before Russia I pleaded with her to come with us.

"You never saw a happy day in your life with my monster-father. Come with us. I'll show you a happy life, Polia! I'll take care of you! I owe this to you because you allowed me to call you Mama when I most needed to! Come with me, Mama! Let me look after you!"

She looked down, shaking her head over and over.

"No, Janna! I cannot! I am too old to go there. I will stay on my own until I die. Don't worry about me! Go! And take this with you!"

She handed me her beautiful crystal vase. "Please keep this as a memory of me, and don't sell it even if you need the money for bread. This is the one valuable thing I owned after the day I came to your father's house and you called me Mama. Don't worry about me. Go!"

Epilogue

When I decided to tell this story, it took me a year and a half to get to the point where I could write about my leaving Russia. I simply couldn't pull myself together to do it. I asked myself why this was the case hundreds of times, along with the question "Do I really want to live those agonizing memories all over again?"

Most of the time the answer was a resounding no!

Now—a year and a half after first making that decision—I've done it. All I have to write about is that one simple episode: my actual departure from Russia by plane on February 21, 1974, at ten o'clock in the morning.

And what's so difficult about it? One simply arrives at the airport, checks the luggage, waits for the boarding to begin, and then the plane takes off.

That's it, it's done. It's so simple. Yet if it were actually simple, why would I find writing about it so painful? On the other hand, if I didn't write about it, this last chapter would be left unfinished and I wouldn't be able to start writing the next part—about my new life. I'd have to leave it hanging. And for how long? My mind is already set to talk about my new beginnings in the unknown, my adventures in the new world.

Can't I just forget about this part? No. I have to tell it just as it happened.

I dreaded actually living those moments too, but I went through with all of it in spite of my dread. I had no choice but to board the plane on that date and at that hour, and, painful or not, I now have to jump through the last hoop and paint the picture of my departure from the USSR—from Moscow—even if I don't want to.

That last lonely ride to the airport with Raya—just Raya and me. We are silent, full of inexpressible sorrow, staring straight ahead, holding one another's hands—frozen. Two seated statues...

Everyone else—Max, his brother, and Aleksei—is following us, and Slava is in the third taxi. All are lost in their thoughts, except Aleksei who is excited.

He loves the car ride. It's his passion to be driven. His first word at age one was "drive." And this will be his first airplane ride, which fills him with excitement, but he's reserved about showing it. He is just eight years old, and we celebrated his birthday only eight days ago. Such a serious boy. Who knew that fifteen years later he would become a commercial pilot?

My little boy, we made this decision for you. Did we do the right thing? Who knows?

Now I'm on the airport balcony. My last foothold in Russia, from which I can wave to all my friends, standing there waving back at me and blowing kisses. How many are there? I don't know...I can't see very well. My eyes are blurred with tears. Those last bitter tears...

Why forever? Why? Oh God! Why?

I Never Met My Mother.
By Janna Sosensky

Janna and Polia Seventeen Years Later

"Will I Ever See You Again, Polia?"

Moving Forward

Made in the USA
San Bernardino, CA
20 May 2013